Philosophizing the Body

Philosophizing the Body

Physical, Social, Psychosomatic & Spiritual Dimensions

Papers Presented at the 40th Annual Research Seminar of ACPI held at Vijnananilayam, Janampet, Eluru, 22-25 October 2015

Edited by

Nishant Alphonse Irudayadason

Christian World Imprints ™

&

Association of Christian Philosophers of India

ACPI Annual Philosophy Series No. 17

Series Editors: Keith D'Souza, John Peter Vallabadoss & Kurian Alumkal

First Published in 2016 by

Christian World Imprints™
Christian Publishing & Books from India
H-12 Bali Nagar, **New Delhi-110015**
info@christianworldimprints.com
www.ChristianWorldImprints.com
Phone: +91 11 25465925

&

Association of Christian Philosophers of India
Vijnananilayam, Janampet, Vijayarai PO
Eluru-534475, West Godavari Dt., A.P.
president@acpiindia.com
www.acpiindia.com
Phone: +91 881 2225340

ISBN: 978-93-5148-181-2 (HB) ISBN: 978-93-5148-182-9 (PB)

Cataloging in Publication Data--DK
Courtesy: D.K. Agencies (P) Ltd. <docinfo@dkagencies.com>

Association of Christian Philosophers of India. Annual Research Seminar (40th : 2015 : Eluru, India)
Philosophizing the body : physical, social, Psychosomatic & spiritual dimensions : papers presented at the 40th Annual Research Seminar of ACPI held at Vijnananilayam, Janampet, Eluru 22-25 October 2015 / edited by Nishant Alphonse Irudayadason.
pages cm. -- (ACPI annual philosophy series ; no. 17)
ISBN 9789351481812 (HB)
ISBN 9789351481829 (PB)

1. Human body (Philosophy)--Congresses. I. Irudayadason, Nishant Alphonse, 1971- editor. II. Title. III. Series: Association of Christian Philosophers of India. Annual series ; no. 17.

B105.B64A87 2015 DDC 128.6 23

Printed in India.

Editorial

A contradiction about the body runs through our culture. On the one hand it is highly valued; the ambient materialism attests to it. But, on the other hand, it is relativized as regards its ontological status, anthropological significance and ethical implications.

Globally, never more so than today, defining relationship through "biological" or "genetic" evidence has become increasingly important. In case of dispute, this piece of evidence carries the last word. Yet simultaneously, we all share a common ideology, namely what makes relationship is essentially will and love.

The opposition between "organic" and "voluntary" creates insoluble contradictions. It is this opposition that must be challenged because the body is more than something merely biological. The substantive challenge is to articulate what mind and body means.The human being is the articulation of these two realities. Two dangers now lurk in all walks of life including our everyday discourse: mind without body and body without mind.

As Christian philosophers of India, we need to address this substantive challenge. As Christians, we have some confessional reasons to valorise the body. First, we acknowledge the unity of mind and body in our creation narrative. In Genesis 2:7 we read, "The Lord breathed into his nostrils the breath of life; and the man became a living being" (NRSV). The Hebrew phrase used for "living being" is *nefeshhayyah*, which can also be rendered as "living soul" as preferred by some translations.The soul in this sense is that which animates the body, itself being led by the *nishmathayyim*, the breath of life. The soul is the life of the body and the breath of God is the life of the soul. Behind *nishmathayyim*, at its source stands *ruah*, the breath of God; this in Greek is translated as *pneuma* and in English as "Spirit." The English biblical scholar J.A.T. Robinson says, "The Hebrew idea of personality is that of an animated body, not (like the Greek) that of an embodied soul."

Secondly, we believe in the incarnation of Christ. In the words of Louis Evely, "Through incarnation, God has shown us that the body is a good conductor of the divine." Already St. Paul has affirmed that the body is the "temple of the Holy Spirit" (1 Cor. 6:19). John Paul II, in an Ash Wednesday catechesis, declared that "the body is the primordial sacrament."

Thirdly, Christianity asserts not the immortality of the soul (in the Platonic sense) but the resurrection of the body. We must note here the corporeal nature of our relationship with Christ. For the baptized, the link to Christ is not only spiritual in the sense of the "intangible," but it is also primarily corporeal: through the sacraments, concrete signs and gestures are made on the body amidst the community of believers called the Church, which is the Body of Christ. As the theologian Urs von Balthasar says, "to have a body is to touch the body of Christ."

As philosophers, when it comes to the question of the body, it seems reasonable to adhere to metaphysical realism. It is obvious that our spiritual and intellectual life depends also on our physical and neuronal conditions. It is therefore evident that the "objective" body is important for the experience of the "subjective" body. It is the same subject that thinks and lives a body. "I think with my body," says a character in one of the novels of Henri Bosco. Insofar as the human person is real, the body is real. The purely spiritual soul devoid of a body is a mythological assertion. This abstract soul, contrary to the concrete body is vested with abstract characteristics like unity, simplicity, immortality. But the body is a concrete reality, which experiences hunger, pain, suffering and death. Death is a reality that we cannot escape; in as much as death is real, the body is real.

Another philosophical reason to value the body is the idea of the infinite in the finite: towards aa phenomenology of the sensible. The French moral philosopher Joseph de Finance holds that in sense experience, there is something that pure thought will never find completely. This is perceived in health, dance, sports, art and light, as well as in the experience of birth, parentage and death.

From the Indian point of view, it has been generally held that the body is not considered important in mainstream philosophical discourses. However, as part of our everyday living which is predominantly religious, the body occupies an important place. This is evident in the practice of yoga, dances, popular religious ceremonies and folk festivals. Indian wisdom considers the whole universe as a cosmic body. Rekha Menon, Professor of History of Art, evokes the relationship of the lived body to the outside as follows: "The body is always in excess of itself, always expressive and hence trans-body," a body that goes beyond its limits. We exist in the world with and through the body, an existence which is an opening and a sight to the world. In the process of philosophizing the body, faith, reason and wisdom converge, each with its own arguments, depending on the context; what happens in the body is not everything, nevertheless, it is not 'nothing.'

Hence, as Christian philosophers of India, we deliberated on the challenges and opportunities of Philosophizing the Body and several papers were presented at the 40th Annual Research Seminar of the ACPI held at Vijnananilayam, Janapet, Eluru, in the State of Andhra Pradesh, from October 22 to 25, 2015. These research papers are edited and published in this work in four parts.

The first part dwells on the subject from phenomenological and existential perspectives; the second part addresses the social, political and gender issues in philosophizing the body; the third part discusses the approaches of science and technology in philosophizing the body; and the final part focuses on the spiritual dimensions of the body. Hence, this work approaches the question of philosophizing the body from multi-disciplinary perspectives.

The first part contains six research essays. The first essay titled "Modernity and Exile of the body" by Nishant Alphonse Irudayadason, while discussing at length how the Cartesian philosophy was instrumental for the exile of body from philosophical discourse, shows how the contemporary phenomenological approaches have given its rightful place to the body by valuing the embodied existence. The second essay by Keith D'Souza tilted "Liberating the Body: Mythonomologic Resources" discusses three resources, viz., mythos, nomos and logos, to liberate the body from an oppressive understanding of the body. The third essay titled "Humans as Bodily: A Phenomenological Probe" by Johnson Puthenpurackal argues that from the phenomenological perspective, the body is an essential dimension of being human and he offers reasons for his position through an in-depth discussion on the three concrete manifestations of bodiliness: laborality, linguisticality and sexuality. Felix Fernandes, the author of the fourth essay titled "Body, Desire and Insatiability" elaborates Levinas' phenomenological notion of the 'face' to affirm that the other remains elusive and insatiable. The fifth paper titled "Body, Gaze, Shame and Counter-Gaze" authored by Victor Ferrao is a philosophical attempt to point out the crippling effects of Gaze on the body and the relational dynamism between Gaze and Shame on the one hand, and between Shame and Counter-Gaze on the other, through a meticulous analysis of the works of Derrida, Lacan, Foucault and Deluze. The final essay on Part I by Gregory Mathew Malayil titled "Body and Consciousness: From Somatic Correlates to Causes," through a detailed study of Merleau-Ponty's concept of somatic consciousness offers a valuable insight that the functions of consciousness are possible only with the body as a medium.

Six research papers dwell on the social, political and gender issues in philosophizing the body, which form the second part of this work. The first essay "Body, Bio-politics and Bioethics" by S. Sekar Sebastin offers a general overview on the issues of bio-politics and bioethics related to the body and in particular puts forward the idea of how the body is "othered" with the help of Foucault's analysis. The author of the second paper, James D. Chellappa, in his essay "Caste, Race, Colour and Body" offers a critique of the Indian society in which the impact of caste and colour has led to a reductionist view of the human body. In his essay "Humans for Sale," the author Ashley Miranda laments how in contemporary times, human bodies are objectified, commodified and reified and calls for an ethical engagement to retrieve the intrinsic worth of human beings. The next three essays focus on gender issues. Dolreich Pereira in his essay "A Medieval Perspective on the Body," through a careful analysis of question 92 on the sexual difference in Summa Theologiae of Thomas Aquinas tries to show that Aquinas, far from being a misogynist was in fact a feminist of his times since he had affirmed gender equality in many subtle ways. Challenging patriarchal perspectives, Gayatri Mendanha in her essay "In Search of Woman: Re-making Ourselves" with the help of Women thinkers Simone de Beauvoir, Judith Butler and Toril Moi offers a philosophical basis to probe into the ideas of gender, sex and body and explores the possibilities and challenges that lie in re-making ourselves differently. In his essay titled "Body, Gender and Sexuality in Family," A. Pushparajan, taking insights from Gandhian philosophy, puts forward an integral approach to the body, gender and sexuality in order to provide a strong base for family life.

The third part contains three essays. Stephen Jayard in his essay "Is Body Merely Bodily?" offers reflections on the body discussing issues in bio and medical sciences and arrives at the conclusion that human body is not just 'bodily,' but an essential combination of both 'bodily' and 'something more.' The essay "Redesigning the Human Body in Science and Technology" penned by Noel D'Costa highlights that the blurred distinction between biology and technology calls for a renewed understanding of the body. Francis Arackal, the author of "Body in Media: Organs without Body," exposes the attempts of the media to set unrealistic beauty standards that are often counterproductive and invites us to counter the beauty standards propagated by the media.

The final part of this work explores the spiritual dimension of the body. Thus the essay of Kuruvilla Pandikattu titled "The Body of the Earthlings in *Laudato Si*'" looks at the "precious and precarious" nature of human body and pleads for a "re-membering" of the earthlings. In his essay "Fasting and Feasting: Differing Philosophies of the Body," George Karuvelil not only presents the immense spiritual and physical benefits of fasting in religious traditions, but also outlines a mystical view of the body. John Peter Vallabadoss, in his essay, "Body, Suffering, Death and Afterlife," analyses the meaning of the human quest for understanding life in the body with suffering and death.

Kurian Alumkal, in his essay "Buddhist Concept of the Body," with the help of Śāntideva's *Bodhicāryāvatāra* brings out the insight of Mahayana Buddhism on the body as *upāya* or the expedient means to liberation. The essay titled "Body in Saiva Siddhanta" by Andrew Anbarasu offers a positive approach towards the body as put forward by the tradition of Saiva Siddhanta. The final essay "A Meditative Reflection on the Human Body" authored by James Purathail makes a meditative journey through the reflections on the human body to bring out a positive and spiritual dimension of our bodily existence.

This collection of essays presents in a single volume various approaches and perspectives towards philosophizing the body, each perspective valid in its own terms but not exhaustive or categorical. These multiple complementing and at times conflicting perspectives and approaches only point out to the richness of the philosophical discussion that this topic calls for. No attempt is made to homogenize to offer a single philosophy, but instead possible ways of philosophizing the body from different perspectives, and this open-ended approach is inevitable in our contemporary times where we learn to celebrate difference and embrace heterogeneity. This work reflects novel insights into philosophizing the body. I wish to thank all the contributors for their commitment to be precise and scientific in drafting the final version and meeting the deadline in spite of their various academic commitments. A word of thanks is also due to all the governing body members of ACPI for having confided in me this pleasant task of editing this work. I am hopeful that it will be a valuable resource for any further research with regard to philosophizing the body.

Nishant Alphonse Irudayadason
Jnana-Deepa Vidyapeeth
Pune 411014

ACPI is grateful to "Missionswissenschasftliches Institut Missio, Aachen, Germany," for having empowered it with financial help for printing the first six ACPI books. This initial support has enabled ACPI to go ahead with the publication of its later books. The present volume (ACPI annual series 17) is the eleventh of this kind.

Series Editors
ACPI Annual Series

Contents

Part 1

Phenomenological and Existential Perspectives

1

Modernity and Exile of the Body

Nishant Alphonse Irudayadason
Jnana-Deepa Vidyapeeth, Pune

Abstract: This article tries to outline how Descartes, the father of Modern philosophy due to his obsession with clear and distinct ideas has paved the way for the body to be excluded from the philosophical discourse. The post-Cartesian philosophers till the end of the nineteenth century have followed the Cartesian legacy and have disembodied the self. This article traces a route into thinking about the body since the advent of Modernity with Descartes until the approach of body experience in science. This essay dwells in-depth on the Cartesian philosophy in the first part, to show in clear terms as to how the rationalism of Descartes was instrumental for the exile of the body. In the second part, attempts are made to show that this thinking is often defiant of the corporal condition which is critiqued by some phenomenologists who also invite a renewed understanding of embodied existence.

Keywords: cogito, rationalism, phenomenology, embodiment, embodied existence, knowledge, thought, sense experience.

Introduction

Every utterance about the self formulates an interpretation explicit or implicit about embodied life. This expression, embodied life, drafts a meaning which according to some is ambivalent or even ambiguous: Does the embodiment refer to a locus of a soul or spirit in flesh? Every discourse on the human person, whether in art, science, philosophy or theology, struggles with this concept of embodiment. Wanting to write the history of embodied life is a project doomed to be a failure. The story, moving from the body-prison of some Greek or religious thinkers to the "body am I" affirmed by Nietzsche's Zarathustra, resists any writing. This tenacity shows a non-controllable and an elusive part of the very flesh of the human being.

Is the body only a vain garment for a hidden identity or is it the whole of the human being? Does the bodily dimension have anything to do with what it means to be human? Many, who have given a negative response to this question, hold that the body emerges from folly. Should we "avoid, so far as possible, intercourse and communion with the body, except what is absolutely necessary, and are not filled with its nature, but keep ourselves pure from it" as suggested by Plato (Phaedo, 67a)?

At the end of the nineteenth century Nietzsche vehemently denounced the despisers of the body: it is a great reason, "der Leib ist eine große Vernunft" it is the very self of which the human person takes pride.[1] At the end of the century, new protagonists, most frequently scientists, inscribed the "I" or that which we dare call our identity. We also know the current ethical debates about genetic manipulation; do we not consider such experiments as jeopardizing what is essentially human? All these approaches suggest that we cannot imagine or understand the human person without his/her body. But simultaneously a deep resistance and an ineradicable denial of reducing the human person to a body wells up within us. The return to the hinterland is now forbidden and the gateways to the old metaphysics are forever lost. For many the prefix "meta" is henceforth crossed out from the vocabulary and what remains in only the physical. The materialist monism has succeeded the old pre-modern dualism.

Among the protagonists of this movement, there was Descartes (1596-1650) who occupied a strange position. By asking us to doubt everything, he initiated the rout of traditional metaphysics. His detractors would willingly parody the words of Gavroche, a character in Hugo's *Les Miserables*, singing "This is the Descartes fault," after that of Voltaire and Rousseau. In their eyes, Descartes is the villain who, by taking the mind and body for two things (res) radically distinct, has led us to many difficulties. He is held responsible for the impasses of contemporary philosophy about the carnal condition of the human being; problems of neuroscience and cognitive science to describe the production of thought by the brain; and again the diverse socio-cultural contempt of the body. François Guery writes with humour: "In fact, everyone is against Descartes... Heidegger's *Being and Time*, in 1927, was already a declaration of war against Descartes and his 'substances.'"[2] We can multiply almost infinitely the quotes reproducing sarcasm whose object is the author of *Meditations*. This public knowledge makes Descartes inevitable in any research about the embodied life.

Descartes' Distrust of the Body

Let us recall a famous passage from Descartes' *Meditations* published in 1641 in which Descartes presents his dualistic view which will later be severely criticized:

> I rightly conclude that my essence consists solely in the fact that I am a thinking thing [or a substance whose whole essence or nature is to think]. And although possibly (or rather certainly, as I shall say in a moment) I possess a body with which I am very intimately conjoined, yet because, on the one side, I have a clear and distinct idea of myself inasmuch as I am only a thinking and unextended thing, and as, on the other, I possess a distinct idea of body, inasmuch as it is only an extended and unthinking thing, it is certain that this I [that is to say, my soul by which I am what I am], is entirely and absolutely distinct from my body, and can exist without it.[3]

Much has been written on this text and other similar texts. It is not necessary here to make the exegesis or to summon advocates and opponents. It is sufficient to note that with these lines Descartes broke from a secular tradition: he accorded to the soul the privilege to signify the human being and henceforward to entrust him to thought. The soul is no longer responsible to animate the body which functions on the model of mechanics well admired by Descartes.[4] But this well perfected machine does not bear the specificity of the human person. For proof, it is enough to quote Descartes from the Second meditation: "Thought and thought alone cannot be taken away from me... I am therefore not admitting that I am anything at all other than a thinking thing-that is, a mind, soul, understanding, or reason (terms whose meaning I did not previously know)... I'm not the collection of organs called a human body." The human body is *res extensa*, object, matter, form, extended, etc. that only reason can know clearly and distinctly. The subject is essentially defined by thought: there is identity between me and my thought. The immaterial *res cogitans* can accomplish what the body is incapable of, that is to grasp every form and every dimension. We understand to what extent of insignificance the human body has been reduced. The Cogito Sum unambiguously affirms that personal identity is not related to corporeality. The Cartesian body becomes an object: It is what we have, not what we are. We can better understand the intensity of Nietzsche's proclamation of the body as a great reason. It is therefore instructive to examine the motivations or reasons that led Descartes to formulate this radical dualism. This interrogation will capture what becomes of the body in this dualism and to measure the permanence of this vision of the body until now. This critical effort will open pathways to a renewed understanding of embodied life.

What has led Descartes to distinguish so vigorously body from mind? His ambition was to provide an independent basis for undeniable knowledge. This desire was driven by a vivid awareness of some of the implications of the scientific discoveries of his time. Astronomical Research in particular had revealed to Descartes that the bodily senses are misleading. Everyday trivial experiences can testify to this. We read the following in his *Discourse on Method*: "After all, it is possible I may be mistaken; and it is but a little copper and glass, perhaps, that I take for gold and diamonds."[5] But above all the body does not feel the motion of the earth and induces us to judge that the sun rises and sets. Still again it makes us admit that the sun has the grandness perceived by our eye.[6] What many have called the Cartesian contempt of the body is a result of taking seriously a devastating experience: the world is not such as the body makes us see or feel. This revelation is essential to the development of Cartesian metaphysics. An important lesson that Descartes draws from this is the obligation to be wary of what is given to us by the senses. Renouncing the scholastic maxim that "there is nothing in the understanding which has not first been in the senses,"[7] he agrees resolutely to doubt all knowledge that would not have reason as its foundation. "Whatever I have so far accepted as supremely true, I have learned either from the senses or through the senses. But I have occasionally caught the senses deceiving me, and it's prudent never completely to trust those who have cheated us even once."[8] Descartes emphatically underlines indeed that "many experiences gradually destroyed all the faith that I had in my senses."[9] In Descartes lies a real master of suspicion demanding a permanent distrust of the senses, body and beliefs. This disintegration of trust goads him throughout his writings into a search for truth in the sciences. Methodic doubt becomes indispensable in the path towards clear and distinct knowledge and to the evidence of reason is given the role of firm foundation of all knowledge as is the case in mathematics and geometry. The Cartesian body, therefore, is not only an object, but also an object of distrust. It is no longer an intermediary between the world and the subject. The knowing subject truly knows the real only through his/her faculty of judgment insofar as the bodily senses continually risk to submit him/her to error.[10] The mind alone is capable of an indubitable knowledge of reality while the material body is an object of knowledge. The body is the other vis-à-vis the knowing subject, but as it is a source of confusion and illusion, it is a threatening other and more alienation of the knowing subject reveals that otherness. This Otherness, in clear and distinct knowledge, is to be constantly reduced to an object and submit itself to the "master and owner" according to a famous phrase of Descartes.

And because the most certain knowledge for the author of the *Meditations* is one developed by the mathematical-geometric sciences, mechanics is the heuristic paradigm of experimentation and explanation of bodily experience. Descartes considers the body to be the most advanced machine.[11] However, his wonder is not without terminals: he regrets the inaccuracy of the body compared to the clock, for example, "which is made up of only wheels and springs, can count the hours and measure time more exactly than we can with all our art."[12] Again, this assimilation of the body to the machine reiterates the distrust of the body. This body mistaken for a machine also announces the modern biological and cognitive sciences or sometimes surprising explorations of psychosomatic experience: the current molecular biology knows the body now as inaccessible to the senses and the science called artificial intelligence works for constituting a mind freed from the support of a living body. Others prefer a mind that can override the body and hope for its perfection through the transgenic. We remain the embarrassed heirs of Descartes. Is it not Descartes who opened the way for the autonomy of reason, inaugurated modernity, "and resolved no longer to seek any other science than the knowledge of myself?"[13]

However, we must agree that the Cartesian conquest of self and subjectivity is accomplished at the cost of exiling the body, flesh and sense experience. The transformation or reduction of the living body into an object with extension or graspable form paradoxically signals the loss of the body: it disappears, vanishes in this seizure. Identified substantially and completely to its thought the self is disembodied. What is the impact of this disembodiment? It is both the annihilation of a relationship of trust and the refutation of otherness. Descartes' ambition to arrive at a firm foundation of knowledge has necessitated, as we have seen, in a detour through mistrust and transformation of the real, of what is different, starting from the body, into a manageable object. The embodiment is the encounter with the unsurpassable otherness of tangibility itself in a permanent tension, irreducible between distrust and trust. From this perspective, the body is not insignificant in the project of becoming and to be oneself. Admitting the relevance of the flesh is the challenge in understanding who we are. We will address this challenge by contesting the Cartesian heritage.

The Exiled Body

Despite the constant discomfort caused by his dualism, Descartes entices us: the cogito, the guarantor of self-certainty, includes a pretention almost of an unlimited knowledge; the cogito is as the foundation of all proofs, even that of God. We are all his legatees. But which itinerary shall we follow? Marc Richir, a contemporary French phenomenologist in a short essay entitled *Le corps*, works out a trajectory linking Plato, Aristotle, the Stoics, Epicureans, underscoring the essential place of Christian thought in the West and ending with Descartes, Nietzsche and Husserl's phenomenology. Throughout this journey, Richir, attentive to questions that do not deplete the corporal condition, is guided by the conviction that philosophical effort has tirelessly meant an excess of body, frequently hypostatizing this supplement in a soul or in a separate entity.[14] Fontaine suggests with regard to the thinking of the body a circuit inaugurated by Descartes, continued by Kant (1724-1804) and Maine de Biran (1766-1824), before Henri Bergson (1859-1941), Jean-Paul Sartre (1905-1980) and Maurice Merleau-Ponty (1908-1961) arrive on the scene.

What do we learn from this post-Cartesian philosophical storyline? It is easy to see that in the 18th and 19th centuries, the discourse on somatic modality became shipshape. The sovereignty granted to reason has led to a quasi-silence, as if the question of the body was settled once and for all. Thus, although Kant had deconstructed Cartesian metaphysics, he nevertheless radicalized the gap between soul and body. Descartes used with great caution the metaphor of the soul "lodged in the human body exactly like a pilot in a ship."[15] For Kant, the problem of localization is now gone out. Fontaine wrote that the question of the body as "seat of the soul" not only makes no sense, but is even self-contradictory. The experience of the subject in his/her embodied condition is a construct, an elaborate representation. The self is a representation accomplished by the "I think." The Kantianism deepens the Cartesian deprivation of the body. Despite the revalorization of the senses, the cogito is disjoint from its carnal modality. Reason must distance itself from all givenness of individualization of which the body is a part. This is what is strongly evidenced by Durkheim a century later. He writes:

> For [Kant], the keystone of the personality is the will. The will is the faculty of acting in conformity with reason, and reason is that which is most impersonal in us. For reason is not my reason; it is human reason in general. It is the power the mind has to rise above the particular, the contingent, the individual, to think under the form of the universal. So, it can be said from this point of view that what makes a man a person is that whereby he is identical with other men, that which makes him a man, and not a certain man. The senses, the body, in a word everything that individualizes is on the contrary considered by Kant as the antagonist of the personality.[16]

This interpretation of Kantianism illustrates the gap between mind and body. Personal identity is totally delinked from corporeality; becoming human requires the overcoming of the body. Even more, to be oneself is equated with the impersonal of reason.

In the context of the rationalism and idealism of the nineteenth century, the reflection of Maine de Biran on the body does not fail to surprise us. This context also explains as to why little attention is given to his work. His philosophy seeks to anchor the cogito in the body. Valorising the living experience of an immediate test of the self in action, Maine de Biran notes that to be active is the irreducibility of the self. He refuses to delink the "I think" from the "I can" inscribed in the body. These intuitions will only appear through the recent work of phenomenology of the body.[17]

The Rediscovered Body

The 20th century seems to have reinstated the exiled body in intellectual discourses of the West, in particular in the Phenomenology initiated by Husserl. The stage for this breakthrough has been prepared by many thinkers including Darwin, Freud, Nietzsche and Marx. The rediscovery of the body is remarkable in contemporary culture, science and phenomenological investigations initiated by Husserl. We shall briefly look at the content and the ambiguity of this new attention given to the somatic mode in the works of phenomenologists and the distance it has maintained vis-à-vis the Cartesian thought.

Phenomenology, from the work of Husserl onwards, has been confronted with the issue of the corporal dimension of the human person. Many analyses have been devoted to it. It is enough to mention a few major works along these lines in the continental tradition such as *Being and Nothingness* by Jean-Paul Sartre, *Phenomenology of Perception* by Maurice Merleau-Ponty, *Philosophy and Phenomenology of the Body* by Michel Henry, *Philosophie du corps* (*Philosophy of the Body*) by Claude Bruaire and *Freedom and Nature: The Voluntary and the Involuntary* by Paul Ricœur. These researches patiently pick up and explore the challenges posed by somatic existence: is the body what we have or what we are? Following the semantic distinction made in German between *der Körper* and *des Leib*, these authors have proposed various names more or less conformed to the referred reality: body-subject and body-subject, own body, living body, psychic body, flesh, etc. Attempting a synthesis of interpretations of carnal experience in these works would be pretentious. Their diversity shows the inexhaustible semantic wealth and irreducibility of the embodied life. This impossible reduction is already amply clear in the ambivalence of 'having' and 'being' offered by the somatic condition. Ricœur sums this up when he writes: "two language games are no longer juxtaposed but superimposed, following the relation that prevails between the concept of person and that of body and which makes us say that persons are bodies as well."[18] We can still aggravate this ambiguity by stating that the body is also what we have: it is that by which we act and we are. These phenomenological approaches to the body happily propose ways to resist the various occlusions for which the body is the object of thought. They also allow us to face the disembodiment of the human person and the distrust of his/her personal relationship with the world without returning to the old metaphysics.

Endeavoring to explore and describe the living experience, phenomenology deploys this openness to the same carnal structure in the living human person. Through sensation, affection, affectivity, passion and thought, the lived body is constantly on its way to otherness. Already in feeling and in perception is manifested, "the tendency of the body to disappear in things;"[19] through sight, hearing, touch, etc., the body, in the words of Marc Richir, is in excess of itself. In its ability to be affected, it deepens the breach towards the other than itself: it not only discovers the sensible (hot-cold, hard-soft, etc.), it also experiences pleasure, displeasure, pain, etc. and vibrates to the various aspects of the world (it is bright or dark, or surprising or dull, etc.). The subject lives in coincidence with his/her body; in it he/she expresses his/her relationship to the world: he/she blushes, trembles, turns pale, etc. Passion, another modality of this openness to otherness, despite me, makes me fully corporal: it is then what possesses me or what I am in my inability to take distance with respect to what seduces me, calls me outside of me: am I then a prisoner of the exciting object or carnal instinct?

Together with thought, the body dramatically attests its escape towards the other than oneself: it "spiritualizes" itself. Thought takes us to the immaterial and the incorporeal, giving rise to the dualities of body-soul and material-spiritual, in which humans try to hold on often lopsidedly to their roots in the flesh and the impossibility of exhausting them totally. But while claiming to live a life dispensed from the body, thought bears the scars of its anchorage in the body: it wants to see clearly, to conceive and envisage; it retains the marks of this body, it inhabits in as much as it makes the body its home to exist in the world, in the not-self. The human body becomes the self in its openness to what it is not; it is even able to give rise to thought, thus engendering the other.

In its various modalities of orientation towards otherness, in this excess of itself, the body gives witness to what characterizes it in the heart of the living. Phenomenology encounters here a fundamental intuition of cultural anthropology. The human person in his somatic condition distinguishes himself/herself from the entire living world by his/her indeterminacy: he/she is an "imperfect" being, that is to say, he/she is not rigidly adapted to a specific environment; he/she is made in his/her very flesh for a relationship of infinite openness to the world.[20] Unlike animals determined in their responses, adjusted perfectly to their environment, to their biotope, the embodied human person faces the constant challenge of creating a world that is habitable. The invention of tools, transmission through learning, establishment of mediation and traditions through language, a common life regulated by laws, etc., testify this ongoing creative work required by his/her exceptional situation of embodiment in the living universe.

The German philosopher and anthropologist Helmuth Plessner makes a similar interpretation on the specificity of the embodied life of the human person. Animals reacting to environmental queries in a preprogrammed manner are in a quasi-unchangeable concentric position related to their adherence to the biological role that has been set for them once for all. The human person, on the contrary, in his/her relation to his/her body, is in an eccentric position: unconstrained in his/her responses, he deals with the world and with his/her corporal conditions of reciprocal relationships.[21] The human person is not centred on himself/herself; he/she does not definitely hold all solutions to the demands from outside. This incompetence, ignorance of the human person is intrinsically linked to his carnal existence; it leads him/her constantly outside of himself to go towards the self. In this reciprocity, he/she is his/her body in his/her original way to own it in the mode of reception responsible for his/her possibilities as well as for his/her somatic limitations. The coincidence with oneself is not given in the doubting and disembodied cogito; it happens in openness to otherness inscribed in one's corporeality. The body is the primary figure of this breach to the other insofar as I am because there is this other: for the other, am I not always my body?; in my actions, does not my body keep its powers at my disposal?; through its limitations and also through its forms of expression such as laughing and crying, for example, does not my body have power over me and to which I can also give myself?

Conclusion

The body highlighted in the contemporary period often conceals a Cartesian distrust of it; it is an object that must be mastered and owned. Phenomenology develops a different perspective. It outlines a secret link of trust experienced at the flesh itself. Helmuth Plessner explicitly names this link: "Knowing to speak, act, and create: this not only means having certain organs, but also mastering a sense, and trusting this power."[22] This trust is not intended to control or to transcend the bodily condition. On the contrary, it is in this trust that we live. Clinical observation of children emotionally deprived (isolated children, those born of incest, those deprived of mother, those placed care institutions, etc.) revealed that they do not secrete growth hormones in such situations. Placed with foster families where they can extract the emotional nourishment they need to grow, they begin to secrete growth hormones, in the very evening of their arrival in the host family. We are at the very elementary and fundamental level the development of the human being. Regardless of culture, a child needs affective nourishment to express its genetic program.[23]

This example highlights the unsurpassable roots of every spiritual experience in the somatic condition. The self is not a purified consciousness disconnected from the flesh. It is not exhausted by an indubitable knowledge. The advent of the self happens in the trust of the one who invites it to become true in its corporal condition. This trust, which need not be hypostatized in a soul, is affirmative both of the impossible control and of the impossible reduction of the body, and signals towards an embodied freedom.

Notes

1 Here, we may recall some lines of his speech: "Body am whole, and nothing else, and soul is only a word for something in the body. The body is a great reason, a plurality with one sense, a war and a peace, a herd and a pastor. Instrument of your body is also your little reason, my brother, whom you call "spirit," little instrument and toy of your great reason."

2 François Guery, "The word of Descartes: Master and owner ...," *Magazine Literary* 342 (1996): 34f.

3 René Descartes, *Meditations*, Sixth Meditation.

4 See René Descartes, *Discourse on Method*, Part V.

5 Descartes, *Discourse*, Part I.

6 See Descartes, *Discourse*, Part IV.

7 Ibid.

8 Descartes, *Meditations*, First Meditation.

9 Descartes, *Meditations*, Sixth Meditation.

10 See Descartes, *Meditations*, Third Meditation.

11 See Descartes, *Discourse*, Part V.

12 Descartes, *Discourse*, Part V.

13 Descartes, *Discourse*, Part I.

14 See Mark Richir, *Le corps* (Paris : Hatier, 1993), 77.

15 Descartes, *Discourse*, Part V.

16 Emile Durkheim, *Elementary Forms of the Religious Life* (New York: The New Press, 1995), 306.

17 The thought of Maine de Biran was later developed by the French phenomenologist Michel Henry.

18 Paul Ricœur, *Oneself as Another*, trans. Kathleen Blamey (Chicago: The University of Chicago Press, 1992), 66.

19 Richir, *Le corps*, 10 (translation mine).

20 See Franck Tinland, *La difference anthropologique: Essai sur les rapports de la Nature et de l'Artifice* (Paris: Aubier-Montaigne, 1977), 72 and 124.

21 See Helmuth Plessner, *Laughing and Crying: A Study of the Limits of Human Behavior* (Evanston: Northwestern University Press, 1970), 38. On page 36, he writes: "The human position appears as an eccentric position. Just as the world and my own body are revealed to me and leave me in control insofar as they enter into a relationship with me as a center, they retain, on the other side, their supremacy over their inclusion in this perspective, because they are a different order and include me in reciprocal relations."

22 Helmuth Plessner, *Laughing and Crying: A Study of the Limits of Human Behavior* (Evanston: Northwestern University Press, 1970), 210.

23 See Boris Cyrulnik, *De la parole comme d'une molecule* (Paris: Seuil, 1995), 43 and 47.

2

Liberating the Body
Mythonomologic Resources

Keith D'Souza
St. Pius X College, Mumbai

Abstract: The human body is a complex text understood via the means of differing interpretive frameworks. While there are many interpretive aspects of embodied life that are cause for cultural and personal celebration, there are also many aspects that are the cause for severe cultural and personal wounds. It is both possible and necessary to heal many of these socially constructed, interpretive wounds of the body. The second part of the essay attempts to redress these wounds with the help of various resources: mythic, nomic and logic. Mythos-based resources may be found within various scriptures, foundational texts and cultural traditions. Nomos-based resources are found in healthy socio-political structures and practices, and legal frameworks. Logos-based resources rely on the use of communicative, explanatory and critical processes to negotiate between rival interpretive positions. These three resources need to be used creatively, critically and productively in order to mitigate the many forms of oppressive interpretations governing the body.

Keywords: mythos, logos, nomos, mythonomologic, liberation.

The Body as Blessing and Curse

The body may be interpreted as blessing, curse or a myriad other estimations within these two extremes. The body may be interpreted as blessing when it is recognized or celebrated as the site of joy, pleasure, or any experience of human wellbeing. The body may be interpreted as curse on account of its physical limitations and ailments, and whenever it is experienced as the site of pain, shame, unhealthy guilt and powerlessness.

The Body as Beauty and Blessing

What is singularly distinct of the human species is the power to create vastly divergent conditions which prevail over the satisfaction of both primary and complex personal and social needs. Human beings are highly creative when it comes to even basic drives such as eating and drinking. There are an enormously wide variety of recipes the world over which governs the process of ingestion. The material intake of the goods of the earth has become a fine art, especially for those who can afford to indulge in such pleasures. At the level of clothing too, there seems to be no limit to the variety of styles which govern the simple act of sheathing one's skin. Body accessories too are in abundance, such as rings (finger, ear, nose, toe and other places), bangles, bracelets, chains, *mangalsutras*, *bindis*, tattoos, wigs, perfumes, deodorants, etc. The human homestead – primarily intended to provide protection from the environment and physical security – could range from a frugal hut to an opulent palace.

Beyond the satisfaction of these simple needs of food, clothing and shelter, the human body finds expression in various creative forms. These include athletics and games, which demonstrate bodily prowess or agility; song, which uplifts the human spirit; dance, which manifests grace and dexterity; and drama, which reveals various emotions in mime and narrative.

From all of the above, it can be seen that the nature and aptitude of the five senses are all put to good use – for survival or satisfaction. However, the body and its senses are also a necessary entry point and vehicle for human knowledge in general. This is because the human person is best understood to be an 'embodied spirit' – a belief which finds erudite and systematic articulation in the writings of Thomas Aquinas, inspired by the anthropological presuppositions of Aristotle and the Semitic presuppositions inscribed in the Scriptures. The Cartesian forgetfulness of the body has been rather short lived, and today feminist writers – among others – accentuate this point in a radical manner, indicating how differently gendered bodies process knowledge differently[1] – a claim which may be extended to include other biological differentials such as race, age, physical disability, etc.

The Christian tradition too, in different ways, lays emphasis on the body as something beautiful and blessed. To begin with, the Incarnation stresses the bodily aspect of the divinity of Christ – a notion which has been traditionally accepted, albeit using technical Greek philosophical categories, in the first centuries of the Christian tradition. Because, salvation has an "already, but not yet" flavour to it, the bodily aspect of human development is an important feature of wholesome wellbeing. This concern for bodily wellbeing has had an impact on the social manifestation of ecclesial faith, facilitating care for the hungry, sick, naked, homeless, and the "poor" in general – a signifier for those who in many ways are vulnerable, dispossessed or marginalized. Finally, Christians do not believe in the resurrection of the soul but instead the "resurrection of the body," further indicating the significance of embodiment, in time and eternity.

The Body as Lack or Curse

Whenever the body is experienced as a site of inconvenience, pain, shame, guilt and powerlessness, what is experienced is some form of lack or curse. The satisfaction of basic desires related to food, clothing and shelter for all human beings seems a distant possibility. A huge mass of humanity still struggles with one or other of these bodily dimensions of human life. Besides these limitations, hardly anyone can totally avoid falling physically sick, while many suffer from some form of physical addiction or substance abuse or the other. No one can avoid the process of ageing – though contemporary technology seems to invest a considerable energy in prolonging life and even promising extreme forms of longevity.

What is far more vexing than these physical limitations of the body, however, are many oppressive social forces which cause horrendous and often untold suffering. The cosmetic and medical industries are never short of a market on account of largely artificially induced needs that are created, mostly based on a psychology of shame and fear, respectively. The need to dress up appropriately – and fashionably – may also be a manipulative mechanism, as it creates a false need of social approval, and in some cases, the need to parade one's beauty in an exhibitionist manner. Here gender discrimination also rears its ugly head, as more expectations related to beauty are imposed upon women – though, not surprisingly, in the animal kingdom, the 'law of attraction' is reversed, as the males of most other animal species need to be better looking that their female counterparts.

The process of 'othering' is another way of inducing bodily-related shame. In the words of Sherry Shapiro, "Body in all its materiality is socially marked and identified as black, woman, handicapped, old, lower class, fat – as the language of "other." The first clue to identity is the skin you wear."[2] The "skin you wear" was the apparent basis of the *varna* system, which underlies the caste – or more appropriately, the *jati* – system, in India.[3] Kancha Ilaiah vividly describes the repugnant nature of caste differentiation in the following anecdote, remembered from his childhood:

> Surprisingly, whenever a Goudaa friend came to my house he would eat with us, but sit slightly apart; when we went to Kaapu homes their parents would give us food but make us sit a little distance

> away. While eating we were not supposed to touch each other. But later we could play together and drink together from the rivers and streams. If we had carried our mid-day food to the cattle field, we sometimes attempted to touch each other's food, but suddenly the rules that our parents had fixed would make their appearance: we would speak insultingly of each other's castes and revert to eating separately. Within moments, however, we were together again.[4]

This process of shaming and guilt inducing – sometimes reinforced by much more horrifying and degrading narratives – between the castes has been carried on in India for millennia, and in various forms of discrimination in other parts of the world. In many cases, it has obtained the blessings of religious sanction, but otherwise cultural and political interests have served to retain these gross prejudices.

Perhaps worse than the more subtle violence undergone because of caste and similar mechanisms of social degradation is the powerlessness brought about in various situations of bodily victimization and torture, such as corporal punishment in schools and homes, molestation and rape as a form of pleasure or power, unjust incarceration and violence in prisons, etc.

Shame and unhealthy guilt are especially prevalent in the area of sexuality. Human history has borne witness to innumerable sexual taboos – some of which are justifiable and some unnecessarily imposed. The sexual liberation movements in Western society – now reaching significant proportions in India as well – are a rejection and a reaction to repressive – rather than integrative – mechanisms employed in these societies. The internet today has led to an explosion of voyeurism, not only, but perhaps to a large extent, due to the repressive forces that most societies have chosen to adopt regarding the potent, and often frightening phenomenon of sexual power. However, modernity seems to have enabled communities to move from repression to permissiveness – both extremes that are personally and socially dysfunctional.

Emancipatory Possibilities

Having presented some of the *challenges* concerning the interpretation of the body in the last sub-section, we now explore *opportunities* for more positive and productive interpretations. What are the various resources one may tap in order to employ "emancipatory possibilities of resistance, as a tool and a strategy?"[5] I propose the neologism "mythonomologism" as a framework containing primary sites from which interpretive strategies may be sourced. *Mythonomologism* shares a family resemblance with Panikkar's "cosmotheandrism," as both of these entail three different, discrete, but nevertheless intertwined domains: hermeneutical in the case of *mythonomologism* and ontological in the case of cosmotheandrism.

Mythos-based resources may be found within foundational texts of communities and cultural traditions. Nomos-based resources are located in healthy social frameworks and practices. Logos-based resources rely on the use of communicative, explanatory and critical processes to negotiate between rival interpretive strategies. Mythos has to do with *purpose* and *passion*, nomos with *praxis* and the *polis* and logos with *principle* and *process*. Mythos is the realm of the cultural *projection* of presuppositions, which taken together, often constitute an operative cultural paradigm. Nomos is the field of socio-political *construction*, giving rise to productive and stabilizing social processes.[6] Logos is the sphere of reflection and communication, leading to requisite *deconstruction* and *reconstruction* of the lifeworld and social practices, giving rise to new and refined presuppositions. Given the four major hermeneutical concerns of understanding, explanation, critique and application, mythos would best correspond to 'understanding,' nomos to 'application' and logos to 'explanation' and 'critique.'

Any recourse – ideological or otherwise – to only one or two of these resources may not be adequate to deal with oppressive interpretations and actions associated with the body. Such limited strategies find themselves often rejected by those who favour other dimensions of the hermeneutical triad. Besides this, a sole focus on each of these dimensions may turn out to be rigid and counter-productive, leading to severe social problems. Mythos-limited thinking may lead to various forms of fundamentalism. Nomos-restricted thinking may lead to "bureaucratization" and a resultant system of impersonal relations, as feared by Max Weber,[7] and what Habermas calls "the colonization of the lifeworld"[8] and "systemically induced lifeworld pathologies."[9] Finally, postmodern thought and feminist critique have alerted us to the limitations and aberrations of "logocentrism." For positive change to materialize, interplay between these three dimensions of human consciousness is imperative. Such interplay may take place at a personal level, or within a community, or between persons and communities.

The "Golden Rule" straddles all of these types of discourse: mythic, nomic and logic, and is a reliable functional standard or norm by which one may judge the nature and extent of liberative concerns to be employed in the realm of body interpretation. This rule – called "Golden," because of its ubiquitous presence in various religious and cultural traditions – has both positive (obligatory) and negative (interdictory) formulations, e.g., "treat others as you would like them to treat you" (Lk. 6:31), and Hillel's "do not do unto your neighbour what you would hate him to do to you" (Babylonian Talmud, *Sabbath*, 31a). Paul Ricœur argues for its adoption as a comprehensive deontological standard, especially as it allows for affective dimensions and contextual considerations related to practical action, unlike other formulations of right-based moral reflection.[10]

Mythos-based Resources

Human beings are not just rational animals, but more so, social and emotional animals. These social and affective dimensions of humankind are most often influenced by traditional ways of thinking, behaving and relating. Religion and culture are two of the most powerful social forces that provide inspiration, direction and purpose to individuals and communities.

There are numerous foundational texts and practices within different religions and cultures which give meaning and purpose to their adherents across time and space. It is important to locate specific texts and traditional practices within each religion and culture which may feature liberating interpretations related to the body. In what follows, I shall mainly focus on Christian foundational narratives – which are heavily indebted to, and in continuity with Jewish foundational narratives – in order to indicate instances of salubrious interpretations of how the body may be estimated.

To begin with, the Exodus towards the Promised Land – as registered in the *Tanakh* and commemorated generations later – was a turning and defining point for the Jewish community. The Exodus was primarily liberation from the slavery of bonded labour.[11] For Christians, however, the 'Promised Land' is more transcendent, based on the foundational experience of the Resurrection of Jesus. This too was understood as a liberating action – a freedom from the limitedness of death, leading not towards a spatio-temporal blessing, but one valued even more so: an eternal blessing in Paradise, where one is born again, not as a resurrected soul, but a "resurrected body."

On the negative side of body interpretation, one of the most controversial issues which stem from mythic resources is that of "purity laws" – a problematic theme even in contemporary India, featuring various restrictions and bans on what one eats, how one behaves and what one produces aesthetically. It is both possible and necessary to take recourse to equally strong examples in religious and cultural traditions that demonstrate liberating mind-sets with regard to many of these purity issues. For example, there are numerous instances in the Gospels where Jesus had to defend the violation of perceived purity laws before the religious authorities of his time. His strong condemnation of ritual purity (e.g., Mk. 7:1-22) demonstrated a revaluation of these laws in terms of an interiorization of spirituality. On account of his "table-fellowship" and his liberal attitude towards food and drink, he was called a "glutton and a drunkard," and one who eats with "tax collectors and sinners" (Mt. 11:19; Lk. 7:34). Jesus nevertheless demonstrated a relatively broadminded attitude with regard to these two purity considerations, namely, what he consumed and with whom. Even in the most puritanical Christian communities today, the fact probably goes unnoticed that Jesus chose an alcoholic beverage (wine) as one of the elements used for sacramental communion. If not for the dream of Peter

(Acts 10) – which not only made Peter more liberal about what he ate, but even with whom he ate – Christians would be restricted, like Jews and Muslims, about what they could or could not eat. Thanks to Jesus and Peter – and many others who interpreted scripture in more liberating terms – Christians stand out as a religious community with few dietary restrictions. Even during the fast, Christians are urged "not to look gloomy" or to make the fast seem like a farce (Mt. 6:16).

Jesus demonstrated a liberating standpoint even in the area of sexual morality – one of the most contentious moral issues, especially in heavily patriarchal societies. In the famous incident of the adulterous woman (Jn. 8:3-11), he uses a variation of the 'Golden Rule' to thwart attempts at her life. Similarly, with the woman who washes his feet with her hair (Lk. 7:36-50), he uses the principle of munificence.

It is these sources of inspiration that are based in scripture and tradition which need to be tapped in order to aid contemporary attitude-formation and action towards a more salubrious interpretation of, and attitude towards the body. However, even though we have indicated some of the more liberating anecdotes and interpretations related to the body, there are other aspects of mythos that could as well lend themselves to stringent, rigid and even dysfunctional interpretations, from a contemporary perspective. There has been ambivalence about the nature of the body as a suitable instrument for salvation in the history of the Church, with both ascetic and liberal interpretations abounding.[12] According to Sherry Shapiro, "the body in Greek thought has been the focus of the struggle between form and desire (between Apollo and Dionysus). Christianity inherited this viewpoint, but darkened it by seeing the flesh as the symbol of the Fallen Man and irrational denial of God."[13] In the Bible, the body – especially the feminine body – has sometimes been placed at the level of property.[14] Also, it is possible to find texts in the Bible which harbour patriarchal assumptions and prejudices governing the female body – a reflection of the culture during the time of their composition.[15] This is why, besides taking recourse to mythos in order to arrive at a holistically liberating approach to the body, there is also a need to take recourse to nomos and logos.

Nomos-based Resources

Nomos has to do with the day-to-day experience of being-in-the-world, governed by social norms and practices. It entails the interpersonal, social and practical dimension of consciousness, as compared to mythos (more ideal) and logos (more transcendental). The recourse to 'nomic' means of liberating the body may take numerous forms, influencing cultural, political and economic conditions in order to promote liberating forces or processes. Changes at the nomic level often take place as a result of the interplay between the mythic, nomic and logic aspects of consciousness – at intrapersonal, interpersonal, communitarian and inter-community levels. As a development of this interplay, notions of social rights and duties get better clarified. Many of the commonly-perceived and held rights that we now take for granted were at one time considered to be privileges enjoyed by only a few.

The establishment of law and order in social settings has taken place in various forms from the inception of social life – from the least organized nomadic tribes to the most organized nations. Both Plato and Aristotle presented systematic evaluations of different forms of political systems. However, it is only during modern times that constitutionalism and egalitarianism has overtaken otherwise more totalitarian, monarchical or politically stratified forms of governance and social order. The introduction of the discourse of modernity into the public sphere lies at the foundation of contemporary nomic development, especially in materially and scientifically developed societies. It is this discourse that has emphasized the notion of 'human rights' and helped to now design a 'human development index' – precious movements in the direction towards the recognition of the satisfaction of basic bodily needs and the rescuing of the body from otherwise primitive or privileged systems of oppression.

There is a far greater recognition of the need to legislate strict laws to punish those who mutilate the body unjustly. Besides laws, there needs to be a good system or order of implementation. Nomos basically has to do with "law and order," and how this takes root in human consciousness via attitude-formation, "internalization" or "socialization."[16] At a deeper level, nomos has to do with how power is negotiated in a community. According to Meenakshi Thapan, "power operates from within us and has taken root in the form of general dispositions in our ways of thinking, knowing and seeing so that we perceive as we are meant to and thus know of our embodied selves as we are expected to . . . It is through forms of symbolic violence that culture as systems of meaning and symbols are imposed and experienced as legitimate."[17]

To overcome the negative tendencies of power inscribed within the matrix of social construction, one must be able to first recognize the ways in which power is inscribed before actually strategizing to resist such inscriptions. "The nature of resistance will vary depending on social position, privilege and status and other assets that serve as markers of inclusion and exclusion."[18] Within social hierarchies, it is possible to have nuanced relationships in which power is apparently wielded by some, while it is actually wielded by others. According to Pierre Bourdieu, for example, "even when women do wield the real power . . . they can exercise it fully on condition that they leave the appearance of power, that is, its official manifestation, to the men."[19]

The nomic life is ridden with latent and more obvious forms of abuse with regard to the body. Each culture and community has had its ups and downs in its interpretation of the body at the nomic level. Today a tectonic shift is taking place with regard to caste, tribal and gender differentiation and discrimination in India. While the mythic and sacrosanct acceptance of caste seems almost untouchable – even to a great leader like Gandhi – laws against untouchability and in favour of reservation (affirmative action) have been gradually introduced and implemented. As a result, vulnerable sections of society have now greater recourse to the fulfilment of basic rights, including physical security and dignity. Urban locales would seem to be more successful than rural ones at putting into practice these new norms of behaviour.[20]

The need to develop strong legal frameworks, just laws and surety of implementation is imperative for physical security. In this context, it is a shame that practices of bodily mutilation or amputation are still considered as legal or juridical compensation in some parts of the world, and that capital punishment is still practiced in many countries – though the most materially developed seem to have gradually done away with these forms of bodily punishment.

At the level of the life-world, there seems to be an increase in the influence of "bureaucratization," resulting in a plethora of timetables, diets and exercise regimens. These are often bolstered by fear and mimicking mechanisms, tied to culturally competitive and economic models of success and failure. No wonder that a simple act of Pope Francis embracing a man with a serious facial deformity makes so many waves, as we are programmed to look pitiably upon disability. The same applies to Mother Theresa of Kolkata looking after numerous categories of social rejects: here the ethics of care and of gratuitousness take preponderance over the ethics of right and of duty. The Church has striven to alleviate bodily limitations over centuries, as a result of its well-organized institutions that attend to different bodily ailments – and numerous mental and spiritual ailments which take their toll on the body. This results in an institutionalization of charity or care, which springs ultimately from its mythic presuppositions. Christianity may be better interpreted in terms of a *karmamarga* rather than a *jnanamarga* – or even a *bhaktimarga*.

Today, the most urgent nomic reform needed is at the global level, in terms of a new economic order. We live in a gilded age, in which the bodies of a very few are privileged the world over, while a vast majority of humankind struggles to satisfy basic bodily needs. Unless new economic norms and practices are put into place, mythos alone would not be sufficient to redeem us from this shame of gross global imbalance. The role of logos as a mediating instrument to reform nomos is imperative, especially at the transnational and transcultural (transmythic) level of discourse.

Logos-based Resources

While mythos represents tradition and nomos social practice, logos represents the realm of rationality, communication and negotiation. Logos has typically tended to manifest itself in an overvaluation of the soul, the mind and the will, and an undervaluation of the emotions and the body. This is reflected across time, from powerful images like Plato's chariot allegory in the *Phaedrus*[21] to more contemporary social currents influenced by rationally powered modernity. Arguing against this tendency, Dani Cavallaro contends that, "In repressing the body, civilization has made us ashamed of our instincts and denied our creativity ... *Hatred for the body is a product of the desire to make everything practical, comprehensible and exploitable*."[22]

However, logos need not only be understood in cognitive or rational terms, as communication and negotiation also involve non-verbal and affective dimensions. To some extent, the Thomistic influence within the ecclesial intellectual tradition – largely inspired by Aristotle's realism as against Plato's idealism – has been providential in obliquely supporting many movements and projects which affirm bodily and this-worldly development. However, it is mainly over the last few decades that there has been a greater recognition of the way the body influences knowledge processes themselves. Elizabeth Grosz contends that, "Knowledges [*sic*] ... misrecognize themselves as cerebral, a product of ideas, thoughts, and concepts, forgetting or repressing their own corporeal genealogies and processes of production."[23]

In Western culture, Nietzsche has pointed out how the Apollonian emphasis has overtaken the Dionysian one, resulting in a suspicion and suppression of the body and its drives.[24] The three "masters of suspicion" – a term coined by Paul Ricœur , referring to Marx, Nietzsche and Freud – were instrumental in pointing out hitherto unnoticed or repressed dimensions of consciousness and rationality. In particular, it was Freud who stressed the role of sexual and emotional forces[25] and Nietzsche who stressed the voluntary – and often irrational – dimensions influencing personhood. These critical theorists have had a great influence on postmodern and especially feminist thinkers. Sherry Shapiro points out that,

> Both among feminist and postmodern writers, there has been a determined attempt to see all knowledge as emerging from human beings situated in very particular places, cultures, languages, and histories. Nobody speaks or knows with a God's-eye view. This assertion of situatedness can be seen as a form of materialist philosophy, which starts, not with modes of production, but with the body itself – the ultimate material presence in the world.[26]

In line with this thinking, Elizabeth Grosz supports Luce Irigaray's thesis of the "sexualization of all knowledges" and accordingly riles against the "phallocentric and patriarchal models" of knowledge production.[27] According to Grosz, even great critics of mainstream discourse such as Nietzsche,

Foucault, Freud, Lacan, Merleau-Ponty and other critical thinkers are "guilty of abstracting and reducing the body to a singular masculine model" of knowledge production.[28]

Akin to this feminist critique are several other forms of critique based on various types of cultural discrimination, based on race, class, caste, colony, etc. Critical theorizing from each of these subaltern spheres of discourse easily point out to thinking and theorizing that has featured dominant modes of intellectual production, often based on material and bodily considerations.

While logos no doubt finds itself hermeneutically constrained in terms of the context which gives rise to thinking, it nevertheless continues to offer promise of social change, in some form of the other. This is because logos is not only to be understood restrictively in terms of actual processes of knowledge production, but more appropriately and comprehensively, in terms of a transcendental or common *capacity* to engage in communication and to produce discourse. In this meta-discursive sense, logos is the main resource for both systematic and rational explanation (especially important to comprehend mythos) and deconstruction and social critique (especially relevant for reinterpreting mythos and for bringing about a change within nomos). Explanation and critique aid the "hermeneutics of suspicion" – a role fundamental to logos – and in doing so help to challenge prevalent mythic and nomic presuppositions and assumptions which denigrate the body.

Logos is thus the sharpest critical tool that one may use at the service of liberating the body, both in terms of challenging mythic and nomic presuppositions and assumptions, and in combating alternative beliefs and explanations at the cognitive level which seem dysfunctional in terms of respecting the body. The "discourse ethics" of Habermas,[29] limited as it is on account of its communicative idealism, is one possible way of critiquing and guiding discourse and development. Such an ethical process enables different voices to find expression on various issues, enabling alternative viewpoints to at least be seriously considered, if not accepted. Keeping in mind Habermas' proposal to create healthy public spaces where such encounters between ideas may be staged, Victor Ferrao argues for the need for the emergence of necessary "counterpublics," which "can become new sites from where we can creatively deconstruct the social construction of our bodies and reconceptualise the marginalized biological dynamism, and thus influence our discursive and material practices."[30]

Conclusion

Liberating the body is an ongoing task. Positively considered, the goal is to affirm the goodness and the beauty of the body based on salubrious mythic interpretations, and to create increasingly free and just societies at the nomic level, so that the scope for the nurturing and celebration of healthy bodily existence may be heightened. Negatively speaking, the goal would be to overcome repressive interpretations at the mythic realm, and repressive social practices at the nomic level, in which the body is marginalized and violated, resulting in shame, unhealthy guilt, and the adoption of unnecessary superstitions and taboos. The mediating and critical role of logos as a negotiating instrument in interpreting mythos positively and proposing healthy nomic life needs to be bolstered and suitably employed.

Within the general backdrop of *mythonomologic* consciousness, there is a need for continual discernment, in order to identify and support influences coming from either mythos or nomos or logos which enhance the experience of bodily existence as beauty or blessing and help minimize this experience as lack or curse. This discernment needs to take place at various levels: personal, interpersonal, communitarian and inter-community. When this happens there will be greater likelihood for embodied blessing to overcome embodied curse.

Notes

1 See Linda Alcoff and Elizabeth Potter, ed., *Feminist Epistemologies* (New York: Routledge, 1993). This volume is an anthology of feminist literature that largely critiques epistemological thinking and theories largely produced by men, often ignoring the issues of gender and social context which underlie the production of these reflections and theories.

2 Sherry Shapiro, *Pedagogy and the Politics of the Body: A Critical Praxis* (New York: Garland Publishing, 1999), 54.

3 The Sanskrit word '*varna*' is etymologically a physical designator, meaning description, cover or outward form or appearance. While *varna* is a broad designation of the fourfold caste system, the *jati* system is far more complex, and is in effect the more real social designator, which differentiates and positions one sub-community in relation with others.

4 Kancha Ilaiah, *Why I am not a Hindu* (Kolkata: Samya, 1996), 2.

5 Meenakshi Thapan, *Living the Body: Embodiment, Womanhood and Identity in Contemporary India* (New Delhi: Sage, 2009), 164.

6 The term 'nomos' has been used in a similar manner by various authors in diverse fields. Cf. Peter Berger, *The Sacred Canopy: Elements of a Sociological Theory of Religion* (New York: Doubleday, 1967), 19 ff.; Rober Cover, "Nomos and Narrative," in *Harvard Law Review* 97, no. 4 (1983-84): 4-68; Susan Jarratt, *Rereading the Sophists: Classical Rhetoric Refigured* (Carbondale: Southern Illinois University Press, 1991), 41 ff.; and Carl Schmitt, *On the Three Types of Juristic Thought*, trans. Joseph Bendersky (Westport: Praeger: 2004), 49 ff.

7 Max Weber, *Economy and Society: An Outline of Interpretive Sociology* (Berkeley: University of California Press, 1978), especially Vol. 2, Ch. XI, "Bureaucracy."

8 Jürgen Habermas, *The Theory of Communicative Action*, Vol. 2, trans. Thomas McCarthy (Boston: Beacon Press, 1989), 331.

9 Ibid., 197.

10 See Paul Ricœur, *Oneself as Another*, trans. Kathleen Blamey (Chicago: The University of Chicago Press, 1992), especially Studies 6-9, wherein the author argues for the legitimacy of the Golden Rule as a comprehensive practical principle, focused on the 'rightness' of moral reflection rather than the 'goodness' of ethical projection.

11 This mass migration which is part of the inspirational heritage of Jews, Christians and Muslims, has its echoes in the massive contemporary movements of individuals and families (economically and politically 'forced' migrants or "refugees") towards greener material and social pastures.

12 See James Keenan, "Christian Perspectives on the Human Body," *Theological Studies* 55 (1994): 330-46.

13 Shapiro, *Pedagogy and the Politics of the Body*, 44.

14 See Margaret Kamitsuka, ed., *The Embrace of Eros: Bodies, Desires, and Sexuality in Christianity* (Minneapolis: Fortress Press, 2010), 19 ff.

15 See A. Metti, "The Female Body in Hebrew Scriptures: A Critique," *VJTR* 68 (2004): 177-95.

16 See Peter Berger and Thomas Luckmann, *The Social Construction of Reality* (London: Penguin, 1967), where the authors describe how social reality is constructed and internalized.

17 Thapan, *Living the Body*, 166.

18 Ibid., 168.

19 Pierre Bourdieu, *Outline of a Theory of Practice*, trans. Richard Nice (Cambridge: Cambridge University Press, 1977), 41, as quoted in Thapan, *Living the Body*, 165.

20 This is why Ambedkar encouraged Dalits to migrate to cities, so that they may experience less of the social scar of caste, given the anonymity characteristic of city life.

21 See *Phaedrus*, trans. R. Hackforth, in *The Collected Dialogues of Plato – Including the Letters*, ed. and intro., Edith Hamilton and Huntington Cairns (Princeton: Princeton University Press, 1996), Section 246a-254e.

22 Dani Cavallaro, *The Body for Beginners* (Hyderabad: Orient Longman, 2001), 65, original emphasis.

23 Elizabeth Grosz, "Bodies and Knowledges: Feminism and the Crisis of Reason," in *Feminist Epistemologies*, 204.

24 Cavallaro, *The Body for Beginners*, 66.

25 See Sigmund Freud, *Civilization and its Discontents*, trans. and ed. James Strachey (New York: Norton, 1962). According to Strachey, "the main theme of the book [is] the irremediable antagonism between the demands of instinct and the restrictions of civilization" (p. 6).

26 Shapiro, *Pedagogy and the Politics of the Body*, 19.

27 Grosz, "Bodies and Knowledges," 210.

28 Ibid., 204.

29 See Jürgen Habermas, *Moral Consciousness and Communicative Action*, trans. C. Lenhardt and S. Nicholsen (Cambridge: MIT Press, 1990), for an outline of the features of discourse ethics.

30 Victor Ferrao, "Politics of Body: Enabling and Ennobling Our Embodied Selves," *Jnanadeepa* 12, no. 1&2 (2009): 290.

3

Humans as Bodily
A Phenomenological Probe

Johnson J. Puthenpurackal
Vijnananilayam, Janampet

Abstract: The paper begins with some preliminary clarifications, followed by a phenomenological probe into corporeality, and a look into the threefold corporeal manifestation of human corporeality. Phenomenological method, as developed by Husserl, brings together the subjective act (*noesis*) and the objective content (*noema*) by means of the theory of intentionality. It considers reality as intentionally perceived by consciousness. Phenomenology looks at body as an essential dimension of the human. 'Worldliness' and 'bodiliness' are closely interrelated; one becomes the link to the other. In its intentional meaning, I am essentially *bodily* as well as *spiritual*. My 'placement' in the world is determined through my body, which shows itself as the 'door' – the possibility of opening and closing. My being *bodily* shows itself as the 'door' by means of which I can reveal as well as conceal myself. The body both *opens up* and *limits* possibilities – I can and I cannot. The body is both a *burden* and a *blessing*, insofar as it shows itself both as distanced from and synchronized with me. The study finally looks at three concrete manifestations of bodiliness: laborality, linguisticality and sexuality. As corporeal, humans show themselves primarily as workers – the dimension of laborality. Work is creative of a better nature and a better human. By means of work humans communicate themselves. Although the hand is a living tool, humans find the need to make other tools as 'extensions' of human hands. Work is a social phenomenon, as it links me to other humans. Through work humans are in a never-ending process of transcending. Secondly through corporeality humans show themselves as communicative or linguistic. Humans do not create, but only enable language to emerge by their listening-responding. When human subjectivity controls the response, it turns out to be manipulative language. Finally as corporeal, humans are sexual as well. From a phenomenological point of view, *relationality*, *complementarity* and *creativity* are the threefold meaning of sexuality. The original and intense *relationality*, *complementarity* and *creativity* in sexuality are extended to embrace all the realms of human existence.

Keywords: body, complementarity, creativity, linguisticality, phenomenology, relationality, sexuality, work.

Introduction

This paper on 'Humans as Bodily' is to be seen as a study carried out from a phenomenological perspective in the context of the research seminar on "Philosophizing the Body: Challenges and Opportunities." Philosophizing in the contemporary period cannot be thought of apart from phenomenology,[1] a philosophical method that brought about a revolution in western thinking. We begin this paper with a preliminary clarification of the phenomenological method and of body-soul relation, before we make a phenomenological probe.

Preliminary Clarification

It was Edmund Husserl, who, after having passed through an intellectual search and struggle through different phases, developed phenomenology as a method. In this paper we refer only to those features that are specific to the phenomenological method. The term phenomenology[2] brings to our mind the Kantian distinction between phenomenon and noumenon; but Husserl does not accept such a distinction. According to him there is only phenomenon; reality is phenomenon – the way in which reality shows itself to consciousness. Here we have a hint at the necessary relation between the act of consciousness and its objective content; Husserl works it out through the theory of 'intentionality,' according to which the subjective act (*noesis*) and the objective content (*noema*) belong together – one implies and involves the other. The intentional object is not the brute factual object, but what is constituted *in* and *by* the intentional act. The intentionally constituted phenomenological object is the 'essence'[3] or 'meaning' of reality. Reality in its meaning comes about in the 'meeting' of the noetic act and noematic content. In the intentional act of my *getting frightened*, something is constituted as *frightening*. Thus phenomenological meaning is neither what is empirically experienced by the senses nor what is conceptually arrived at with reason, but rather what is intentionally perceived by consciousness. Thus the phenomenological probe, here, does not consider 'body' as a physical object or as a concept, but as an intentional object that 'speaks' to and is 'perceived' by consciousness. This introductory clarification of the way of our approach becomes clearer as we begin our journey of the phenomenological probe.

The question of the body refers to its relation to the spirit or soul. In western philosophy the 'body' has been considered as different from and subordinate to the 'soul,' which came to be known as the *Cartesian dualism*. Body was given only as much importance as mere matter. As a result of the exclusive and exaggerated emphasis on the 'spiritual' and the 'rational,' traditional western thought failed to give adequate importance to the *bodily* dimension of the humans.[4] In the twentieth century there was a shift in the understanding of the human: the human is now taken as a person, as a psychosomatic unity of bodily-spiritual being, without any inferior-superior approach that tends to view "either that a human being is an animated body or that [s]/he is an embodied soul."[5] Merleau-Ponty presents this question through his theory of 'body-subject,'[6] which is hailed as the victory over the 'either/or' of Cartesian dualism. We take spirit and body as the two essential dimensions – and not two parts[7] – of the human without any priority for one or the other.

With this preliminary clarification we are prepared to launch ourselves into a phenomenological reading of human corporeality or bodiliness.[8]

Phenomenology of Human Corporeality

Being corporeal or bodily is an integral dimension of the human; being human necessarily implies being *worldly* and *bodily*. My 'worldliness' and 'bodiliness' are so interrelated, that "*my* body is the transition from *me* to my world."[9] It is through the 'body' that I link myself with the world, and the world shows itself to me. "My corporeity [corporeality] is that by which the world manifests itself to me and that by which I project myself on the world... Because, it is inseparably subjective and objective, my body mediates between my 'I' and the world of things..."[10] My 'body' and my 'world' come to be and cease to be together. "When my body begins to disintegrate, my world also 'goes to pieces,' and the complete dissolution of my body means...the end of my being as a conscious being-in-the-world, the end of my being-[hu]man."[11] Thus human existence in the world necessarily implies its corporeal character as well – human existence *in* the world *with* body,[12] that is to say, the human exists as *worldly* and *bodily*.

We now ask the question as to how corporeality manifests itself in its intentional meaning. As there is no conclusive or definitive meaning in phenomenology, we shall let human corporeality speak aloud in our phenomenological reflection. In keeping with the phenomenological way of philosophizing, we consider 'corporeality' as an essential way of *my* being-in-the-world – the ontological characterization of *my* being *bodily*. That brings us, in the language of Marcel, to the 'mine-character' of body. In phenomenology we take an involved actor-approach, which enables us to look at body as *mine* – body with a personal possessive pronoun.

The use of the possessive pronoun can give the impression that body is 'something that I possess.' Far from it; it rather refers to a meaning of '*personal dimension*' and not '*personal possession.*' Making use of the distinction between 'being' (*être*) and 'having' (*avoir*),[13] Marcel throws more light here. Body can be considered neither exclusively as *having* nor as *being*. It is not anything that I possess or have. What I *have* is at my disposal; and I can dispose it off without ceasing to be what I am. What I possess is not constitutive of my being. Thus the body is not anything that I *have*. Although my body is not a *having* in the strict sense of the term, it is the condition for all having.[14] Nor can we say that I *am* my body. As body has an ambivalent position of *being* and *having*, it is more appropriate to use the expression: I am *bodily* or *corporeal*. I am essentially *bodily* as well as *spiritual*. The 'I' (person) unifies the *bodily* and the *spiritual*. Even when we refer exclusively to physical or to spiritual functions, we never refer to the body or the spirit as the *subject* of those functions; the 'I' or the person is the subject or the agent of both physical and spiritual functions. Thus, we say 'I am hungry' and 'I know the solution,' and not 'my body is hungry' and 'my spirit knows the solution.'[15] Thus, my being bodily, just as my being spiritual, belongs to my very Being.

My 'placement' in the world is determined through my body; I have a 'place' in the world because of my body. The 'world' stands for the condition of human relationality, and it is through my 'body' that I am set in relation to the environment (things) and to society (persons), and my 'position' is defined in relation to them.[16] Hence, corporeality has to be taken not in its brute objectivity, but in relation to the total situation of relations and perspectives, that constitute one's horizon. I, through my body, am the centre of a vast circle of horizon. One's movements and relations, communication and composure, actions and gestures, appearance and apparel...constitute one's situation, in relation to which 'corporeality' shows itself.

In the phenomenological sense, the body shows itself as the 'door'[17] – the possibility of opening and closing, of welcome and rejection, of entry and exit. The body as the 'door' is primarily open and transparent. I encounter the other and the other encounters me through body. The body is that through which I show the inner of mine to the other, and the other to me. The clutched hands point to one's 'tension,' the open arms show the attitude of 'welcome,' etc. Besides being the medium of mutual openness and revelation among persons, the body is the intermediary of concealedness as well. I can make use of my body as a means to hide my genuine self. Thus when I show the commonly accepted gesture of welcome, it need not necessarily reflect the inner of my being; I can hide my real self under the mask of my body. Thus, my being *bodily* shows itself as the 'door,' by means of which I can reveal as well as conceal myself.[18]

The above-mentioned dual character of the body as *revealing* and *concealing* manifests itself in yet another form of the *opening up* and *limiting* of possibilities. My bodiliness both *enables* and *disables* me to have various possibilities. Because, of my body I am *able* to walk, play or dance, etc. – indefinite number of possibilities! At the same time, because of my body I am *unable* to walk faster, *unable* to do so many things…an indefinite number of impossibilities! As being-in-the-world, I am thrown into the irrevocable *facticity* of embodiment, and I am blessed with the indefinite *possibility* of embodiment.[19] The body thus *enables* and *disables* me; I *can…* and I *cannot*; every 'can' of mine is accompanied by some 'cannot.' Thus, corporeality both opens up and limits possibilities.[20]

The dialectical way of corporeal manifestation is also evident from the way the body shows itself both as a *burden* and as a *blessing*. Although I experience my body as *mine*, I feel myself distanced from my body; I recognize it as radically other than myself insofar as it does not 'function' as I would like. It does not move along with me: it does not sing and dance as I want. The recognition of the body as a burden grips me when I experience my life with its ontic limits – experience of pain, fear, tension, stage-fright, bodily processes, inability, etc. – and I would rather desire not to have such a body! I feel that I am at the mercy of my body; and it shows itself as a curse, as a burden that is imposed on me: my experience of the body as a boundary-symbol! But I also experience my body as a 'grace' or a 'blessing.' I experience my body as fully synchronized with me; it sings and dances along with me. I do not see any distance between me and my body; and I feel identified with my body, and I am happy with it. Thus, I find my body both as a burden or curse and as a grace or blessing. So profound is the intentional meaning of *bodiliness*!

We have shed some preliminary light on the phenomenological meaning of 'body' as *being* and *having*, as *revealing* and *concealing*, as *possibility* and *facticity*, as *grace* and *burden*: the mystery of being *bodily*!

The Ways of Being Corporeal

The above-given phenomenological insights on human corporeality become more focused and concrete as we focus our attention on three of the prominent ways in which humans show themselves in their corporeality: work, communication and sexuality.

As Corporeal Humans Are Workers

As corporeal, humans show themselves primarily as workers. The phenomenon of work can be seen only in relation to the two related dimensions of the humans: the 'worldly' and the 'bodily' dimensions. The human being is essentially 'worldly' and 'bodily,' and 'work' is that specific way of human existence as *worldly* and *bodily*.[21] Marcel refers to the close relation between my *être incarnée* and *être-au-monde* as 'participation.'[22] Through work I participate in the world with my body.

Work, as characterized above, is specifically human, and it is a *creative* activity, accompanied by thought and vision. Thus, what the machines, animals and slaves do cannot be referred to as 'work' in the strict sense of the term. When work is seen purely in terms of production and profit, it is reduced to a physical activity. We take 'work' not as a physical activity, but a personal activity, emanating from and constitutive of the *whole person*.

A human being is *creative* through one's work. By the *refining* touch of work the nature is made more beautiful, more refined, more homely, etc;[23] and thus the world gets created, enabling the constant movement from *chaos* to *cosmos*.[24] Along with creating a better earth, work is *creative* of better humans as well. This 'bettering' at the instance of work – *bettering* of the earth, and *bettering* of the humans – is differently referred to: work *humanizes* humans, and *animates* nature. When the human 'will' is imposed on nature, it is devastated and disfigured. As humans are truly *humanized* by work, they will truly *animate* nature as well.

Work is one of the ways in which humans communicate themselves. The work that one has done is a pointer to the type of person that one is. Just as a 'book' is a pointer to the person of the author, so also is the case with any work. Thus the garden becomes the 'book' that the gardener has written. Work expresses what is spoken of in the work, and the one who enabled the work to come to be; in the sculpture the sculptor carves his own 'image' together with what is intended by him. In the statue of Mahatma Gandhi we see the image both of Gandhi and of the sculptor.

Although humans insert themselves into the world by means of their 'bodily' dimension, human *hands* stand out prominent with regard to dealing with things through work. I handle reality through my hand, since my hand is fully 'handy' for me, as it can be easily handled to handle things. The kind of work that one has done speaks for the kind of *hand* that one has, and the kind of person that one is.

Although a hand is a living tool, humans do find the need to make other tools to facilitate their work. Humans began to develop and use tools, not in place of their hands, but as an extension of their hands. Scheler[25] has rightly pointed out that the superiority of humans over animals is not because they develop and use tools, but because of their capacity to form *the concept of a tool*. Developing the concept of a tool is made possible by the twofold awareness of humans: the inability of one's hands, and the ability to surmount this inability. I realize that my hands are vulnerable, but I am aware of my ability to overcome the limitation of my hand. From this twofold awareness tools got formed as 'extensions' of human hands. With the introduction of tools, the gap between *what I want* and *what I am able* is narrowed down.

Although tools are referred to as the 'extensions of the hand,'[26] we can find that almost every part of the body is made to be extended by means of some tools. Are not the spectacles the extensions of eyes? Our legs by which we walk are extended in the form of various vehicles; are not the computers the extensions and facilitations of our brains? Even the 'heart' as an organ can be extended. All the above-mentioned types of extensions are only extensions of the various organs that are physical parts of the body. But no tool can extend these organs in their phenomenological meaning. Heart, as a physical organ, can be extended by means of technological devices; but the 'heart' as the centre of love, decision, relation and action cannot be extended by means of any tool!

Work is a social phenomenon, even though in work I deal primarily with things with the help of my hands and their extensions (tools). Humans work in togetherness with others overtly and covertly. I am *horizontally* related to others through my work, mainly because I stand in need of other workers in order to carry out the work that I do. My work relates me with other humans *vertically* as well, since the work that I do today is based on what has been done in the past, and the consequences of my today's work have bearing on the workers of the future. Thus the work-fellowship is extended not only to the present, but also to the past and to the future, and thus it embraces the whole of humanity. Although what is said above is true of any work, when the work is intensively more meaningful it will embrace an extensively wider humanity: a parallel correspondence between depth and width: the greater the depth, the greater the width.

The human is in a constant process of moving from what one is *already* to what one is *not yet* by means of work. The secret of human and cultural growth consists in the fact that humans can work *creatively* and *responsibly.* I am constantly addressed by indefinite possibilities: "you can…," and when I respond to them by my work with an "I will," I become responsible. In responding to the situation in work, humans become *responsible.* This process of responding and transcending is never at an end.

By one's work every human being is in a process of humanization and transcendence in togetherness with others, and human hands are extended to embrace the whole world of things and persons. This concluding note on the phenomenon of work is a disturbing reminder to every human being about one's challenging responsibility to create a better oneself and thus a better world.

As Corporeal Humans Are Communicative

It is through the corporeality that humans show themselves as communicative or linguistic.[27] As communal beings humans are communicative. The human communicates through the whole of one's existence; s/he communicates not merely by means of the words that one utters but also through the words that one does not utter at all; not only with the signs and symbols that one makes, but also with what one does not make; not only with what one has produced, but also with what one has not produced. Silence and absence too speak! In short, the whole of human existence is communicative or linguistic.

Through the various modes of existence – using of words, being silent, showing of signs, doing any work, etc. – humans communicate or speak. Does human speaking constitute language or communication? It appears as though language is created by a human's 'speaking' in its various modes. Language comes to be through the primordial 'speaking' (*Sprechen*) by reality and the corresponding speaking (*Ent-sprechen*) by humans.[28] In its coming-to-be reality speaks, and in this silent speaking there is present a call to the humans to 'speak' – to *speak in response* to the reality speaking. Humans, by attuning themselves to the tune of reality, bring the soundless 'speaking' to the sound of human language. Thus, a human is neither the creator of language, nor even the speaker of it, but only the 'responder' to the primordial speaking by reality.[29]

The original human response may take various forms, such as poetic sparks, bodily gestures, significant silence, works of art, expressions of wonderment, etc. A poet gives out poetic sparks in response to one's *being gripped* by reality; one gives 'sound' to what one is *touched* with; and this 'giving sound' is human speaking, and one's *being touched* or *gripped* is one's being spoken to by the primordial speaking of language. *The humans are able to speak only insofar as they are enabled to speak.* We listen by letting ourselves be spoken to. Thus Heidegger uses the expression '*ent-sprechen*' (cor-responding) for the human speaking in response to the primordial 'speaking' (*sprechen*).[30] When a professor values the answer-papers and gives a particular grade for a student, s/he is in fact listening and responding to what the answer-papers speak to him/her.[31] When one is conscientious in making a just valuation, one experiences struggle within oneself, not knowing whether one has rightly 'heard' what the answer-papers have spoken!

Since the humans do not 'create' the language, but only enable it to emerge, it has an independence and autonomy from the human 'speaker' or 'writer.' Language thus can yield meaning that was not originally envisaged by the so-called 'creator' of language. Hence, the meaning of a text goes beyond what may have been intended by the human speaker or writer. It is not the humans that speak through the language, but rather language 'speaks' – the way it speaks – to the humans to 'cor-respond' to it, by which language comes to be or emerges.

Just as the human body, language too is diaphanous or revealing. Through linguistic communication the other manifests oneself to me, and I to the other. On the other hand, language conceals as well. It can disfigure, manipulate or even hide the *real* from me. The language of propaganda and advertisement is an explicit example of manipulative communication that conceals. When language emerges without humans' manipulative control, it will be more of revealing; when human subjectivity plays a manipulative role, there is more of concealing!

Human language is a response to the primordial speaking of language in reality. Humans respond to it in *various* ways; by 'variety' we refer to the different levels of response with regard to its primordiality. '*Mythical* language' is more primordial a response than '*logical* language.' The *mythos*-centred[32] language as the primordial language or 'aboriginal language' shows itself in various modes: poetic sparks, insightful sayings, profound proverbs, mythical stories, spontaneous expressions of art-forms, etc. Eventually mythical language is made to be logically precise, as a result of which its poetical profundity is replaced with conceptual clarity. The mythico-poetic language functions as evocative *pointers* rather than informative *concluders*. When we give greater clarity and more precision to language, the farther removed it is from the original response of humans! In order to give thought to this forgotten 'mother-tongue' – the original response of the humans to the speaking of reality – we need to take a 'step-back' to our original being human: the metaphysically uncontaminated purity of ourselves.

As Corporeal Humans Are Sexual

Sexuality is an existential phenomenon enveloping the whole person. It is closely linked to human corporeality; as corporeal the human is sexual as well. As an existential phenomenon, sexuality could best be defined as the drive towards relation and love; as foundational to sexuality, love is its source, force and goal. "Sexuality is love actualized in the corporeal sphere which can become incarnate and fulfilled in sexual activation as well as in sexual abstinence."[33] Hence, as sexual a human being is oriented towards a relation with another.

Sexuality as the intense relation of love may be explained as a relation of *ek-stasis* ('standing out' of oneself) and of *eis-stasis* ('standing into' the different). The different inter-penetrate each other and stand out into a unity – mutual openness and nakedness! Sexuality is a total sharing of being, merging into the unity of being-with-the-other. As the mutual *ek-stasis* and *eis-stasis* sexuality is intimately *inter-subjective* – subject standing out from subject into another subject – a face-to-face relation – a relation between persons with 'face' or individuality.

The Biblical story of Adam refers to a mate being given to him, not so much for the continuance of the human race, but that he may have a 'helper': "It is not good for the man to be alone; I will make him a helper fit for him" (Gen. 2:18). This Biblical reference shows that sexuality stands for relationality, complementarity and creativity – a helper is given so that Adam could *relate* himself to the helper, so that the helper could *complement* what is lacking in Adam and vice versa, and so that out of this complementary relation between them the human race keeps on *creating* itself. From a phenomenological point of view, *relationality*, *complementarity* and *creativity* are the threefold meaning of sexuality.

Sexuality is the basis for all human relations. Sexual relation as an intense form of human relation goes beyond the relation between the male and the female. The limited meaning is widened so as to include all forms of human relations – among siblings, student-companions, co-workers, co-players, etc. The Biblical saying, 'It is not good for man to be alone,' does not mean that one should have a sexual partner, but that the human is necessarily relational. Relationality is extended not only to other humans, but even to God.[34] Sexuality as the drive towards union is intentionally extended to all relations.

Secondly, sexuality means *complementarity*.[35] The sexually different male and female complement each other in the various aspects of their life – physical, psychological, emotional, etc. The meaning of sexuality as complementarity is not to be limited to that between the male and the female; this archetypal complementarity is extended to almost all dimensions of the human: social, religious, cultural, philosophical, moral, etc. Just as the 'male' and 'female' complement each other, so the whole humanity is in a situation of mutual complementarity. No social group, no cultural values, no religious or moral doctrine, no philosophical or theological thought is so complete and self-sufficient that no complementary help is required from the other. Thus, rightly can we say: *everybody has something, and nobody has everything*!

Sexuality implies *creativity* as well. From out of the merging of the different, something 'new' emerges. It is through the sexual merging of the male and the female that a 'new' is born! It is the primary reference of sexuality as creative. It can be given a phenomenological extension of meaning. Only as a result of the interaction of the different, there takes place creative growth. Humans have grown in almost all aspects of their life with novel and creative thoughts and actions, insofar as they have been open to be touched by the 'different' – the different outlook, different culture, different religion, ... Democracy is generally considered as valuable and useful since it functions with an opposition of a different outlook. Any system that does not tolerate the different is condemned to stagnation. Thus, sexuality as creativity is the basis for all creative development and progress towards all new-ward growth.

After having considered corporeality in general from a phenomenological point of view, we dwelt at some length on three of the concrete corporeal expressions: laborality, linguisticality and sexuality. We have no claim that these three dimensions exhaust human corporeality. These are not three parts or functions of human bodiliness; rather the whole person is laboral (creative), linguistic (communicative) and sexual (relational). The phenomenological meaning of the whole person as laboral, linguistic and sexual got developed by widening the perspectival limit of 'hands' in work, 'tongue' in linguisticality, and 'sexual organs' in sexuality. Although primarily the three dimensions are focused on one or the other corporeal part, phenomenologically they are extended so as to embrace the whole person.

Taking a close look at the three dimensions of laborality, linguisticality and sexuality, we can find some similarity. In the ordinary understanding, these dimensions refer to three exclusively different realms. But existentially and phenomenologically these dimensions refer to the same existential process – the process of creating, relating, cooperating, widening, transcending. Is not laborality an invitation to work-fellowship in order to create a better cosmos? Does not linguisticality make humans more social by their existential communication? Is not sexuality a call to humans to relate and complement themselves towards creative growth? As genuinely laboral, linguistic and sexual, humans are gradually becoming cosmic persons.

Notes

1 The monolithic structure of western thought with its claim of absolute certainty with universal and perennial validity has been triumphantly marching forward until the twentieth century; Nietzsche challenged it with his twin-proclamation of the death of God and the decadence of reason, Husserl proposed a philosophical method suitable for a philosophizing without any absolute claims, Heidegger developed a philosophy of finitude, and postmodernism has established it in contrast to modernity.

2 The term 'phenomenology' was used for the first time by J. H. Lambert (1728-77) in his *Neues Organon*. Thereafter the important thinkers who used it in their philosophy are: Herder, Kant, Fichte, Hegel, and Brentano. With Husserl the term gets a definitive meaning. See *Historisches Wörterbuch der Philosophie*, Bd., 7, s.v. "Phänomenologie."

3 Only Husserl uses the term, 'essence'; later philosophers use 'being' or 'meaning.'

4 It is to be noted that although there was a neglect of the bodily dimension in traditional western thought, in the contemporary period we notice a reversal – a cult of body in the world of capitalism and globalization!

5 John Macquarrie, *In Search of Humanity: A Theological and Philosophical Approach* (London: SCM Press Ltd, 1982), 53.

6 Merleau-Ponty proposes the theory of 'body-subject' in his *Phénoménologie de la perception*, and mainly in an address of his, entitled, *L'homme et l'adversité*, delivered in Geneva on 10 September 1951.

7 The term 'parts' points to a division in the human, whereas 'dimensions' cannot be divided as parts; they are complementary.

8 What is presented in this study is part of an elaborate probe into the human by the present author: *Human Existence as Home-Coming: An Approach in Reflective Phenomenology*. Bangalore: Asian Trading Corporation, 2015.

9 William A. Luijpen, *Existential Phenomenology* (Pittsburgh: Duquesne University Press, 1969), 58 (emphasis mine).

10 E. Barbotin, *The Humanity of Man* (New York: Maryknoll, Orbis Books, 1975), 53-54.

11 Merleau-Ponty, *Phénoménologie de la perception,* 14th ed., (Paris, 1945), 327; as cited by Luijpen, *Existential Phenomenology*, 59.

12 Just as 'in' cannot be taken in the physical sense of the 'inside-ness' of something with respect to something else (water 'in' the bottle), so also 'with' has to be understood here not in the sense of 'side-by-side-ness' of something with respect to something else (walking 'with' him), but in the phenomenologico-existential sense of 'way of being.'

13 Marcel deals elaborately with this question in his celebrated work: *Être et Avoir* (Paris: Editions Montaigne, 1935).

14 It is because I am bodily that I am able to possess or to have anything, and thus it is my foundational 'having.' But for my body I would not have been able to possess anything.

15 Macquarrie, *In Search of Humanity*, 48.

16 Battista Mondin, *Philosophical Anthropology* (Rome: Urbaniana University Press, 1985, Published in India by TPI), 234.

17 For an intuitive and phenomenological understanding of the 'door,' see Richard Lang, "The Dwelling Door: Towards a Phenomenology of Transition," in *Dwelling, Place and Environment*, ed., David Seamon and Robert Mugerauer (Dordrecht: Martinus Nijhoff Publishers, 1985), 201-13.

18 Although, we said that body is the means of one's opening or closing, strictly speaking body only reveals. Even concealing or closing is a mode of revealing; one reveals oneself as concealing.

19 Heidegger speaks hardly anything on the question of body; but the inspiration for our explanation here is none other than the earlier philosophy of Heidegger as delineated in his *Being and Time*.

20 This is true of every 'givenness' of mine; every givenness is a limit from which something *begins*, and at which something *ends*; it *enables* and *disables*. The givenness of my being an Indian *enables* me to have the many possibilities that are part of my being an Indian; at the same time, as I am an Indian the possibilities that are of the British people are denied to me – I am *disabled.*

21 I base this section of study on another article of mine, "The Phenomenon of Work: The Way of Human Existence as Worldly and Bodily," *Divyadaan* 17, no. 2 (2006): 137-49.

22 Gabriel Marcel, *Du Refus à l'invocation* (Paris: Gallimard, 1940), 33. As cited by Richard Zaner, *The Problem of Embodiment: Some Contributions to a Phenomenology of the Body* (The Hague: Martinus Nijhoff, 1964), 42.

23 Although, we have presented 'work' in very mild terms as the 'refining touch,' the history of humankind shows something that is totally different. Humans have been involved in the manipulation and exploitation of nature for profit.

24 This is in perfect agreement with the Biblical and Christian understanding of work. God created the world, and He gave a responsible privilege to the humans to continue the creation by means of their work.

25 He is a German phenomenologist who has focused his attention on 'person.' See Scheler, *La posizione dell'uomo nel cosmo* (Milan: Fabbri, 1970), 106-07; as cited by Battista Mondin, *Philosophical Anthropology*, 176-77.

26 There is a great difference between tools and technology, and the difference consists not in that of size and complexity, but in the way they are extended. Tools are the extensions of the human; and hence the human controls the tools, whereas technology controls the humans.

27 Aristotle's definition of the human as "*zóon logon echon*" has been traditionally translated as 'rational animal.' Today philosophers are inclined to render it as *linguistic animal*, by looking into the original meaning of '*logon*.'

28 Just as the world worlds (*Welt weltet*), thing things (*Ding dingt*), so also language languages – language speaks – (*Sprache spricht*). In German '*Sprache spricht*' shows the close relation between the noun and its verbal form. In English it is normally rendered as 'language speaks.' But in Heideggerian meaning and style, we have to use the expression: 'language languages.'

29 Johnson Puthenpurackal, *Heidegger: Through Authentic Totality to Total Authenticity*, 219.

30 It is significant to note the relation between the terms: *sprechen* and *ent-sprechen*. The prefix 'ent-' has a twofold meaning: it can mean a 'negation' (eg. 'binden' = to bind; 'entbinden' = to unbind, to dispense, etc.), or it can emphasize the meaning 'in response to' more clearly ('bieten' = to offer; 'entbieten' = to offer in response to). In the case of 'ent-sprechen' the second sense is highlighted. In our use of the English rendering 'to correspond' it is intended to mean 'to give a response, corresponding to the original speaking by reality.'

31 When the judges make a judgment on a person – as guilty or innocent – they are giving a united 'sound' to the way that person shows oneself with regard to a particular case.

32 For a discussion on the profound meaning of *mythos*, see *Historisches Wörterbuch der Philosophie*, Vol. 6, 281-318.

33 *ACPI Encyclopedia of Philosophy*, s.v. "Philosophy of Sexuality."

34 It is very much present in Bhagawan Rajneesh (1931-90) who developed an eclectic doctrine of Eastern Mysticism with individual devotion and sexual freedom.

35 Sexuality has not always been understood in terms of complementarity. There have been three philosophical positions: 'no significant differences between man and woman' (Plato), 'men are superior to women' (Aristotle), 'sexual complementarity" (Augustine and Hildegard von Bingen).

4

Body, Desire and Insatiability

Felix Fernandes
Divyadaan, Nashik

Abstract: The theme at hand is treated from the perspective of the philosophy of Emmanuel Levinas. His magnum opus of 1961, *Totality and Infinity: An essay on Exteriority* deals with an analysis of what he famously calls the 'face-to-face' relation. This brief study here dwells on the said theme, considering Levinas' language significantly constitutive of terms such as Totality (the "Same"), Infinity (the "Other"), Need, Desire, the Face, Insatiate Desire (Insatiability). The Face, or the body, signifies much more than what we can see or perceive. The lesson that comes home to us is that the human person is transcendent in nature. There is in him the play of both, immanence and transcendence, the human and the divine. Knowing cannot contain him or take hold of him by way of concepts or ideas. The Other forever escapes the grasp of epistemological and ontological categories that try to describe or define him. Thanks to the dimension of infinity and mystery, the Other remains ever elusive. In Levinas' words, he continues to be an enigma. In the final analysis therefore, we submit that Desire for the Other remains evermore insatiable.

Keywords: Totality, Infinity, Other, Alterity, Need, Desire, Face, Ontology, epistemology, caress, voluptuosity, signification, transcendence.

Introduction

I choose to treat the theme at hand from the perspective of the philosophy of Emmanuel Levinas. His *magnum opus* of 1961, *Totality and Infinity: An essay on Exteriority* deals with an analysis of what he famously calls the 'face-to-face' relation. In this brief study we shall dwell on the theme, considering

Levinas' language significantly constitutive of terms such as Totality (the "Same"), Infinity (the "Other"), Need, Desire, the Face, Insatiate Desire (Insatiability).

Totality (The "Same")

In Levinas' terminology, Totality refers to the narcissism of the knowing 'I' and the compulsive need to possess the Other[1] and reduce it to a copy of itself. Like Narcissus the handsome Greek who fell in love with himself upon seeing his own reflection in the pool, Totality feels at home with itself, with sameness. It abhors difference. Levinas' claim is that Western philosophy, with its Greek categories favouring universalism, has consistently practised a suppression of the Other. It rests on the indissoluble bond between the One and Being, where Unity alone is ontologically privileged.[2] It has always sought the return to, and the fusion with Unity. Ontology and epistemology have, embedded in them the seeds of violence, he states. Comprehension of the Other amounts to taking hold of the Other, in accordance with ontological categories. It is the way of domination. The Other is perceived as a threat and as a source of allergy, thanks to his/her foreignness. In all honesty, I need to humbly accept the fact that "the Other is not a new edition of myself."[3] The other person enjoys a separate existence, independent of me.

Infinity (The "Other")

Infinity is about *infinition*. The idea of the Infinite, as Descartes calls it, overflows thought and remains ever exterior to it.[4] Significantly, all knowing qua intentionality already presupposes the idea of Infinity, which is pre-eminently *non-adequation*. Whereas intentionality follows the way of *adequation*, Infinity exceeds all *adequation*. Here, the surplus of Infinity crosses the barriers of immanence.[5] He persists in saying that one of the principal thesis of *Totality and Infinity* is that the *noesis-noema* structure is not the primordial structure of intentionality.[6]

Infinity refers to alterity and its radical otherness, as different from the Same. Infinity is totally distinct and separate from totality. It is not that it is merely different from totality, but distinct from it. The two do not belong on the same plane together, nor do they belong to a common genus. Levinas' claim is that the Other is not knowable. The Other exceeds all grasping from the part of the knowing self. Whereas the theme of totality subordinates life to representation, the fact is that not everything in life can be made an object of representation. The dimension of Infinity is one that just cannot be represented by thought.

Yet another area that Levinas considers in his attempt to speak of the Other, of alterity, is the area of fecundity. He starts by asserting that the structure of fecundity is not limited to the biological fact.[7] It goes beyond it.

Significantly, fecundity speaks of the child who is similar and yet distinct, from the parent. The child, mine in a certain sense, but not exactly me, refuses to fall back upon my past to fuse with it, thanks to its newness and alterity.[8] This is reminiscent of Kahlil Gibran who in his book *The Prophet*, while speaking of children, says to the parents: "Your children are not your children. They are the sons and daughters of Life's longing for itself. They come through you but not from you. And though they are with you yet they belong not to you."[9] This speaks of the total otherness of a given person, even with respect to one's own parent. Thus, far from the world of the self-centred ego, with its consequent suppression of the Other, Levinas challenges us to respectfully listen to the voice of the Other.

Need

"We live from 'good soup', air, light, spectacles, work, ideas, sleep, etc.... These are not objects of representations. We live from them,"[10] affirms Levinas. He describes this situation as enjoyment (*jouissance*), wherein the self's needs are met and satisfied by the world. The self *lives from* or *lives on* the world and its material resources. And all along, the self is happy for its possession of the world.[11] In food, for example, energy which is to be found in something outside of myself is transformed into my own energy. Levinas explains: "Nourishment, as a means of invigoration, is the transmutation of the other into the same, which is in the essence of enjoyment: an energy that is other, recognized as other, recognized, we will see, as sustaining the very act that is directed upon it, becomes, in enjoyment, my own energy, my strength, me. All enjoyment is in this sense alimentation."[12]

Levinas says clearly that "life is *love of life*, a relation with contents that are not my being, but more dear than my being: thinking, eating, sleeping, reading, working, warming oneself in the sun."[13] Enjoyment (*jouissance*) names the process by which the subject makes itself at home in an environment where otherness in not a threat to be overcome, but a pleasure to be experienced. Need, in this sense, is not be defined negatively; it reveals the dependence of the self on the non-self, as also the ability of the self to find satisfaction and happiness in the encounter with the *other* which the world is.[14] He claims that, "happiness is accomplishment: it exists in a soul satisfied and not in a soul that has extirpated its needs, a castrated soul."[15] He affirms again: "The suffering of need is not assuaged in anorexy, but in satisfaction. Need is loved; man is happy to have needs. A being without needs would not be happier than a needy being, but outside of happiness and unhappiness."[16]

We need to remember however that it is the 'other', and not the 'Other', that is taken into the same as a source of *jouissance*. The distinction between 'other' and 'Other' (*l'autre*, or its personalized form *autrui)*, even if it may appear trivial, is nevertheless indispensable to Levinas' thinking. The Other, who is the absolutely other, paralyses all possession from the part of the same. This, he is able to do because he comes from above, from a height, in the epiphany of the Face. The other may be incorporated into the same whereas the Other never can be. Not even murder can bring the Other under the possession of the same. One may succeed in killing the Other physically, in annihilating him, however the Other can never be dominated over by the Same.[17] The Other always succeeds in escaping the clutches of the Same. Whereas the latter confirms totality, the former reveals infinity.

Significantly, Levinas views Husserl's phenomenology as a culmination of the entire Western tradition of philosophical reflection, which is a tradition that has been 'a destruction of transcendence.' A movement of intentionality originating within the subject, perceiving the external object, and then returning to itself is fated to fall back into immanence, he claims.[18]

Desire

Appreciably, Levinas considers an analysis of Desire to speak of Infinity. He begins by claiming that Desire is very different from need. There is a sharp distinction between the two. Whereas need might reveal a lack or an absence which can be filled, Desire is insatiable. Whereas need is a lack that satisfaction can make good, Desire speaks of fullness. And, whereas need, a primary movement of the same, is in my power, Desire exceeds me at all times. Levinas captures the distinction well when he says that "in need I can sink my teeth into the real and satisfy myself in assimilating the other; in Desire there is no sinking one's teeth into being, no satiety, but an uncharted future before me."[19]

Levinas insists that Desire cannot be satisfied. He claims that Desire in some way nourishes itself on its own hungers and is only augmented by its satisfaction. He describes it by saying that "Desire is like a thought which thinks more than it thinks, or more than what it thinks. It is paradoxical structure, without doubt, but one which is no more so than this presence of the Infinite in a finite act."[20]

This Desire, which is an aspiration that does not proceed from a lack is the Desire of a person, states Levinas.[21] The Desired here is the Other in an eminent sense. The Other, who is metaphysically desired, is not an "other" like the bread I eat or the land in which I dwell. Surely, I can "feed" on these realities and satisfy myself, knowing that their *alterity* becomes part of me and my identity as a thinker or a possessor. However, metaphysical Desire desires *something else entirely*; it desires the *absolutely other*. Levinas reminds us that, "Desire is desire for the absolutely other. Besides the hunger one satisfies, the thirst one quenches, and the senses one allays, metaphysics desires the other beyond satisfactions, where no gesture by the body to diminish the aspiration is possible, where it is not possible to sketch out any known caress nor invent any new caress."[22] This Desire remains unquenchable simply because it asks for much more than food.[23] It desires remoteness, alterity and exteriority of the Other. This alterity, which is non-adequate to the idea, is understood as the alterity of the Other and of the Most-High. Metaphysical desire opens up here the very dimension of height.[24]

The Caress and Voluptuosity

In the final section of *Totality and Infinity*, 'Beyond the Face,' Levinas discusses Desire, the most intense form of which is found in erotic love. The beloved may be caressed but not possessed, he affirms. Analysing the caress, he tells us that the caress transcends the sensible. The caress seizes upon nothing, constantly soliciting that which ceaselessly escapes it to move into a distant future, that which slips away from it. The caress reminds you of a virgin who remains ungraspable, forever swooning, and withdrawing into her unanticipated future. The caress aims at neither a person nor a thing; rather, it aims at the tender who has no longer the status of an existent or an object. There is a certain delicacy and gentleness that characterizes the caress. On the other hand, voluptuosity is a profanation. It discovers the hidden as hidden, and uncovers it. In that sense, there is violence involved in voluptuosity. Again, inasmuch as voluptuosity has at heart not the Other but its voluptuosity, it is a voluptuosity of voluptuosity itself. In other words, it is love of the love of the other.[25] It seems suggestive of a certain amount of opportunism and utilitarianism here. Thus, we see that whereas voluptuosity proceeds from intentionality with one's own pleasure and satisfaction in mind, caress proves to be respectful of the alterity of the Other. Unlike voluptuosity, caress chooses not to possess and grasp the Other.

Hence, we see that Desire is situated beyond satisfaction and non-satisfaction. It is beyond the satisfaction of an unsatisfied need. As we have seen above, no voluptuosity can fulfil it, nor close it. Levinas claims that only the relationship with the Other, or the ideal of Infinity, accomplishes it.[26]

In trying to explain insatiable Desire as totally different from need, Levinas refers to the Platonic myth which describes love (*Eros*) as the offspring of abundance (*Poros*) and poverty (*Penia*). Certainly then, this is not the desire of what one has lost, but absolute Desire.[27] Again, citing Plato's *Symposium*, he speaks of the myth of the androgynous being as presented by Aristophanes. Aristophanes' theory was that the human being was once androgynous in nature, until the moment Zeus split it into two, into male and female. Ever since, the two halves are supposed to be seeking each other, with the nostalgic hope of fusion and completeness once again. Plato however rejects the myth of the androgynous being as presented by Aristophanes, in effect catching sight of the non-nostalgic character of Desire.[28] True Desire, says Levinas, is that which the Desired does not satisfy. It is not about a lost fatherland or plenitude, nor is it about homesickness or nostalgia.[29] What Desire desires is transcendence, exteriority, the alterity of the Other. This is desire for the Other, which cannot be satisfied, rather than need for the other, which can be. Desire differentiates itself from the poverty of need; the Desired does not fill it, but deepens it.[30]

Desire is produced as the Infinite in the finite, the more in the less. It is a Desire perfectly disinterested, goodness itself.[31] It is a Desire that withdraws from its satisfaction as it draws near to the Desirable. It desires after what is beyond satisfaction; it does not identify, as need does, a term or an end. It is a Desire without end, coming from beyond Being, and is characterized by transcendence, and disinterestedness. It is a desire for the Good.[32] Levinas puts it simply: "Desire is desire for the absolutely Other."[33] Besides, this Desire for the Other, this goodness liberated from the egoist gravitation of the ego, retains a personal character to it.[34]

The 'Face-To-Face' Relation

Levinas claims that the whole of *Totality and Infinity* aims to show a relation with the Other not only cutting across the logic of contradiction, where the other of A is the non-A, the negation of A, but also across dialectical logic. The Same and the Other are exclusively different, and simply do not belong to the unity of a common system. In such a situation, the welcoming of the Face answers to the unquenchable Desire for Infinity.[35]

Face as Signification

Of all Levinas' terms, *visage* (face) is perhaps the best known. However, the word *visage* is perhaps also the most mysterious, because it both does and does not refer to real human faces. According to Levinas' account, the Face should not be confused with the part of the head where the eyes, nose and mouth are to be found. It is that, and much more. Levinas declares that in the Face, the Other is presented to me directly and as absolutely external to me.[36]

The Face is that part of the human body which is most readily visible, and is also the most expressive part of the body. However, the Face is not simply *seen*. *Seeing* the Face would be to make of it an intentional object of the perceiving consciousness, thus reducing its absolute otherness.[37] The Levinasian Face is not anything we might see, thematise and appropriate. He explains that 'what is specifically the face' is that which cannot be reduced to perception.[38] This is what ensures its otherness, its alterity.

> The face is not the mere assemblage of a nose, a forehead, eyes, etc; it is all that, of course, but takes on the meaning of a face through the new dimension it opens up in the perception of a being. Through the face, the being is not only enclosed in its form and

> offered to the hand, it is also open, establishing itself in depth and, in this opening, presenting itself somehow in a personal way. The face is an irreducible mode in which being can present itself in its identity.[39]

The Face is not an object of "experience in the sensible sense of the term."[40] It refuses to be a content or object that can be seen or touched by me, for in the act of seeing and touching, its alterity risks being enveloped and grasped. The Face simply refuses to be contained by me.[41] Thanks to its exteriority, the Face never becomes an image or an intuition. In this sense, the Face cannot be ranked as a meaningful manifestation.[42] In its transcendence, the Face exceeds all categories of meaning.

Signification without Context

Levinas says that "the face is signification, and signification without context."[43] He insists that the Face is meaning and signification all by itself, and that the relation to the Face is straightaway ethical.

> The face is signification, and signification without context. I mean that the Other, in the rectitude of his face, is not a character within a context. Ordinarily one is a "character": a professor at the Sorbonne, a Supreme Court justice, son of so-and-so, everything that is in one's passport, the manner of dressing, of presenting oneself. And all signification in the usual sense of the term is relative to such a context: the meaning of something is in its relation to another thing. Here, to the contrary, the face is meaning all by itself. You are you. In this sense one can say that the face is not "seen." It is what cannot become a content, which your thought would embrace; is uncontainable, it leads you beyond.[44]

The Face signifies *otherwise* than merely what is seen. Its infinite resistance to our power is affirmed precisely in opposition to the will to murder that it defies. Being completely naked – and the nakedness of the Face is not a figure of speech – it means by itself. It is not relative to anything. Levinas sets the signifying of the Face in opposition to understanding and meaning grasped on the basis of the horizon of meaning.[45] The novelty lies in Levinas' claim that the Face of the other man is the original locus of the meaningful.[46]

The Face presents itself directly, outwardly and eminently. Levinas calls it as the epiphany of the Face, a manifestation, a revelation. Now, the expressing of the Face is language all its own. The Other, revealing itself by its Face, is the first intelligible. This epiphany washes itself of, and indeed precedes, cultures and their allusions. The Infinite in the Face does not appear as a representation (re-presentation). It is not a derivation of knowledge or self-knowledge.[47]

Levinas insists that the Face directly signifies the ethical dimension and that it cannot be reduced to an object of perception:

> I wonder if one can speak of a look turned toward the face, for the look is knowledge, perception. I think rather that access to the face is straightaway ethical. You turn yourself toward the Other as toward an object when you see a nose, eyes, a forehead, a chin, and you can describe them. The best way of encountering the Other is not even to notice the colour of his eyes! When one observes the colour of the eyes one is not in social relationship with the Other. The relation with the face can surely be dominated by perception, but what is specifically the face is what cannot be reduced to that.[48]

The eruption of the Face of the Other is the original site of the sensible. The Face's meaning is simply the proximity, the presence, of the Other. This meaning goes beyond those plastic forms which forever try to cover the Face like a mask. In any case, the Face always shows through these forms.[49]

Transcendence of the Face

It is transcendence, that greets me in the Face of the Other. The Face breaks the system. The ontology of Being and truth just cannot ignore this face-to-face structure, that is, this structure of faith.[50] In his complete otherness, the Other appears as without a history, as outside the system. As interlocutor, the Other remains transcendent in expression.[51]

The eruption of the Face denotes the way in which the presentation of the Other to me exceeds all idea of the Other in me. The proximity of this face-to-face relation cannot be subsumed into a totality; rather, it concretely produces a relation which cannot be described as a totality.

Levinas claims that it is the approach of the Face that leads us to the Infinite. "In the access to the face there is certainly also an access to the idea of God. In Descartes the idea of the Infinite remains a theoretical idea, a contemplation, a knowledge. For my part, I think that the relation to the Infinite is not a knowledge, but a Desire,"[52]

Without doubt, Levinas' analysis of the Face, revealing simultaneously both, the mastery and the poverty of the Other, is an important analysis. "It is the presupposed in all human relationships. If it were not that, we would not even say, before an open door, 'After you, sir!' It is an original 'After you, sir!' that I have tried to describe,"[53] stresses Levinas. Faced with the Other, it is an experience of awe and respect that prompts me to grant him preference before myself at all times, even in a simple daily act such as entering a door.

Conclusion

Thus we see that the Face, or the body, signifies much more than what we can see or perceive. The lesson that comes home to us is that the human person is transcendent in nature. There is in him the play of both, immanence and transcendence, the human and the divine. Knowing cannot contain him or take hold of him by way of concepts or ideas. One forever escapes the grasp of the epistemological and ontological categories that try to describe or define him. Thanks to the dimension of infinity and mystery, the human person remains ever elusive. In the final analysis, Desire for the Other remains evermore insatiable.

Notes

1 For Levinas, the Other, with a capital 'O', refers to the actual, immediate person facing the self. The Other is not a concept or a representation of man/woman in general, but an actual neighbor, here and now.
2 See Levinas, *Totality and Infinity: An Essay on Exteriority*, trans. Alphonso Lingis (Pittsburgh: Duquesne University Press, 1969), 274.
3 Emmanuel Levinas, "A Religion for Adults," in *Difficult Freedom: Essays on Judaism*, trans. Sean Hand (Baltimore: The John Hopkins University Press, 1997), 17.
4 Levinas, *Totality and Infinity*, 25.
5 Ibid., 27.
6 Ibid, 294.
7 Ibid., 306.
8 Ibid., 271-72.
9 Kahlil Gibran, *The Prophet* (London: Penguin Books, 1992), 22.
10 Levinas, *Totality and Infinity*, 110.
11 Ibid., 110.
12 Ibid., 111.
13 Ibid., 112.
14 "The primordial relation of man with the material world is not negativity, but enjoyment and agreeableness [agrément] of life," says Levinas. Ibid., 149.
15 Ibid., 115.
16 Ibid., 146.
17 Ibid., 171.
18 See Michael B. Smith, "Translator's Introduction," in *Emmanuel Levinas, Outside the Subject*, trans. Michael B. Smith (London: The Athlone Press, 1993), xvii.
19 Levinas, *Totality and Infinity*, 117.
20 Emmanuel Levinas, *Ethics and Infinity*, trans. Richard A. Cohen (Pittsburgh: Duquesne University Press, 1985), 92.
21 Ibid., 299.
22 Levinas, *Totality and Infinity*, 34.
23 See Emmanuel Levinas, "Philosophy and the Idea of Infinity," in *Collected Philosophical Papers*, trans. Alphonso Lingis (Dordrecht: Martinus Nijhoff Publishers, 1987), 56.
24 See Levinas, *Totality and Infinity*, 34-35.
25 Ibid., 257-66.
26 Ibid.,179.
27 Levinas, "Philosophy and the Idea of Infinity," 57.

28 Levinas, *Totality and Infinity*, 63.
29 Levinas, "Philosophy and the Idea of Infinity," 57.
30 Levinas, "Signature," in *Difficult Freedom*, 294.
31 Levinas, *Totality and Infinity*, 50.
32 Emmanuel Levinas, "God and Philosophy," in *Of God Who Comes to Mind*, trans. Bettina Bergo (Stanford: Stanford University Press, 1998), 67.
33 Levinas, *Totality and Infinity*, 34.
34 Ibid., 236.
35 Ibid., 150.
36 Ibid., 193-94.
37 See Levinas, *Totality and Infinity*, 187 and 193. According to Levinas, the act of 'seeing,' already presupposes recognition (re-cognition) and knowledge.
38 Levinas, *Ethics and Infinity*, 86.
39 Levinas, "Ethics and Spirit," 8.
40 Levinas, *Totality and Infinity*, 193.
41 Ibid., 194.
42 Ibid., 297.
43 Levinas, *Ethics and Infinity*, 86.
44 Ibid., 87.
45 Emmanuel Levinas, "Is Ontology Fundamental," in *Entre Nous: On Thinking-of-the-Other*, trans. Michael B. Smith and Barbara Harshav (New York: Columbia University Press, 1998), 10.
46 Ibid., 145.
47 Levinas, "Signature," in *Difficult Freedom*, 294-95.
48 Levinas, *Ethics and Infinity*, 85-86.
49 Emmanuel Levinas, "Ethics as First Philosophy," in *The Levinas Reader*, ed. Sean Hand (Oxford: Basil Blackwell Ltd, 1989), 82-83.
50 See Emmanuel Levinas, "The I and the Totality," in *Entre Nous: On Thinking-of-the-Other*, trans. Michael B. Smith and Barbara Harshav (New York: Columbia University Press, 1998), 34.
51 Ibid., 34.
52 Levinas, *Ethics and Infinity*, 92.
53 Ibid., 89.

5

Body, Gaze, Shame and Counter-Gaze

Victor Ferrao
Patriarchal Seminary of Rachol, Goa

Abstract: This paper attempts to dismantle the power of the gaze over us and proposes to bring about a counter-gaze that can help resist the crippling effects of this gaze. The gaze is focussed on the Body. In fact it produces plural and hierarchized bodies in terms of race, caste, etc. We begin our journey with a kind of a genealogy of the gaze. Next, we scrutinize the relational dynamism of the gaze, self and its other. We then move into an analysis of how the gaze affects and haunts the self and its other as trauma and how the intergenerational transmission of trauma becomes a predicament of humanity. Finally we indicate how the gaze produces shame and seeks a mode of resistance through a counter gaze.

Keywords: gaze, counter-gaze, shame, discourse, signifier, desire, trauma, 'objet petit a,' cryptonomy, Oedipus complex, unconscious, metaphysics of presence, mirror stage.

Introduction

The metaphysics of presence is also a metaphysic of gaze. The metaphysics of presence claims the original privilege of self-transparency and plunges into immediacy. As we subscribe ourselves to the metaphysics of presence, our being-in-the-world comes under its gaze and we become presence-centric in all our thinking and being. Perhaps, we might trace an intertwined entangling space between Derrida, Foucault and Lacan. Indeed, the metaphysics of presence holds it sway over us by becoming a gaze in both a Foucaultian as well as a Lacanian sense. The Lacanian mirror stage can also open us to the process of how we become enslaved to the deception of the metaphysics of presence. The gaze into the mirror as well as the gaze of the mirror leads to the imaginary presence, the constitution of the Ego. The mirror multiplies into the infant's voice as well as the voice of the care givers, like the mother (acoustic mirror). This means the image that a child views (gaze) in those mirrors become the umbilical cord that shapes much of the early fate of the child. The delusion of the metaphysic of presence influences humans in the very constructions of one's core identity which is ultimately a lacking self. There is something in the self that cannot be presented (the Real of Lacan). It is this that makes the self a lacking self. This lack in the self is the *raison d'être* of human dynamism as-beings-in-the-world. Yet even as a lacking self, we cannot get out of the metaphysic of presence because the subject, though the master signifier still remains largely Phallocentric. Hence, perhaps the Deleuzian insight of the riding of desire might open ways of allowing a counter gaze that might enable us to resist the power of the logo-centric gaze.

This paper attempts to dismantle the power of the gaze (a form of metaphysic of presence) over us and proposes to bring about a counter gaze that can help resist the crippling effects of the gaze. We begin our journey with a kind of genealogy of the gaze and scrutinize the relational dynamism of the Gaze, self and its other.

The Birth of Gaze

The gaze cannot simply be subjectivized. It is not as if we are gazed upon by a big brother. In fact, we are dealing with an empty, a-priori gaze. It is a point that ruptures our visual field. It is a point that returns the gaze. It is this object which returns our gaze that becomes the possibility of our seeing anything at all. Though Lacan did not use the word gaze in his mirror stage essay, we can try to anticipate his latter treatment of the same in our study because it allows us to link the gaze, the ego and the body right from the time of our infancy. This approach can further assist us to understand how the gaze triggers desire which paradoxically can never be fulfilled. This is because the subject cannot completely comprehend the gaze. The gaze is a lost object that the subject never really had. Hence, there is nothing to recover. This why desire can never really be fulfilled. Besides, the gaze is not just visual. It is auditory and sensual. Hence, we shall consider the relation of the gaze and the voice.

The Gaze of the Mirror

Lacans's essay on "the Mirror stage as formative of I function, as revealed in the Psycho-analytic experience" was delivered in 1949.[1] Lacan brings the close ties between the gaze and the body and the formation of ego in that essay.

He argues that the first sense of ego emerges in an infant by looking into the mirror and relating it to its body between the sixth and eighteenth month. The child's experience of rupture of having a fragmented body leads to a sense of mastery by way of the mirror. It is the mirror that disrupts the gaze of the child and returns it bestowing an illusionary sense of mastery over its fragmented body.[2] It is an illusion or fantasy because wholeness of the body is felt in a way that is not experienced. This is certainly misrecognition of the Image as real since it involves a sense of mastery over the body which the child does not enjoy.[3] The sense of lack that a child feels as a subject leads to the formation of the ego. In a way the return of the gaze via the mirror dupes the child into not seeing what is missing in it and its world experience. Thus, the mirror stage effectuates what Lacan has christened as the Imaginary. The imaginary is at once both visual and illusionary. Lacan teaches that the imaginary often works to conceal the functioning of other categories that constitutes our experience which he calls the Symbolic order and the Real. The imaginary belongs to the order of what we see (the world of Gaze); the symbolic order is the one that supports and regulates the visible world. This means that the symbolic belongs to the realm of language and as such structures our experience and our identities. A person experiences being thrown in a symbolic order and becomes subjected to it but feels that h/she is reaching an actualization in the identities/subject positions given by it. Though there is never a complete realization of the same, this gap is hidden by the sense of ego that h/she derives through the functioning of the imaginary. Thus, hiding the incompleteness of the symbolic order, the imaginary also hides what Lacan calls the real. We might understand how the minorities in our country are pushed by a sense of being not Indian enough to become 'Hindians' by joining the symbolic order of the majority. The same is true about narrow exclusionary nationalism which is also a reactive response to the symbolic order of the colonizer. This is how the self/ego covers its sense of lack and nullity and feels a self-presence which remains within the logo-centric underpinnings of the metaphysic of presence indicated by Derrida.

The Gaze as an *Objet petit-a* (object cause of desire)

Lacan presents the gaze as a point of disruption, a lacuna in the field of vision. It is not the look of the seemingly omnipotent look of the subject at the object but the gap in which desire manifests itself in what we see. The desire distorts the field of vision. Gaze is an "*objet petit-a*"[4] of a scenic drive. It is the drive that motivates us to look. The *objet petit-a* in Lacan is always a lost object, an object from which the subject marks its distance and emerges as a desiring subject.[5] It is the loss of the object that triggers the process of recovery that desirers it. Loss becomes the basis of desire. This in turn reinforces the subject as a lacking self because it does not have the object and the object only exists in so far as it is missing. The object is the object cause of desire and not the desired object. Thus, it induces a chain of actions which seeks the object of desire that may indeed obtain some object of desire but the *objet petit-a* lacks any substantial status and remains unattainable. This means it does not exist prior to it being lost. The '*objet petit-a*' compels the subject to see because it offers him/her to see the unseen or to reverse the side of the visible. It promises to allow the subject to peep into the secret of the other but paradoxically the secret exists insofar as it remains hidden. Thus, the point of disruption that we have considered here becomes for Lacan the point at which the subject gets involved with the object of gaze and actively distorts the field of the visible in pursuit of the desire that is triggered off indicating a complete loss of mastery on the part of the subject. Thus, the gaze becomes a point where the subject loses his/her subjective privilege and becomes subjected to and embodied in the object. The imagination produces an illusionary sense of mastery in the subject but the gaze being an encounter with the real cannot offer any resembling mastery. From our Indian experience, the gaze of the colonizer is still afflicting us. The colonial gaze has disrupted the angle of our vision and we can trace how in the context of an apparent cultural, religious and political superiority, the colonizer has led us (and continues to lead us) to become clones or mimic men of the colonizers. Hence, we have edited versions of colonizers who seek to assert a singularized version of culture and pose it as the pure Indian culture, the unification of various religious Indic cults and sects under the banner of Hinduism in the 19th century, and even singling out the Bhagavad Gita from other sacred books as the holy book. Hence, the real India and its culture and religions continue to be a lost object of desire.

Gaze and Voice

Besides gaze, Lacan takes up voice and places it along Freud's 'partial objects' like the breast, phallus and faeces. These partial objects are not on the side of the looking/hearing subject but are on the side of what the subject sees and hears. Lacan teaches that when we are talking of it, it is an answer to the primordial address by the other. It is as if we are already addressed but paradoxically the address is vacuous. We cannot locate the addresser. The addresser remains a blank, empty a-priori, formal condition of the possibility of speaking. Just like the object returning a gaze becomes the formal condition of seeing anything at all. Thus, in our every experience, we exclude what Lacan calls *objet petit-a*, and enter into what we believe to be the normal way of living as humans. This means that for a normal access to reality something must be primordially repressed and excluded. In some way we are condemned to be logo-centric. Like the object of the gaze is a blind spot within the gaze, so also the object of the voice is a silence within the field of the audible. We can only speak in a silent vacuum. But this silence has to be silenced in order that we speak and be heard. This does not mean that silence is a ground from where the voice emerges but on the contrary the reverberating sound itself renders visible the figure of silence. We can hear the voice with our eyes. When we look at the painting of the screaming women in distress, we seem to hear the scream. The figure of silence speaks. Lacan teaches us that the moment we enter the symbolic order, there emerges and unbridgeable gap between the body and 'its' voice. He teaches us that the voice acquires a spectral autonomy and never really belongs to itself. It is as if the speaker's own voice hallows him/her out and in a sense speaks by itself through him/her. Moreover, this points towards the gap in the visible, towards the aspect of what eludes our gaze. That is why Zizek says, 'ultimately we hear things because we cannot see everything.' We must further say that we hear what we cannot see as well as see what we cannot hear (as in the case of the picture of a screaming woman in distress). Hence, in the very hearing of oneself speaking and seeing oneself as looking, the gaze returns as a self-mirroring reflection to the immediacy of the vocal self-affection. Thus, the gaze makes us see in the mode of hearing. It is at this point that logo-centric metaphysics breaks down.[6] This is so because the primacy of seeing is derailed but we are into the mediation of the voice; the age of phonocentrism and still another spiral of the metaphysics of presence.

Gaze and Self and its Other

We have already, considered how the subject's imaginary identity lies literally outside of himself/herself. The ego in this sense cannot be identified with the subject. The encounter with the other, particularly with primary care givers like the mother becomes the mirror that leads the infant to imagine a kind of mastery over a fragmented experience of its body. This mirror experience continuously and indefinitely influences the subject due to the relationships of the self with its other.

Lacan teaches that ego is related to the subject but cannot be identified with the subject. It is a necessary function of the imaginary of the subject. This means that the subject's imaginary identity lies literary outside of itself. The ego lies outside what is generally thought to be the self-contained identity of the ego. The ego is eccentric. It is the subject's imaginary identity. In fact ego emerges as a splitting and alienating identification of the image in the mirror with which the self mistakenly identifies itself. This identification is not an imitative relationship of a pre-existing ego. In fact, the ego comes into being only because the image irremediably traps the subject. This is why the ego becomes the most intimate other of the self. This means that the ego is the primary other in which the self identifies itself. We have already studied the original alienating misidentification when we discussed the mirror stage. The mirror stage establishes the basis for the psychic journey of the subject for its several successive imaginary identifications. Therefore, we might say that at any given point in time the ego is nothing but a sum total of all the misidentifications. Hence, due to the alienating psychic dynamism, we might understand why Ashish Nandy calls it, the most intimate enemy.[7] The subject jubilantly misidentifies itself in the otherness of the specular image. In doing so, the subject undergoes a redoubling. On the one hand, it objectifies itself in the mirror image and on the other hand it identifies itself with the imaginary other without recognizing the other as other. This means that the ego finds itself at the place of the other and fails to recognize its own alienation from the self. In some way the ego lives what Descartes viewed as madness, that is, madness consists in believing oneself to be other than what one is.[8] Thus, in some way, it builds a permanent rivalry of the narcissistic images created by the lure of the mirror with the subject. Within our country we can trace how a majority community is born through the mirror image under colonization and how Indians steadily became what might be called 'Hindians.' This migration of self into an imagined 'Hindia' lays a demand on the minorities to join this new symbolic order.

The Gaze of the Signifier

Words have great power over us. It is as if words condense the power of the Gaze. Words have a performative power. They bring into being what they signify. Words affect the way of our being in the world. The symbolic horizon evoked by words determines our life and being in the world. The world of words determines our inter-subjective roles. It pushes us to identify with the fore-closed symbolic order(s). It is this symbolic order(s) that embed the inter-subjective circuit. The signifier belongs to the body of images. But when the image acquires an interlace of relations with other images, it produces semantic resonance which takes us into the symbolic register. Within the symbolic register, it is the speech itself that speaks in and through us. Hence, we become a speaking body and the one spoken to. The speaking and the spoken to dimensions of our body are based in the libidinal (*Jouissance*) drive. This means the empire of the signifier is grounded in the experience of *Jouissance*. The speaking body is also a spoken body. Lacan situated these dynamic roots of speaking and the spoken body in the unconscious. This takes us to the gaze of the unconscious which interlaces and controls the life and being of the speaking and spoken body. In fact, Lacan views the body as an image that emerges at the mirror stage wherein *jouissance* is injected in the Body. It is this playful identification of the mirror image while the body is still trapped in its motor impotence that gives an impression of unity from outside. This image (signifier) acquires in the symbolic register the function of signifying. Hence, the body gets trapped and exists in the body of images that relates as a complex system of signification.[9] In some ways we are born into the gaze of the signifiers. Our bodies are trapped into a body of images (signifiers) and their signifying dynamism. Lacan further teaches that signifying dynamism becomes the very stuff of symptom that torments us.[10]

Unconscious as the Discourse of the Other

With the death of the Cartesian subject, the subject with a substantively rational inner world was deconstructed. This opens us to think that the subject is not primarily what is within but what is without. This takes us not to the question 'who I am' but 'where I am.' This means that the subject or the self is de-centred and eccentric. The subject is elsewhere. Hence, it is not 'I think therefore I am' but it is that the 'it thinks there I am.' The subject is constantly displaced by the thinking it. Therefore, we have to agree 'I think where I am not' or 'I am where I think not.'[11] Hence, there is an It with respect to I. This It is the unconscious. It is an occulted I. Lacan teaches that this unconscious is structured like a language. It is said to come into existence with the person's insertion into the symbolic order. It in some way impels and impacts the self. Lacan further teaches that the unconscious is the discourse of the other but the other does not exist. Lacan establishes the radical exteriority of the unconscious. It is produced as a gap that opens up between nature and culture. The subject occurs at the moment of non-recognition. When one stops to think, one loses hold over one's being. Lacan places Cogito between thought and being. The cogito is the unconscious. Descartes had substantialized the cogito as *res cogitans*. Cogito thinks but it cannot be followed by an 'I am' of Descartes. Lacan's Cogito thinks but loses hold on the being. Cogito becomes a forced choice between thought and being. It is in the place of loss, the loss of being. The subject is then located in the gap. One cannot choose oneself as a subject. One can only remain a subject by holding on to something else, a positive element of sense which paradoxically entails the disappearance of the subject. The cogito is structured by the unconscious and the unconscious is structured as language. This means that the unconscious is discursive. The unconscious thus can be viewed as the gaze of the discourse of the other. Following Heidegger's view, Lacan posits that language is the house of being but is the torture house of being.[12] The trauma comes from the fact that Lacan's subject does not fit the language. Hence, he says, 'the letter kills the body.' This is why he confronts us with the real which resists language. Thus, he moves beyond the horizon of language which otherwise is thought to limit the horizon of being.

Gaze, Haunting and Self

Gaze has a haunting dimension. Often the signification systems – particularly meaning embedded in a painful past – slides, slips, and is distorted and digressed. Such a past can become part of the symbolic order that sometimes returns to haunt the self of another generation who have little or nothing to do with that past or the signification system. The capacity of the past or a signification system to be affected and that affects us can be viewed as a gaze that operates on our embodied life.

The Gaze of Cryptonymy

Nicholas Abraham and Maria Torok state that language is perceived as a system of expressive traces. These expressive traces can generate a catastrophe that can initiate a process of repression on words. This is called cryptonymy which inhibits the generation of meaning by concealing a segment of associative path that normally lets one to freely move from one element to another in a verbal chain.[13] Thus, cryptonymy operates as a gaze that disinvests meaning (signifier) from a signified. This hollowing of the word is done through the process of encrypting. This brings us to Lacan's notion of the subject which is marked by an indelible lack in being and as such is linguistically rendered as an irreducible separation or barrier between a progressive chain of interlocking signifiers and stable meanings (signified).[14] Cryptonymy admits the progressive dynamism of the chain of signifiers but focuses on the obstruction or the barrier that serves to separate the chain of signifiers from their potential meanings (signified). What is obstructed in cryptonymy is not meaning but a situation whose interpretation precisely depends on its very resistance to meaning. As a situation or condition, a cryptonym provides hidden cohesiveness to the self. The crypt is a locked topographical space, with neither a dynamic unconscious nor ego of introjections. Indeed, it is an enclave between the two, a kind of artificial unconscious.[15] That means, it allows us to understand how the gaze of obstruction operates and separates the chain of signifiers from the potential signified. That is, a disruption of the significatory chain opens up the trauma that breaks the potential links with the signifier. This allows the self to slip into a mask and become faceless. Perhaps, 'who' in the word Hindu obstructs its inclusive embrace by all Indians and can itself become a point to understand how a traumatic past suppresses and constrains its meaning, while at the same time, one can notice some people encrypting an identity into it. Hence, by giving a genealogy to it, we can deconstruct it and manifest that it is not original. This is why Hindu as a subject will always remain haunted by the unhomeliness of the term Hindu because it is striving to reclaim a past that it does not own. Hence, the unspeakable secrets are already put into words that reveal, exorcise and expel.

Trans-generational Haunting Gaze

There is a Gaze that operates in the summoning of the past. This Gaze of the past can live as a haunting presence in our present which seeks to possess the self. The spectral presence of this trans-generational haunting Gaze can be viewed with Lacan's notion of the unconscious as the discourse of the other. The spectral presence of the trans-generational haunting gaze becomes more intense when the historical mirror is viewed as cracked. Perhaps, Nicolas Abraham and Maria Torok's work might illumine what is the nature of a trans-generational haunting gaze which is under our consideration over here. Abraham and Torok mark the distinctions between psychoanalytical terms like introjections and incorporation to manifest trans-generational haunting. Introjections and incorporation are viewed by them in terms of the psychodynamics of loss and its aftermath. They present introjections as a successful steady psychical assimilation of something lost and view incorporation as a form of swallowing the whole of something lost. They caution us that it may appear to be assimilated but would burst through symptoms in language. This means in principle it can be carried from one generation to another, resulting in being haunted by a secret once incorporated. These incorporations of losses can irrupt and disrupt our life when precipitating historical conditions that may provide a stimulus for their emergence.[16] Thus, in the context of colonialism, we might trace how some colonial ideals apparently available but not actually unavailable to the colonized people are mourned as loss of an ideal. The trace of such incorporation is important for any understanding of the present and the future because of the present that haunts.[17] The psychic effects of concealment and the unspoken make the past refuse to ossify in the past but remains ever-present to the present moment of the people haunting them. Haunting is a symptom of trauma whose cause cannot be represented by language in a linear temporal narrative. In fact the trauma of the past gets transmitted through the cultural inscription to which we are condemned. The haunting gaze instigates verbal stirrings of the secrets and burdens of the past just allowing a glimpse at them through the redeeming act of narration.

Gaze of the Post-memory

The painful memories of the past come to haunt us in the present. Often the past that haunts us is not merely temporally represented to us but becomes spatially alive to us. The painful past registers itself through geographical and psychological touchstones. A painful past travels through disrupted geographies like the breaking down of the Babri Masjid or the temple in Goa. The landscape of the holocaust or the Gujarat Carnage refuses to shed off its geographical trace. But there are complexities to these events. On one side the disruptive events of the past were attempts to erase rather than commemorate a particular traumatic past. Most of these traumatic geographies evoke complex memories of both triumph and loss. Hence, what becomes a memory of triumph for one becomes a counter memory for the other. The painful traumatic memories migrate and multiply by registering themselves in writings of history, literature, building of monuments, photography, films, paintings etc. Somehow everyone has to deal with the after effects of the traumatic past even if one is born into a later era. The complexity of the intergenerational transmission of trauma requires representations in narrative and images that are profoundly geographical and produce divergent iterations of our relationship with the past. Within this haunting of spatially laden memories, we have to understand what is described as post-memory by Marrianne Hirsch. Hirsch christens the relationship that a generation after those who witnessed cultural or collective trauma bears to the experiences of those who came before that access, only by means of stories, images and behaviours among which they grew up. Hence, post-memories do afflict and affect us like a does the term "gaze leading" make sense? our thought, feeling and action.[18]

Gaze and Shame

The experience of our body is not merely physical. There is a profound phenomenological experience of the Body. The body can be experienced through? different registers. We have an experience of the body as erotic, beautiful, casteist, racial, and political besides the predominant biological one. Body therefore, pre-exists as well as is created. Indeed, all these various dimensions interlace with one another depending on the dominant gaze that is operative on us. Hence, this interlocked experience can produce a self-consciousness (internalized gaze) ranging from triumph on the one hand to guilt and shame on the other. Bodily practices are diverse and embedded in the gaze of politico-socio-religious and economic-scientific cultures. We seem to be living in Schizo bodies.

The frailty of our bodies makes us feel that our bodies are broken. Bodies seem to be emptied and imperfect. We seem to hollow the body and treat it as a body without organs. Thus, a masochist body cannot be populated by anything but intensities of waves of pain. This means that a masochist is seeking a body that only pain can fill. The same is true of a drugged body which seeks to fill itself it with pleasure. Thus, we have diverse body practices that seek to experience a body without organs. But these Schizo practices paradoxically, instead of filling the bodies, end up emptying them. The casteist body, the racialized bodies arise from schizolizes (body practices) that wish for a body without organs. The body without organs is construed in such a way that it can be occupied and populated by intensities, which are circulated and come to pass. These intensities circulate in space that does not have extension. The body without organs is the field of the immanence of desire.[19] The immanent field of desire is not internal to the self. The self is flowing in a schizophrenic process of desire that produces all that is egoist and heroic in humans. Schizolysis assists us to dismantle the gaze of the yoke of Oedipus. It de-territorializes the body. The yoke of Oedipus was a resolution of the original shame. Shame is scenic. It draws us to close our eyes as well as escape the gaze of society.

The final self-blinding of Oedipus in shame also indicates the scenic nature of shame. But falling away from the symbolic order, the oedipal economy brings in a gaze of the law of the father triggering shame and the need to run away from that gaze. Jean Paul Sartre also construes the shaming dimension of Gaze. The voyeur looking through the key hole disturbs the persons objectified by the gaze and overwhelms him with the feeling of shame. Schizolysis becomes a counter gaze since it no longer views the subject as a lacking subject and also does not construe desire as a drive to acquire the lacking object. Desire thus becomes a process of constant becoming as well as an opening to infinite possibilities. This means desire is a flux that overcomes barriers and codes (symbolic orders). Desire is a name that does not designate any ego. Desire thus is liberated from the lacking subject and the object of lack. In this context therefore, desire never stops. It never territorializes. The self that does not have a closed, fixed or stable identity but one that stays metamorphosed in the flow of desire. This means that the self stays in the constant process of becoming.[20]

Desire for a Body without Organs

The view of Deleuze and Guttari on desire as production becomes a great resource to develop a counter gaze. Deleuzian body is often ordered according to the order of things (symbolic order) reigning in a particular society. The boundaries of our bodies are set by these orders of things. This means our bodies are bound by the territorialisation emerging from the order of things in our society. Hence, the bodies are ordered as pure, impure, *satvic*, *tamasic* or *rajasic* based on the hierarchical order reigning in our society. This symbolic order has a rigid hierarchy inscribed in it and as such produces an effect of shame that afflicts those who are pushed to the lower side. Desire when viewed as production becomes unbound and cannot bind our bodies to the order of things. It can de-territorialise our bodies from the bondage of the order of things and thus operate as a counter gaze. Hence, the desire to become a body without organs deconstructs the monoliths imposed by the specific symbolic orders embedded in different cultures.[21] All bodies experience affects and has the power to affect. Hence, the counter gaze flowing from this view can re-territorialise bodies in other symbolic orders and thus, become salubrious to our embodied existence. The counter gaze of desire frees us from being prisoners of the configuration of the oppressive symbolic orders of our society; though desire somehow assembles (territorialises) into a dynamic stabilization. These stabilizations always remain in flux, always coming together and moving apart. It is this possibility of de-territorialisation and re-territorialisation that allows us to ride our desire and deconstruct the waves of symbolic orders, which constrict and restrain our embodied life. Thus, it is possible to contest and dismantle the symbolic order that racializes and outcasts our bodily existence.

Riding the Wave of Desire as a Counter Gaze

The Deleuzian and Guttarian notion of the subject is that it continuously becomes a radical counter gaze that can resist the gaze of the order of things and symbolic orders that otherwise bring about a process of subjectivation. We are not merely tossed and structured by the (m) other, our tradition and culture with which we share dynamic relations. We do not simply fit in the mould of our society. We are in a constant process of crossing our own spatio-temporal boundaries (de-territorialisation). Deleuze teaches that this process can be psychologically put as becoming the other in the process of individuation. This means that we do not have any stable pre-existent identity. Our identity is constructed in the dynamic process of individuation. The individuation is dialogical and is always populated by the order of things in our society. The process of individuation is in constant dialogue with the structure of the order of things in our society and is artistic and creative and may bring about a metaphoric death of the subject, which becomes the condition of the possibility of becoming someone other than the present self. Deleuze and Guttari introduce their notion of the rizomatics as a process of forging multiple connective lines, thereby constituting what he calls the immanent plane of consistency. This means that the Deleuzian subject is in a constant process of becoming-other. Hence, the anti-Oedipus in the subject rises beyond the closed boundaries of the symbolic order and desires to become a body without organs.[22] Thus, the notion of self comes very close to the dynamic notion of non-self in Buddhism. Allowing the subject to think through reason and affect can enable the self to resist the gaze of the symbolic order(s) and lead us to carve out transformative and liberative identities. This allows us to de-territorialise several symbolic order(s) and allows us to create self-validating and egalitarian planes of consistencies that can challenge caste, creed, gender and other fanatic identities.

Conclusion

No one can live without being under a gaze. The gaze in several ways shapes our embodied lives. The body is an object of gaze and is affected profoundly by it. But our bodies have the capacity to affect and return the gaze as a counter gaze. The gaze can bring us to shame and the counter gaze can redeem us from oppression and exploitation. As Indian Christian thinkers, we are challenged to allow the counter gaze of Indian-ness and Christian-ness to influence our thinking and being in our society.

Notes

1 Jacques Lacan, *Ecrits*, trans. Bruce Fink et alia (New York: W.W Nortan, 2006), 75-81.
2 Ibid, 76.
3 Ibid., 80.
4 'a' here stands for *autre* (other). *Objet petit* differentiates from the grand other.
5 Jacques Lacan, *Eratum of the Four Fundamental Concepts of Psychoanalysis*, ed. Jacques-Alian Miller, trans. Alan Sheridhan (New York: W.W Nortan, 1998), 83-90.
6 See Slavoj Zizek, "'I hear you with my eyes' or the Invisible Master," Renata Salael and Salvoj Zizek, eds., *Gaze and Voice as Love Objects* (London: Duke University Press, 1996), 91-95.
7 See Ashish Nanady, *Loss and Recovery of Self under Colonization* (Delhi: Oxford University Press, 1983).
8 Lorenzo Chiesa, *Subjectivity and Otherness: A Philosophical Reading of Lacan* (London: MIT Press, 2007), 16.
9 https://www.congressoamp2016.com/uploads/75e14c5d4818bbf03a465f38184718d7dd3cf45d.pdf (accessed August 12, 2015).
10 Darwin Leader and Judy Groves, *Introducing Lacan: Graphic Guide* (London: Icon Books, 1995), 36-37.
11 http://wayanswardhani.lecture.ub.ac.id/files/2013/04/Lacan-3.pdf (accessed September 3, 2016).
12 The symbolic order houses the law that regulates desire (Oedipus complex), lack, conscience, morality and religion. Within this view, unconscious also becomes unstable and non-substantive. Unconscious is not a place holder of repressions but a dynamic relation of the self to the social world (symbolic order) of law, morality, religion and conscious.
13 Nicholas Abraham and Maria Torok, *The Wolf Man's Magic Word: A Cryptonymy*, trans. Nicholas Rand, *Theory and History of Literature*, Vol. 37 (Minneapolis: University of Minnesota), lix.
14 Ibid., lx.
15 Jacques Derrida, "Forward" in Abraham and Torok, *The Wolf Man's Magic Word*, xiii.
16 http://www.inter-disciplinary.net/at-the-interface/wp-content/uploads/2014/02/lydatrpaper.pdf (accessed September 3, 2015).
17 Ranajana Khana, *Dark Continents: Psychoanalysis and Colonialism* (Dhuram: Duke University Press, 2004), 295.
18 Brett Ashley Kaplan, *Landscapes of Holocaust Postmemory* (New York: Routledge, 2011), 5.
19 http://topologicalmedialab.net/xinwei/classes/readings/DeleuzeGuattari/1000Plateaus06BWO.pdf (accessed August 22, 2015).
20 http://www.borges.pitt.edu/sites/default/files/Ogut.pdf (accessed August 25, 2015).
21 Dani Cavallaro, *The Body for Beginners* (Chennai: Orient Longman, 1998), 162-164.
22 Gilles Deleuze and Felix Guttari, *Anti-Oedipus: Capitalism and Schizophrenia*, trans. Robert Hurley et alia (Minneapolis: University of Minnesota, 2000).

6

Body and Consciousness
From Somatic Correlates to Causes

Gregory Mathew Malayil
Dharmaram Vidya Kshetram, Bengaluru

Abstract: Consciousness and its functions in the body have always posed an enigma to scientists and philosophers. Somatic philosophers of the twentieth-century successfully outlined a number of nuances of consciousness expressed by many of our bodily actions. Their interests are mainly the functions or expressions of consciousness through the body, such as reflective and unreflective consciousness, inhibitive consciousness, etc. They remain silent on what consciousness is or on the mechanism by which it is generated. The philosophical perspectives of Merleau-Ponty on somatic consciousness are discussed in detail. It is clear that the philosophical discourses alone will not provide any deeper insight into what consciousness is. A holistic approach taking into account the quantum-brain sciences would answer the philosophical issues related to consciousness and the body. Consciousness being a multidisciplinary issue, a philosophical approach to the findings of quantum-neuro-brain sciences may unravel the mystery behind it. The question as to whether consciousness is a construct developed in the history of philosophy is also to be addressed.

Keywords: consciousness, mind-body relation, somaesthetic, somatic, neurology, awareness, qualia.

Introduction

The body is the medium through which we observe the environment, receive sensations and accomplishments. In the present culture, people from every walk of life face tension in one or other way. Enhanced body consciousness and sound knowledge of phenomenal consciousness can relieve these problems. Focused attention to our body, its feelings and movements, have long been criticized as a harmful distraction.[1] But such charges are refuted by the most influential twentieth century somatic philosophers. Rather than going over intractable ontological debates on the mind-body relation, most of these philosophers pragmatically reorient their study towards the crucial nexus between body and consciousness.

Explicit discussions on consciousness dating from the seventeenth century and the early part of the eighteenth century are scarce.[2] By the end of eighteenth century, consciousness was understood as a form of relating to one's own self.[3] However, it has to be distinguished from self-consciousness, the consciousness of a self or subject or I.[4] The twentieth century British psychologist Stuart Sutherland once defined consciousness as "a fascinating but elusive phenomenon: it is impossible to specify what it is, what it does, or why it evolved. Nothing worth reading has been written about it."[5] Although consciousness is indeed hard to define, most people have an intuitive idea of what it is. It encompasses two different concepts: the notion of a self and the feelings of which the self is aware, especially qualia, our raw sensory experiences.

Body Consciousness as an Enigma

The major intention of this work is to explore the body's role in generating as well as experiencing various forms and levels of consciousness based on modern somatic philosophy. Anybody who attempts to unravel the enigma connected to consciousness cannot ignore the twentieth century somatic philosophers because they all treated the diverse and complex issues related to body and consciousness in the light of the most powerful western philosophical traditions such as phenomenology, analytic philosophy, pragmatism and existentialism.[6] "The body," according to William James, "is the storm centre, the origin of coordinates, and the constant place of stress in our everyday experience. Everything circles round it, and is felt from its point of view." "The world experienced," he elaborates, "comes at all times with our body as its centre, centre of vision, centre of action, centre of interest."[7] John Dewey passionately exalted the human body as "the most wonderful of all the structures of the vast universe."[8] His *Experience and Nature* celebrates "body-mind" as an essential unity in which the mental life emerges from the body's more basic physical and psychophysical functions. Maurice Merleau-Ponty, who is considered the patron 'saint' of the body, affirms the body's intentionality and essential role in our personal development. At the same time, he resists the concept of reflective body consciousness as a means of enhancing one's powers, emancipatory development, and self-understanding. Though his arguments have limitations, his insights on the primacy of unreflective consciousness were significant and trail-blazing.

Merleau-Ponty on Body Consciousness

Merleau-Ponty insists that the body is the central source of all perceptions and actions. For him body is the core of our expressive capability and thus the ground of all language and meaning. He is well known for his rigorous, systematic, and persistent arguments to prove the body's primacy in human experience and meaning. It may be an irony that Merleau-Ponty typically characterizes the body in terms of silence while celebrating the body's role in expression.

Weaknesses of the Body

Merleau-Ponty considers the weaknesses of the body as an opportunity to analyse its essential and indispensable strength. For philosophy, bodily weakness also means cognitive deficiency. The powerlessness and helplessness of body are daily proven in illness, disability, injury, pain, fatigue, and the withering of strength that old age brings. The somatic impotence is demonstrated finally in the irresistibility of the body to death. The body's imperfect senses can distort the truth and its desires may distract the mind from the pursuit of knowledge.

According to Merleau-Ponty, the body is not a clear object of knowledge. One cannot directly see one's outer bodily surface in its totality, and the body is especially mysterious because its inner workings are always in some way hidden from us. Though we can examine and know our minds through immediate introspection, our bodies cannot be scanned directly, in the way we often assume. At the same time, we should realize that our minds are often impotent to explain discursively what our bodies succeed in performing, and that our minds often fatigue and strike work while our bodies unconsciously continue to function. But despite such recognition of mental deficiencies, the range of what we can do or imagine with the power of our minds still seems far superior to what our bodies can actually perform. Merleau-Ponty's argument for the body's philosophical centrality and value is shrewdly cautious. He embraces the body's essential weaknesses and then shows how these dimensions of ontological and epistemological limitations are necessarily part of our positive human capacities.

Sensations and Consciousness

Merleau-Ponty neglects or resists the role of explicitly conscious somatic sensations which are experiential perceptions of our body. They include distinct feelings, observations, visualizations and other mental representations of our body and its parts, surfaces and interiors. Intellectual focusing or attentive awareness of the feel, movement, orientation, or state of tension of some part of our body would count as a conscious body sensation even when it lacks a significant emotional quality or direct input from the body's external sense organs. Among these explicitly conscious bodily sensations, we can distinguish between (1) those dominated by our more external senses (like seeing, hearing, etc.) and (2) those more dependent on more internal bodily senses such as proprioception or kinaesthetic feelings which relate to stimuli that are produced and perceived within us, especially those connected with the position and movement of the body. Such explicit proprioceptive perceptions can be regarded as somaesthetic perceptions par excellence, because they are not only somaesthetic by invoking mindful aesthesis or discriminating thematised perception, but also by relying essentially on the somaesthetic sensory system rather than our teleceptors, the nerve terminals existing in the eyes and ears and are sensitive to stimuli originating at a distance.

A Critique on Merleau-Ponty's Concepts of Consciousness

The two varieties of explicitly conscious or mindful sensations proposed by Merleau-Ponty and discussed above constitute only a relatively small portion of our bodily understandings and perceptions. On a close examination of the two, it could be found that consciousness exhibits at least four levels as Shusterman points out[9] which we shall discuss in the following paragraphs.

Unconscious Perceptions

When Merleau-Ponty says "that my body is always perceived by me,"[10] he forgets that we are sometimes not consciously aware of our bodies. This is not simply when we are concentrating our consciousness on other things, but because we are sometimes simply unconscious as in deep, dreamless sleep. Even in such sleep, we can discern a primitive bodily perception of an unconscious variety. Consider our breathing while we sleep. If something comes to block our breathing, we will typically turn our heads or push the object away while continuing to sleep, thus unconsciously adjusting our behaviour in terms of what is grasped.[11]

Non-Explicit Consciousness

A more conscious level of bodily perception could be characterized as conscious perception without explicit awareness. In such cases, I am conscious and perceive something, but I do not perceive it as a distinct object of awareness and do not thematise or predicate it as a specific object of consciousness. My awareness of it is at most a marginal one. If my attention is then explicitly directed to what is perceived, I could in turn perceive it with explicit awareness as a determinate, specific and predicative object. But the introduction of such focused attention and explicit awareness would mean going beyond this basic level of consciousness, which Merleau-Ponty celebrates as "primary consciousness," describing it as "the unreflective life of consciousness" and "ante-predicative life of consciousness."[12] Consider two examples of this basic consciousness. (1) In walking through an open door, although I am not explicitly aware of the precise borders of its frame and its relation to my body dimensions and posture, I perceive these spatial relations. (2) Similarly, I can perceive in some vague marginal sense that I am breathing without being explicitly aware of my breathing and its rhythm, style or quality.

Consciousness with Awareness

But perception can be raised to a third level in which we are consciously and explicitly aware of what we perceive, whether such perception is of external objects or of our own bodies and somatic sensations. Just as we can observe the door opening as a distinct object of perception, so that we can consciously perceive (both visually and *proprioceptively*) whether our stance is wide or narrow and whether our arms are extended or close to our torso. We can likewise explicitly recognize that our breath is short or that our fists are clenched; we can even be mindfully aware of the distinct feelings of such breathing or clenching. At this level, which Merleau-Ponty regards as the level of mental representations, we can already speak of explicitly conscious somatic perception or somaesthetic observation.[13]

Reflective Consciousness

The fourth layer is of still greater consciousness in perception and a level that is very important in body-mind attunement. Here we are not only conscious of what we perceive as an explicit object of awareness but we are also mindfully conscious of this focused consciousness as we monitor our awareness of the object through its representation in our consciousness. We will be aware not simply that our breath is short or even precisely *how* we are breathing (say, rapidly and shallowly from the throat or in stifled snorts through the nose, rather than deeply from the diaphragm); we will also be aware of *how* our self-consciousness of breathing influences our ongoing breathing and attentive awareness and related feelings. We will be focused on our self- awareness of how our fists are clenched not only in terms of specific attention to explicit feelings of tightness and orientation of thumb and fingers in the clenching but further to the feelings of that mindful attention itself and the ways such somatic self-consciousness influences our experience of fist-clenching and other experiences.

Merleau-Ponty's philosophy poses a challenge to the value of these two higher (or representational) levels of conscious somatic perception. It does so not merely by celebrating the primacy and sufficiency of unreflective "primary consciousness," but also by specific arguments against body observation and the use of kinaesthetic sensations and body representations. An adequate defence of somaesthetic mindfulness must do justice to the details of this challenge. Merleau-Ponty says that reflective consciousness and somatic representations are not only unnecessary but also ineffective for explaining our ordinary perception and behaviour, which are usually unreflective.[14] From that premise, one might infer that representational somatic awareness is a misleading irrelevancy. But this conclusion does not follow because there is more to explain in human experience than our unproblematic unreflective perceptions and actions. Representational somatic consciousness can help us with respect to cases where spontaneous competencies break down and where unreflective habits are targeted for correction. Moreover, explanatory power is not the only criterion of value.

Limits of a Pure Philosophical Approach

Though the somatic philosophers are providing insights on several nuances of consciousness, it is not explained as an entity. Their concern is actually the expressive or demonstrative functions of consciousness within or through the body. Understanding of the term itself has differences in its nuances. The unreflective consciousness of Merleau-Ponty and his critical attitude to reflective consciousness may be considered as a result of conceptual differences. Such philosophical problems may vanish with an understanding of the mechanism by which consciousness originates. The origin of consciousness, according to the present understanding, is a multidisciplinary issue spreading over psychology, neurology, brain sciences and quantum mechanics.[15]

Certain Unexplained Features of Consciousness

Regarding the relation between brain and consciousness, many scientists and philosophers have the view that consciousness is an emergent property of complex computation among 'integrate-and-fire' brain neurons which interconnect and switch at chemically-mediated synapses. However, the mechanism by which such neuronal computation may produce conscious experience remains unknown.[16] If consciousness is a property of the entire brain, does it 'emerge' when the brain reaches a certain level of complexity? Or are only some parts of the brain conscious? (After all, if we argue that only the brain and no other organs are conscious, why not imagine that only some parts of the brain are involved?) Indeed, neurological evidence suggests that we are unconscious of most of the activity in our brains, for example, heart beating, digestion, posture, and so on, but also the pre-perceptual processing of information from the senses, and the complex task of selecting and controlling the individual muscles that carry out actions.[17]

The *hard problem* that refers to the nature of phenomenal experience of consciousness, and what distinguishes conscious from non-conscious cognition is not explained satisfactorily. Perception and behaviour may be accompanied or driven by phenomenal conscious awareness, experience, or subjective feelings, composed of what philosophers call 'qualia.' Perception and behaviour need not be always accompanied by consciousness.[18] We could have evolved as full-time non-conscious 'zombies' performing complex auto-pilot behaviours without conscious awareness. But we are endowed with phenomenal consciousness, which is an 'inner life' of subjective experience.

Consciousness and Non-Computational Realm

Faced with philosophical conundrums such as the origin, necessity, mechanism of evolution, many neuroscientists have argued that we should simply aim at defining the 'neural correlate of consciousness' – the parts of the brain and the nature and activity of nerve cells that implement conscious states.[19] Consciousness has often been argued to be a sequence of discrete moments. William James described the "specious present, the short duration of which we are immediately and incessantly sensible" though he was vague about duration, which he described a continual "stream of consciousness."[20] The "perceptual moment" theory of Strouddescribed consciousness as a series of discrete events, like sequential frames of a movie.[21] These discrete moments could be interpreted as the result of a process called Orchestrated Objective Reduction (Orch OR) where the fundamental mechanism is the collapse of quantum mechanical wave function as proposed by Penrose and Hemeroff.[22]

Penrose argued that consciousness emerging in a non-computable process occurs in brain for which collapse of quantum mechanical wave function is the possible physical basis. Dissatisfied with its randomness, again, he proposed a new form of wave function collapse that occurred in isolation, called objective reduction. He suggested that each quantum superposition has its own piece of space-time curvature, and when these become separated by more than one Planck length, they become unstable and collapse. According to him, objective reduction represents neither randomness nor algorithmic processing, but instead a non-computable influence in space-time geometry from which mathematical understanding and, by later extension, consciousness derived. Joining with Penrose, Hameroff suggested that the objective reduction takes place in microtubules which are composed of tubulin protein dimer subunits.[23] Furthermore, he proposed that electron condensates in one neuron could be extended to many others via gap junctions between neurons and thus forms a macroscopic quantum feature across an extended area. Collapse of the wave function of this extended condensate results in conscious experience, according to Penrose and Hameroff.[24] Though the foundation of this theory seems questionable, there is an insight into a possible future as well as a break-through for science, especially for Physics. A Philosophical approach to these insights would help us to have more clarity on the origin and function of consciousness. However, since consciousness cannot be simply treated as an outcome of certain Quantum Mechanical processes alone, the roles of neurological as well as psychological and subjective dimensions also need to be investigated.

Conclusion

Though consciousness is fully associated with our body, the problem we face with consciousness is the difficulty to correlate it to any empirical parameter. It cannot be a variable physical quantity like mass, length, time or electric current. However, a clear under-standing of the quantum-neural activities may enable us to enter into the level of evolution of consciousness. This approach would transform consciousness into an empirical problem which could be dealt with experimentally. While searching for consciousness as an entity, we may find it as something caused by certain transitions occurring within the brain. We may then ask 'which parts of the brain are active, or in what special way are they active, when someone does something consciously?' Sometimes consciousness may be a construct gradually evolved in the history of philosophy. What we call as consciousness may be a set of processes taking place in our brain. We may find that the origin of consciousness is beyond the macroscopic realm and like that of matter waves in quantum mechanics. However, it is clear that the origin and functioning of consciousness happen with the body as the medium, and unravelling the details of brain processes would provide us new insights and solution to the differences in various philosophical perspectives.

Notes

1 Richard Shusterman, *Body Consciousness* (Cambridge: Cambridge University Press, 2008), 1.
2 Thiel Udo, *The Early Modern Subject* (Oxford: Oxford University Press, 2011), 6.
3 Manfred Frank, "Non-objectal Subjectivity," *Journal of Consciousness Studies* 14 (2007): 152-73.
4 Thiel Udo, "The Trinity and Human Personal Identity," in *English Philosophy in the Age of Locke*, ed. Michael Alexander Stewart (Oxford: Oxford University Press, 2000), 217.
5 V. S. Ramachandran, "Consciousness," in *Oxford Companion to the Body*, ed. Colin Blakemore and Sheila Jennet (Oxford: Oxford University Press, 2001), 175.
6 Shusterman, *Body Consciousness*, 9.
7 William James, *The Experience of Activity in Essays in Radical Empiricism* (Cambridge: Harvard University Press, 1976), 86.
8 John Dewey, *The Middle Works*, Vol. 2 (Carbondale: Southern Illinois University Press, 1982), 351.
9 Shusterman, *Body Consciousness*, 54.
10 Maurice Merleau-Ponty, *Phenomenology of Perception*, trans. Colin Smith (London: Routledge, 1962), 91.
11 Ibid., 137-139.

12 Ibid., xv.
13 Brian O'Shaughnessy, "Proprioception and the Body Image," in *The Body and the Self*, ed. J. L. Bermudez (Cambridge: MIT Press, 1995), 17.
14 Shusterman, *Body Consciousness*, 67.
15 Bernard J. Bars, William P. Banks and James B. Newman, *Essential Sources in the Scientific Study of Consciousness* (Cambridge: MIT Press, 2003), 1.
16 Cf. C. Koch, *The Quest for Consciousness: A Neurobiological Approach* (Englewood: Roberts and Co., 2004); D. J. Chalmers, *The Conscious Mind in Search of a Fundamental Theory* (New York: Oxford University Press, 1996).
17 Ramachandran "Consciousness," 176.
18 Stuart Hameroff and Roger Penrose, "Consciousness in the Universe: A Review of the 'Orch-OR' theory," *Physics of Life Reviews* 11 (2014): 39-78.
19 Ramachandran, "Consciousness," 176.
20 William James, *Principles of Psychology* (New York: Henry Holt and Co., 1913), 708.
21 J. M. Stroud, "The Fine Structure of Psychological Time." in *Information Theory in Psychology*, ed. H. Quastler (New York: Free Press, 1956), 174-205.
22 Hameroff and Penrose, "Consciousness in the Universe," 39-78.
23 Ibid.
24 Cf. Roger Penrose, *The Emperor's New Mind: Concerning Computers, Minds, and the Laws of Physics* (Oxford: Oxford University Press, 1989); Roger Penrose, *Shadows of the Mind: An Approach to the Missing Science of Consciousness* (Oxford: Oxford University Press, 1994).

Part 2

Social, Political and Gender Issues

7

Body, Bio-Politics and Bioethics

S. Sekar Sebastin
Sacred Heart Seminary, Poonamallee

Abstract: The concern of this paper is to draw attention to bio-politics and bioethics which are involved in ennobling the human body because, of all beings, only human persons can manage the body, train it and render it capable of performing movements of admirable perfections. Even though, it is conceived that the body is a means of pleasure and self-expression which permits the unashamed display of the human body, it is the marvel of politics and ethics with due respect and dignity as it fights against the dualist understanding of body and soul. This paper seeks the aid of Michael Foucault to discuss how the messiness of bodies is often conceptualised and totalised as feminised, and as such is 'othered' in bio-politics. This paper describes the importance of bioethics also, which is the critical examination of the moral dimensions of decision-making in health-related contexts. We should seek the moral common ground basing our moral and political arguments in the public sphere on premises shared by everyone as the body is a means of expressing oneself as it is revelatory and it is the best revealing phenomenon of one's interiority.

Keywords: bio-politics, bioethics, Michael Foucault, bio-power, dualism, beneficence, embodiment, altruism.

Introduction

The body is the most obvious dimension of human persons. It involves any kind of reflection as the body is not merely a natural object but also an object of cultural and political representation and it is being radically rethought in the human sciences. It is pointed out that the body is a means of encoding social values through its shape, size and ornamental attributes. The values embedded in our socializing strategies shape our everyday experiences like sleep and waking, rest and physical activity, hygiene, eating and drinking, reproduction, consumption, entertainment and creativity. Hence, we can assert that the human body is a marvellous spectacle. It is not only due to only external structures but also due to internal structures as well. Thus, the human body is certainly a gift, a symbol of material existence and it is the privileged medium that makes possible the complete expression of our being. We reveal ourselves precisely in and through our body, be it in a smile, in a gesture, in words, in dance and in all the ways possible.

It is also clear that we claim to be superior to animals due to the body we possess. But a Platonic and Cartesian dualism of the body and mind leads to a vanished sense of human identity. It considers the body as an object to possess, to manipulate and to subjugate. Thus, the Manichaean devaluation of the body takes on a new face by condemning the body to gross dehumanisation as there is no recognition of human person in the dualistic tendency. The existing challenges demand us to take responsible initiative to ennoble and dignify the human body seeking the attention of both bio-politics and bioethics which is the concern of this paper.

The Project of Bio-politics and Bioethics

Even though the body is the concern of the field of historical demography or pathology, the seat of needs and appetites and a target for the attacks of germs or viruses; it is also directly involved in a political field. There are power relations that have an immediate hold upon it as they invest, mark, train, torture and force the body to carry out tasks and to perform ceremonies. This political involvement of the body is bound up with its economic use as well. It is a force of production that the body is invested with relations of power and domination, but on the other hand, its constitution as labour power is possible only if it is caught up in a system of subjection. Thus the body becomes a useful force only if it is both a productive and subjected body. The power exercised on the body is conceived not as a property but as a strategy. Its effects of domination are attributed not to appropriation but to dispositions, manoeuvres, tactics, techniques, and functioning.[1]

The current notion of the body as a vehicle of pleasure and self-expression permits the unashamed display. The newspapers and magazines, television channels and social media portray the culture as gradually sneaking into our society and disturbing the minds of the people and it has become a concern of the day. These phenomenological analyses promote self-consciousness to dignify the human body in the context of politics and ethics. Thus, both bio-politics and bioethics take concentrating care to address this issue and find a special attention for preservation of life with a bodily nature. They find the root of this issue in the history of metaphysics as a history of the oblivion of being or the history of ontological affliction which asserts that the truth of the body is kept in exile in metaphysics.[2]

The body is known in its epoch, its fallibility, its objectification and automation, its crucifixion, its rituals of mortification. However, bio-politics and bioethics endeavour to overcome the metaphysical misunderstanding of the human body by overcoming the historically deep-seated guilt, shame and flaming into a terrible hatred of the body. Both argue that the history of mind/ body dualism is the indicative manifestations of a violent, nihilistic rage at the very heart of metaphysics.[3] There is also another metaphysical speculation which asserts that the ascetical ideal of life may be founded on an estrangement from one's body which can actually turn into hatred. This is often expressed in reflections such as the body is the prison of the soul and this can lead to diverse forms of bodily self-torture.[4] Overcoming this dualist understanding of body and soul, biopolitics and bioethics make an effort to establish the human body as the marvel of politics and ethics with due respect and dignity.

A Panoramic Vision of Bio-politics

Bio-politics asserts that although the body is material, it is politically and socially encoded. Hence, we attempt to draw our attention to the social and political production of our bodies. The politics of the omission of the body is one of the issues which occurs in the discursive and material practices as it imposes the social disembodying of our body. The absent presence of the bodily dimension foregrounds the rationalist, white, brahminic, consumerist, male bias that operates as an unmarked norm from which everything else that deviates is seen as unbecoming. This racialization, sexualisation, commercialisation or brahminisation of the body is deeply embedded in the dynamics of politics. This dynamics runs on the wheels of the exclusion of the body, which is looked upon as irrational, messy and passionate. But the white, brahminic, male and consumerist bodies somehow can relate to the ordered, stable, essential, normal, natural and universal and at the same time derive the right to establish order, stability and normalcy everywhere.[5]

It is clear that humans have fallen prey to untold brutalisation of politically constructed bodies. Thus, the notion of bio-politics is used today in many different disciplines and discourses denoting a politics that deals with life and describes the formation of a political domain on the question of biological life. The approach adds a considerable amount of subtle thinking to this field and this project naturally inscribes itself within the process of examining how political power takes biological life as its privileged object of management and control. It is a domain of the practice of politics, aiming at the regulation and steering of life processes. Bio-politics is not the expression of a sovereign will but aims at the administration and regulation of life processes on the level of populations.[6] Beyond the limited domain of specialists, it is also attracting interest among the general public. Bio-politics may refer to questions like the promotion of medical research, legal regulations on abortion and advance directives of patients specifying their preferences concerning life-prolonging measures.[7]

The central claim on bio-politics is that modern politics is characterised by a tight connection between the operations of the state and the phenomena of life, such as health, death, reproduction and so on. Given this, it is surprising that the central problem of how life and politics have combined combined to form a bio-politics has received relatively little attention. Even where it has received attention, the focus has primarily been on the nature of modern politics that takes hold of and controls the phenomena of life.[8] The politics of silence that forbids the discussion on the body has been broken by numerous theorists in the 1990s, influenced by the postmodern thinkers like Michael Foucault. We can discuss how the messiness of bodies is often conceptualised and totalised as feminised, and as such is 'othered' in bio-politics with the help of Michael Foucault.

Bio-power in the Works of Michael Foucault

A relational and historical notion of bio-politics was first developed by Michel Foucault. His concept of bio-politics assumes the dissociation and abstraction of life from its concrete physical bearers and its objects are not singular human beings but their biological features measured and aggregated on the level of populations. The concept of bio-politics maintains a critical distance from theories that view life as the object of politics. According to Foucault, bio-politics does not supplement traditional political competencies and structures through new domains and questions. It does not produce an extension of politics but rather transforms its core, reformulating concepts of political sovereignty with new forms of political knowledge. He planned his multivolume *history of sexuality* as an investigation of modern bio-politics.[9]

In Foucault's work, a conception of the body as a central component in the operation of power relations has occupied a prominent place. Genealogical analysis reveals the body as an object of knowledge and as a target for the exercise of power. The body is shown to be located in a political field invested with power relations that render it docile and productive and thus politically and economically useful. Such a subjection of the body and its forces is achieved through a political technology.[10] Disputing this view, Foucault explains that 'life' and the 'living being' are at the heart of new political battles. He also demonstrates that power and knowledge begin to take into account the processes of life and the possibility of controlling and modifying them.[11]

We can discern three different ways in which Foucault employs the notion in his work. First, bio-politics stands for a historical rupture in political thinking and practice that is characterized by a re-articulation of sovereign power. Second, he assigns to bio-political mechanisms a central role in the rise of modern racism. A third meaning of the concept refers to a distinctive art of government that historically emerges with liberal forms of social regulation and individual self-governance. He not only employs the term "bio-politics" but also sometimes uses the word "bio-power," without precisely distinguishing between the two notions.[12]

One of the first places where Foucault employs the concept of bio-power is in the first volume of the *History of Sexuality*. In part V, "Right of Death and Power over Life," he notes that beginning in the 17th century, a series of political technologies came to be organized around two central poles – one around the body as machine and another around the population as the "species body."[13] Thus, procedures of power were either meant to discipline the human body, to optimize its capabilities, to extract its force while rendering it more docile or to regulate a series of biological processes, such as birth rates, mortality, or life expectancy that would strongly influence and provide control over the population.

Bio-power in the 19th century was, according to Foucault, a complex amalgam of efforts in public health, nationalism, medicine, psychiatry, demography, information sciences and emerging sciences of sexuality and the tentacles of public policing efforts. Today, bio-power is an assemblage that includes genetic technologies, biological weapons, dense global communication assemblages and other newly emergent objects of analysis.[14]

One of the key features of Foucault's account of bio-power is that the central role he gives to normalisation as a form of social and political regulation. As a technique of bio-power, normalisation is irreducible to the institutions and the force of the law and arises from the socio-political authority of statistics.[15] Bio-power brings life and its mechanisms into the realm of explicit calculation and makes knowledge-power an agent of transformation of human life. Bio-power promotes the identification of bodies with politics because of its management as a part of running countries and empires with the life waging on its own political strategies.[16]

The Development of Bioethics

It is true that the problems related to the human body have ethical dimensions as the body is sacred and violation of any part of the body is immoral and inhuman. There are various discoveries and applications outpacing our reflection on the human body and a number of names have been in use to describe the area of study on the body. One of them is medical ethics[17] which studies the human body within the discipline of medicine and medical care. We have a more inclusive term 'bioethics,' which examines the ethical dimension of the problems of technology, medicine and biology in their application to human life. Thus, bioethics is the critical examination of the moral dimensions of decision-making in health-related contexts and in contexts involving the biological sciences.[18]

Bioethics is defined as the science of survival. A more typical definition is offered as "the application of ethics to the biological sciences, medicine, health care and related areas as well as the public policies directed towards them."[19] Bioethics has narrowed the terms of the public debate on the relations between life and politics, since the discussion is mainly conducted in ethical terms and as an argument about values. In his introduction to the first volume the *Encyclopaedia of Bioethics*, Warren T. Reich, the editor explains it as "a composite term derived from the Greek words *bio* (life) and *ēthikē* (ethics). It can be the systematic study of human conduct in the area of the life sciences and heath care insofar as this conduct is examined in the light of moral values and principles."

Major Issues in Bioethics

The activity of bioethics has a fairly short history with a number of issues. A sum of technological advances in medicine in the second half of the 20th century raised acute ethical dilemmas. For example, the development of kidney dialysis brought questions about the allocation of scarce resources to public attention and the development of transplant surgery using organs from dead donors raised questions about how death should be defined and identified. Also the ethics of research on human subjects began to draw attention and many bioethical issues are matters of professional practice as well as law.[20] We cannot neglect different issues related to the human body in bioethics like abortion, reproductive technologies, prenatal diagnosis, new-borns with birth anomalies, organ transplantation, research on human subjects, genetic engineering and patient's rights as well.

Transplant issue is very much in discussion as it is the question of transplantation of human organs, tissues and cells raising a spectrum of ethical concerns, ranging from dominion, ownership and stewardship. This is nothing but respect for the rights of persons and life-saving remedies to allocation of scarce body parts.[21] The moral structure of clinical research reflects the diverse consequences of using medical procedures with human bodies to produce generalizable knowledge. There should be certain ethical principles that should guide research involving human subjects. They are:

a) Respect for persons incorporates at least two ethical convictions: first, individuals should be treated as autonomous agents, and second, persons with diminished autonomy are entitled to protection.
b) Beneficence demands that persons are to be treated in an ethical manner not only by respecting their decisions but also protecting

them from harm with two general rules like 'do not harm' and 'maximize possible benefits while minimizing possible harms.'

c) Justice is relevant to the selection of subjects of research at two levels: the individual and the social. Individual justice requires researchers to be fair, they should not offer potential benefit only to some or choose 'undesirable' persons for risky research. Social justice extends the principle of fairness to groups with their share of the benefits of research.[22]

Another major bioethical issue is the practice of organ donation. How can we morally justify organ donation? As St. John Paul II encourages organ donation as an act of love when it is done in an ethical manner,[23] one can find a way to give himself/herself in blood and body. This gesture allows others to continue to live. At the same time, we must be aware that commercialization has a serious negative impact on many of the medical and ethical values intimately connected with organ donation. Parts of the human body are not to be treated as commodities. Trade in human body is unacceptable, as in any other disrespectful use of the organs or tissues of a living or deceased person. Selling organs or parts of the body for money reduces the value of a person. To use the body as an 'object' is to violate the dignity of the human person. Paid organ donation spoils the spirit of altruism as there should not be material profit in charitable or altruistic organ donation.[24] An inter-human relationship lies at the heart of organ donation, which establishes a relation between the donor and the recipient as not an "I-It" relationship but an "I-Thou" relationship.

The medical technology has introduced new procedures by which the radical remaking of the human body becomes possible. The moralists hold that it is not justifiable to suppress or to destroy any of the basic functions of the human body except to save the life of the whole body. This principle does not forbid the charitable donation of redundant organs such as one kidney or a re-generable part like skin grafts, blood transfusions. A remarkable development of bioethics is concerned with the problems of human responsibility for the proper care of the health of our bodies as individuals and as a society. An ethics of health care which is part of bioethics should not begin with the problems of cure but of the proper care for heath and the development of the body. For example, physical education ought not to be directed toward winning games and breaking records but to the development of a truly useful and delightful body.[25]

Embodiment in Bio-politics and Bioethics

Both bio-politics and bioethics exhort that the disembodying of our body is a social construction and hence a sustained campaign to generate a positive acceptance of our true biological self can truly set us free from slavery. Various means are to be explored to dignify the body, as the violence to our body is growing with terrorism and technologies like genetic engineering. We can also tackle the disembodying of our body through the creation of 'counter publics' that will spring forth a sustained discourse dignifying our biological dynamism with the help of bio-politics and bioethics. They promote embodiment as a possible means to counteract the body which tends to come off as the inferior partner in an uneasy relationship.[26]

Embodiment enlightens us that 'the patient' whose body is manipulated is also a 'person' who is embodied. The self is constituted by the person's materiality as much as by his or her intellectual, spiritual and psychological dimensions. The body enters into the subjectivity of the person, mediates that subjectivity to the world, and is a medium through which the world and other persons interact with the subject as an embodied self because "the body expresses total existence, not because it is an external accompaniment to that existence, but because existence comes into its own in the body."[27] Embodiment endorses that bodies are not just living organisms which as such become the objects of scientific, technical intervention. Bodies are the spatiality and temporality of selves and it is to persons – not only bodies – that all must respond. Thus, embodiment brings a holistic view of the person. In addition to the unity of self and body, the holism extends to a unity of all the physical parts and processes of the body in their personal and social meanings.[28] The spirit of embodiment inclines to see integration as a value and to affirm that the body's contribution to selfhood is not only essential but is also a component of the highest levels of human value and accomplishment, such as love, friendship, moral insight and art.[29]

The social significance of embodiment in bio-politics and bioethics is neither a resignation to human suffering as 'God's will,' nor an absolutization of the individual's 'right to life.' It is the challenge to create a community of solidarity in which suffering and death are healed and avoided where possible, and are recognised as constitutive of human selfhood. All persons in such a community might learn to take their own bodily vulnerability as an occasion for self-transcendence through compassion for the vulnerability of others.[30]

Conclusion

As Christian philosophers, we have to acknowledge that the human being is not a dual being but of unity having an exterior and interior dimension. We may speak of human beings from different perspectives or consider them under different aspects. These perspectives and aspects do not imply any dualism or antagonistic division. We must affirm that the unity of soul and body is so profound that one has to consider the soul to be the 'form' of the body: it is because of its spiritual soul that the body, made of matter, becomes living. Human body is not two natures united, but rather a union forming a single nature. Since the body is good and shares in the dignity of the 'image of God', it is to be valued, loved and celebrated, and not despised.

Both bio-politics and bioethics describe that bodily experiences can become potential sources of insight. The body is meant for the donation and acceptance of persons as gifts for communion and community. This gifting of oneself andunion is not limited to the married state of life alone. All are called to gift themselves bodily according to the calling each has received in life. In their bodily love-giving and life-giving, humans image their creator in self-donation. Since the gift-dimension pertains to the core of our bodiliness, our bodies are not to be simply objectified or made into objects for personal gratification.

The body is a means of expressing oneself. Thus, it is revelatory and it is the best revealing agent of one's interiority. It is due to this fact that in any communication body language is important. Since the history of philosophy manifests an ambivalent attitude to the body with a greater emphasis on the negative aspects, what is called for today is a holistic attitude. It encourages a realistic appraisal of the strengths and weaknesses of the bodiliness of the embodied person. This will enable us to celebrate rather than bemoan our bodiliness, as the angels and nature did when they became aware that the Word had become flesh. As Christian philosophers in India we should seek the moral common ground basing our moral and political arguments in the public sphere on premises shared by everyone. Both bio-politics and bioethics consider the four principles in any decision making. They are, *respect for autonomy* (that is, a person's entitlement to make decisions for him or herself), *non-maleficence* (not doing harm), *beneficence* (doing good) and *justice*.[31]

Notes

1 Frank Bottomley, *Attitudes to the Body in Western Christendom* (London: Lepus Books, 1979), 170.

2 David Michael Levin, *The Body's Recollection of Being* (London: Routledge and Kegan Paul, 1985), 56.

3 Ibid.

4 Ibid., 57.

5 Thomas Lemke, *Bio-politics: An Advanced Introduction*, trans. Eric Frederick Trump (New York: New York University Press, 2011), 1.

6 Ibid.

7 Ibid., 4.

8 Catherine Mills, "Biopolitical Life," in *Foucault, Biopolitics and Governmentality*, ed. Jakob Nilsson and Sven-Olov Wallenstein (Stockholm: Södertörn University Press, 2013), 74.

9 Catherine Mills, "Biopolitical Life," in *Foucault, Biopolitics and Governmentality*, ed. Jakob Nilsson and Sven-Olov Wallenstein (Stockholm: Södertörn University Press, 2013), 33.

10 Anjana Banerjee, *Foucault's Analysis of Mental Illness: A Psycho-pathological Study* (New Delhi: Global Vision Publishing House, 2007), 163.

11 Michel Foucault, *The History of Sexuality*, Vol. 1, trans. Richard Hurley (London: Penguin, 1981), 135.

12 Colin Koopman, "Michael Foucault's Critical Empiricism Today: Concepts and Analytics in the Critique of Biopower and Infopower," in *Foucault Now*, ed. James D. Faubion (Cambridge: Polity Press, 2014), 92.
13 Foucault, *The History of Sexuality*, 139.
14 Koopman, "Michael Foucault's Critical Empiricism Today," 90.
15 Michel Foucault, *Discipline and Punish: The Birth of the Prison*, trans. Alan Sheridan (London: Penguin, 1979), 177-83.
16 Toby Miller, "Foucault, Marx, Neoliberalism: Unveiling Undercover Boss," in *Foucault Now*, ed. James D. Faubion (Cambridge: Polity Press, 2014), 192.
17 Medical ethics is distinguished into clinical medical ethics and institutional medical ethics. The former focuses on ethical issues at the patient-physician interface while the later examines the structural or institutional context within which medicine is practised like issues in health care policy. Also, there is health care ethics focusing on policy analysis or issues related to insurance. See Thomas A. Shannon, *An Introduction to Bioethics* (New York: Paulist Press, 1997), 4.
18 Samuel Gorovitz, "Bioethics and Social Responsibility," *The Monist* 60 (January 1977): 3.
19 Neil Messer (ed.), *Theological Issues in Bioethics: An Introduction with Readings* (London: Dorton, Longman and Todd Ltd., 2002), 1.
20 Ibid.
21 Maria Michejda, "Transplant Issues," in *The Interaction of Catholic Bioethics and Secular Society*, ed. Russell E. Smith (Massachusetts: The Pope John XXIII Centre, 1992), 114.
22 Carol Levine, Nancy Neveloff Dubler and Robert J. Levine, "Building a New Consensus: Ethical Principles and Policies for Clinical Research on HIV/AIDS," in *Bioethics*, ed. Thomas A. Shannon (New Jersey: Paulist Press, 1993), 301.
23 John Paul II, *Evangelium Vitae* (Bombay: Pauline Publications, 1995), 152.
24 Scaria Kanniyakonil, "Organ Donation and Transplantation," in *Catholic Contributions to Bioethics: Reflections on Evangelium Vitae*, ed. Baiju Julian and Hormis Mynatty (Bangalore, Asian Trading Corporation, 2007), 81.
25 Benedict M. Ashley, *Theologies of the Body: Humanist and Christian* (Massachusetts: The Pope John XXIII Centre, 1985), 421 and 425.
26 Lisa Sowle Cahill, "Embodiment and Moral Critique: A Christian Social Perspective," in *Theological Issues in Bioethics: An Introduction with Readings*, ed. Neil Messer (London: Dorton, Longman and Todd Ltd., 2002), 85.
27 Maurice Merleau-Ponty, *Phenomenology of Perception*, trans. C. Smith (London: Routledge and Kegan Paul, 1962), 166.
28 Cahill, "Embodiment and Moral Critique," 90.
29 Ibid., 91.
30 Ibid., 99.
31 Neil Messer, "Christians and Public Debate on Bioethics," in *Theological Issues in Bioethics: An Introduction with Readings*, ed. Neil Messer (London: Dorton, Longman and Todd Ltd., 2002), 264.

8

Stereotyped Bodies
A Christian Critique of the Impact of Race, Caste, and Colour in Contemporary Indian Society

James D. Chellappa
Christian Academy for Advanced Theological Studies, Nagercoil

Abstract: This article is an attempt to bring out the prejudices on the body based on socio-political discrimination such as caste, colour, race and creed. Basing the analysis primarily on the Indian social situation, this article laments how human bodies are hierarchized on the basis of the different status human persons occupy in the society. While pointing out the negative influence of caste discrimination on Christianity in India, the article also makes attempt to show that Christianity can effectively counter such discriminatory practices in order to achieve an egalitarian society in which all humans are treated with dignity and honour.

Keywords: caste, *jati*, *varna*, Dalits, Tribals, Brahminism, nationalism.

Introduction

India in the present era is going through a great crisis. There is political, social as well as ideological unrest. Race/Caste politics based on religious fanaticism and fundamentalism is on the rise. Discrimination based on one's birth or caste is still a reality even in highly educated circles, athough the media has been silent due to the influence of the bureaucracy. A recent case of the discrimination of a young Dalit woman named Soumya Devi (holding a Master's degree from the UK) who applied for a branch manager post in a leading financial institution in Kerala must be brought to notice. It seems that she was assured of the post after her qualifications and experience were considered excellent. But after meeting her in person, those who offered her the post changed their mind for no reason. Hence, she concluded that she was rejected because in their perception, she was not as "beautiful" and "presentable" as they might have expected.[1]

In a generalized sense we can say that all humans are racists. It's true that, "although one may not have racial intent, one's action may nonetheless have racial consequence."[2] We are born in a particular place, a particular caste/tribe or race, and speak a particular language. We are social animals. A struggle for survival exists in all aspects of the human society. The quest for economic excess – where one has to share limited resources with others – becomes problematic. Martin Luther King, Jr., defines racism as a, "doctrine of the congenital inferiority and worthlessness of a people."[3] An important ecumenical body of different Christian denominations known as the World Council of Churches (WCC) has strongly condemned all aspects of racism. A WCC document reads thus:

> Racism is a sin against God and against fellow human beings. It is contrary to the justice and love of God revealed in Jesus Christ. It destroys the human dignity of both the racist and the victim. When practised by Christians it denies the very faith we profess and undoes the credibility of the Church and its witness to Jesus Christ. Therefore, we condemn racism in all its forms both inside and outside the Church.[4]

Caste[5] system evolved in the Indian subcontinent as a rigid system because of the racist and colour conscious attitudes of the invading and immigrant Aryan outsiders. According to K. M. Pannikar, "the first and basic principle of caste is the inequality of [hu]mankind based on birth."[6] Dalit activist V. T. Rajshekar sees caste as, "an indigenous human pyramid, in ascending order of reverence and descending order of contempt, evolved by the Aryans.... is the ultimate manifestation of injustice."[7] The Indian social reformer Jyotirao Phule identifies the Aryans as Iranians/Persians.[8] The Indian synonym for the term caste is *varna,*[9] out of which comes another word *jati*;[10] both give the idea of distinction and discrimination of humans based on the colour of the human body. In the observation of Dunes, "pigmentation is part of caste – the term *varna* means colour and skin coloration manifests social hierarchy too: 'clean' white at the top; 'dirty' black at the bottom."[11] The indigenous people of the land, the aboriginal people became degraded as *dasyus* (slave), *avarnas* (outcastes), *panchamas* (fifth category), *vanaras* (forest dwellers), *rakshasas* (demonic beings), *boodhas* (demi-gods), *asuras* (demons), *nagas* (serpent worshippers), *mlechchas* (non-Vedic), *anaryas* (non-Aryans) and *chandalas* (untouchables).[12] Swami Dharma Theertha says, "India is divided into about three thousand castes and a much larger number of sub-castes... The members of one group are not allowed to intermarry or inter-dine with those of another group. Each group has a caste-name and a fixed place in the hierarchy of castes graded one above the other. One born low cannot, by any means, rise to a higher caste status."[13] Sociologist Pandey is of the opinion that, "the caste system conditioned the consciousness of lower castes in accepting their inferior status in ritual hierarchy as part of the natural order of things."[14] Indian society as a matter of fact is established on the basis of, "graded inequality, which means the elevation for some and degradation for others."[15]

The colour of the person puts his/her body in a definite place in the hierarchy of caste, race conflicts. In the present era, skin colour, English-speaking ability, articulation skills, attire etc. are some of the markers of caste. Since many communities in modern India do not keep caste surnames along with their names, identifying one's caste becomes an inferential game based on the caste stereotype. One can still go wrong in doing so, because all communities in India had all kinds of these markers. If one is from an 'upper caste' community and still dark skinned, s/he is still considered ugly, not because s/he is dark-skinned, but her/his dark-skin represents a lower caste identity. It is clear that, "casteist cultures have constructed binary notions of opposites – positive and negative, inferior and superior – in the vocabulary of the hegemonic upper caste ideology. Notions like 'superior/inferior' and 'divine/profane' rob the Tribals and Dalits of their very humanness."[16] Discrimination based on colour has not left even the animals in India, for example the cow and buffalo categorization; protection and violence.

Body as a Cause of Shame in the Indian Context

The human body can be defined as, "the physical expression of an integrated and unified organism which includes all levels: mental, emotional and spiritual.[17] Kappen says that, "the body is something concrete, visible and tangible. Bodies are unique, each having their own properties, its own specific use value. Hence, they are not exchangeable in terms of equality. The body of an individual can never be substituted for that of another."[18] Indian society due to the influence of Brahminism/caste system even went to the level of constructing identities to particular people groups /their bodies as 'untouchables.' This 'untouchable' status seems to arrive in relation to some traditional occupations confined to menial and despised jobs. They took up jobs like skinning animal carcases, tanning leather, sweeping, removing human wastes, attendance at burial/cremation grounds, brewing toddy, and washing clothes. These occupations gave them a status of "permanent pollution."[19] Kappen further says that, "bodies of persons are ranked according to their ritual purity or impurity. Understandably, the pure has primacy over the less pure and impure.... But one's body derives its status from the family one was born to. Hence, the ultimate determinant of ritual ranking is birth. Since, however, one cannot change one's body or one's parents, ritual ranking is immutable. This explains the rigidity of the caste system."[20]

The caste system has contaminated the Indian psyche to levels unknown. The historian K. M. Panikkar observes that, "caste is not merely a principle of social division, but a comprehensive system of life, dealing with food, marriage, education, association and worship. It is a religion rather than a changing social order."[21] Onesimu identifies untouchability as, "an economic system which is worse than slavery."[22] So, for a person who is born in an untouchable or so called low caste, the stigma attached to his/her caste is from birth to death. The body bears the burns of the injustice perpetuated by the society. This injustice is seen from a spiritual or religious lens and named as one's own *karma* (fruits of one's own deeds). Dr. S. Radhakrishnan condemns the upper caste Indian psyche by saying, "in our relations with one another, we have failed to apply scientific social wisdom. This failure is writ large in our society. Social abuses like untouchability are tolerated simply because the spirit in us is suppressed by the force of custom. They are practised by otherwise kindly people who have ceased to feel and whose understanding is petrified by tradition."[23]

In India, rape[24] is taken as a political tool by the dominant castes and the powerful to inflict pain and humiliation on women and even on the societies to which the victimized women belong. Women suffer double discrimination; one in caste lines and another in relation to gender. By raping the body of a woman the rapist feels as if he sends a message to the entire community of which she belongs. Nuns belonging to Christian community are not spared too; even a 72-year-old nun had to go through such an ordeal.[25] According to the National Crime Records Bureau's (NCRB) latest 2014 report, there were 33,764 victims of rape out of 33,707 reported rape cases in the country during the year 2013. The media is biased on rape cases related to Dalits and minorities. Even the police ignore complaints brought by victims of the downtrodden strata of society. We all know how the media and the Indian society stood up for the victim belonging to the high/forward caste in the Delhi gang rape case.[26] There is also an accusation against Indian caste-ridden patriarchy that, "if a woman is raped by a man of another community, the entire city gets burn with communal frenzy. But the entire community remains a silent spectator when a woman is raped by a man of the same community, as if the community has a right to rape women of their own community.[27]

Many cases of women belonging to the North Eastern states of India featuring Mongoloid racial strains also get molested, raped, abused, and slut shamed all over Indian metros and towns just because of their different looks and costumes. The main reason for atrocities against the Mongoloid communities is because they come in the category of Scheduled Tribals which is counted as part of the lower strata of the Indian society similar to the Dalits. Another visible reason is that the NE Tribals as immigrant workers have taken up odd jobs such as working in hotels as servers or dish washers which are counted as menial by the dominant society and many women working in entertainment industries like massage parlours have even gone to the level of being exploited through the flesh trade by coercion and the promise of unimaginable financial benefits.[28] A Dalit girl was recently beaten by women belonging to the upper caste of her same village because her shadow fell on a man from the so-called upper caste community.[29] Another horrible tale of a Panchayat ordering the rape of two teenage Dalit sisters due to the alleged misbehaviour of their brother towards an upper caste girl can only shame us in the international arena.[30] The Indian psyche is sickened with racist and casteist mentalities to the core, to such an extent that even women become predators of the poor and the oppressed.

The Cow, Buffalo and the Indian

Indians from time immemorial were beef eaters.[31] The beef culture of India is surely pre-Islamic and pre-Christian. Beef politics is a disastrous weapon in the contemporary Indian political scene. Hindutva[32] forces employ beef politics to promote a unique Hindu identity and thus attempt to identify the "other," the "beef eaters" that is, the Muslims, Christians and the so-called Hindu-Dalits, the *avarnas*. Hindutva according to Suchitra Krishnamoorthi, "is a militant imposition of wrongly interpreted tenets of Hinduism. Hindutva is a political tool – nothing to do with the religion itself."[33] Nehemiah Thompson says, "Hindutva is more an economic philosophy for the survival of a privileged minority than a religious phenomenon."[34] Now it is sad to see that the cow, a mere animal, has got more respect than humans do in society and the media. The bodies and the lives of the cows are assumed to have more spiritual worth over the bodies and lives of humans. In 2006, five young Dalit boys were murdered (3 were beaten to death and 2 burnt alive) by a furious mob of 2000 just because the boys skinned a dead cow![35] S. Anand, the famous anti-caste activist, has already expressed his pain concerning this issue in an article written in 2002: "the Dalits account for 165 million of India's one billion-plus human population. The population of cows is pegged at 206 million. There are more cows than Dalits in India. The cows, therefore, have more rights than Dalits. For instance, you can kill Dalits before thousands of witnesses and get away with it. But the imagined murder of a cow will not be suffered. The state promotes the drinking of cow urine and dung, while Dalits are forced to eat the shit and the piss of caste Hindus."[36] Beef related violence has become common throughout India. The worst affected are the minority communities.

The recent gruesome murder of Mohammad Akhlaq[37] in UP's Dadri has made many Indian secularists to raise their voices in protest.[38] The debauchery was sparked by rumours that the Muslim family had killed and eaten a cow. The attack allegedly came moments after an announcement at a nearby Hindu temple that Mohammad Akhlaq had slaughtered a cow.[39] Recently Haryana's Chief Minister Manohar Lal Khattar has said "Muslims can continue to live in this country but they will have to give up eating beef,"[40] joining a growing list of leaders from the BJP and its allies who have weighed in on the issue of cow slaughter. Another mouth piece of the present rulers and a very controversial BJP MP Sakshi Maharaj on Saturday pitched for a law that provides for the death penalty for cow slaughter. Strongly advocating protection of cows, the BJP MP said that "a strong law should be put in place to hang people responsible for cow slaughter."[41] The Indian secular community did various protests regarding this issue and one way of showing dissent was organizing beef fests in many cities of India.[42] The sarcasm is that beef is already banned in most of northern and western India, and there are partial bans in most of the rest of the country.

Kancha Ilaiah sheds more light on this issue when he draws the distinction in his book *Buffalo Nationalism.*[43] Demanding us to critically evaluate the current radical spirituality of our nation, he asks: "why did the cow but not the buffalo become a Hindu spiritual animal?"[44] Ilaiah claims that, "the biggest sufferer of White racism is the world was all that was black, whether humans or animals. In India in the Hitlerite imagination of Aryan racial superiority black human beings and loveable black animals like the buffalo suffered enormous losses of identity. As part of this Aryan arrogance the buffalo, which has the same beautiful colour of the Dravidians, began to be held in contempt. The cow, by and large a white skinned animal, became respectable and beautiful."[45] He further adds that, "the Indian Aryans extended their racism not only to human beings by dividing them into castes but extended it to animals because of which the black buffalo never acquired a spiritual place in the brahminical Hindu mythology."[46] Ilaiah identifies the ideology of Brahminism as, "the most dangerous school of thought that destroyed the meat culture of India by pushing the vast masses into a complex process of self-negation. Those who continue to eat meat are made to feel that they are uncultured."[47] Brahmins were meat eaters which include beef and wine bibbers until the time Jainism and Buddhism challenged their status of supremacy. To counter this threat the Brahmins invented ideas like *ahimsa*, vegetarianism and renunciation focusing on their own survival.[48] Sociologist Dumont is of the opinion that the ideas of purity and impurity are linked with the cow becoming not only non-killable but an object of worship. Killing a cow was equated to the murder of a Brahmin. Assimilating the cow to the Brahmin and it becoming an object of veneration was due to a social circumstance, namely, the opposition of the pure and impure being applied in a social context in which the Brahmin and the Untouchable are at the opposite poles, the latter responsible for the dead cattle, and the former, a paragon of purity, assimilated to the cow.[49]

Indian Christianity and Caste/Race, Colour Issues

One God, one-humanity is the cry of the humanists. Christianity emerged as a humanistic religion which brought out a universal message of love and wellbeing to all humanity. Christianity emerged as a humane religion which saw no distinction between Jew, Greek, and barbarian, the rich and the poor, and between different genders. Christianity's association with India has not been a very successful model per se. Now we can see Indian Christianity too is corrupted and divided based on caste and colour. Contemporary Indian Christian ethos is racist, casteist, and coloured. Churches are divided and congregations scattered is a reality in almost all major denominations.

The New Testament gives ample evidence of Jesus being a tolerant and universalistic Jew. Jesus healed the sick irrespective of whether the person belonged to the Jewish community or not. Unlike his fellow Jews, Jesus dealt with the Samaritans in a very open manner. He even sojourned in their midst and preached the gospel (Jn. 4). Jesus did not have contempt for the sick bodies; there are occasions in which his touch healed them, even lepers (Mt. 8:3). For Jesus all humans are equals and thus respectable. The ideology of Jesus was carried further by the apostles in the pages of the New Testament. St. Paul has reflected the mind of Jesus clearly by saying, "there is neither Jew nor Greek, there is neither bond nor free, there is neither male nor female: for ye are all one in Christ Jesus" (Gal 3:28). This is quite a statement for a once nationalistic Jew to make. Paul understood that God detests racial discrimination. But a lot of terrible things have been done by people in the name of Christianity; the Nazis in Europe, the Ku Klux Klan in America, Apartheid in South Africa, the situation in Northern Ireland, and the list could go on and on – racial bigotry all done in the name of Christianity. The Indian Church has also its share of unchristian endeavours.

There are evidences that the oldest Indian Christians, the Syrian Christians retained the practice of untouchability in order to protect their high caste status. They had limited association with other castes and, "their relations with other groups were governed by rules which were in no way influenced by their Christian beliefs, and they recognized and practiced the whole apparatus of pollution."[50] Missionary/Colonial Christianity of the West too did not fully strive to cleanse social evils from the Christian community. Nehru, the first Prime Minister of India aptly criticizes the Colonial missionary movement by saying, "with the coming of the British power, a new type of missionary came to India. He was attached to British officials and the British army of occupation, and represented British Imperialism far more than the spirit of Christ. It is strange that the gospel of Jesus, the gentle but unrelenting rebel against untruth and injustice in all forms, should be made a tool of imperialism and capitalism and political domination and social injustice."[51] Criticism of the Western Christian impact on Dalit communities is put forth by Indians too. K. Wilson an eminent Indian Christian philosopher clearly scrutinizes the situation. In his words:

The imperialistic and capitalistic nature of the Christian missions has given rise to a new psychology among the Dalit Christians. They have developed a demoralized self-image of themselves. Dependency has increased. Extra-territorial loyalties are either promoted or encouraged preventing the Dalits from seeking local opportunities for self-development. On several occasions everything Indian has been viewed as Hindu and hence detested by average Indian Christians. On the other hand the missions have been successful in projecting their messianic image. Missionary paternalism has eroded every nerve of the Dalit Christians. All this has contributed towards a community of slaves in Churches, and more particularly in mission compounds... The thrust of this whole saga is that missionary service has contributed more towards Christianisation than humanization of the dehumanized Dalit converts. What therefore transpired in the process of religious change is that the depressed Christians have nicely been transferred from the domination of one kind of lordship to another, i.e., from the lordship of the privileged Hindus to the lordship of the imperial and capitalistic Western Christian lords and from Indian social imperialism to Western Christian religious imperialism.[52]

Down the centuries there are manifold disputes in between the Caste-Christians and the Dalit-Christians within all Indian churches. Yet Christians claim to be a casteless society. In this context Chief Justice K. G. Balakrishnan had once asked a question to the Indian Christian community: "would the Christians admit that they practise caste system and that Dalits (among them) face social discrimination requiring reservation to uplift their cause?"[53] Fr. G. Cosmon Arokiaraj, a Dalit priest from Tamil Nadu says, "For Indian Christians, caste is first, Christ is second."[54] Many from the oppressed strata of society are converted to Christianity in the hopes that they would get self-respect, dignity, and equality. But once converted the realities they face are different. It is true that, "the Dalit Christians are subject to atrocities, violence and disabilities solely because they suffer the sigma of Untouchability. Whenever there is any killing or violence, the Caste people do not discriminate between the Hindus and the Christians. Even the Caste Christians do not treat the Dalit Christians as equals."[55] Fr. S. M. Michael identifies a five-fold discrimination that the Dalit Christians suffer in India: "(i) discrimination from the government, (ii) by the caste Hindus, (iii) by fellow Hindu Dalits, (iv) by the upper caste Christian community, and (v) by the subgroups of Dalit Christians themselves."[56]

Christians persecuting fellow Christians is a shame. In Tamil Nadu and elsewhere we have seen Caste-Christians denying the Dalit Christians even a place for burial in the Church's cemetery grounds. The dead bodies are shunned from entering the Caste-Christian streets even if the body is to be taken to the same church cemetery. Dalit Christians have gone up to the level of blaming Church authorities to the UN officials.[57] They see the discrimination against Dalit Christians in the Indian Church as a human rights issue. A desire for justice is overwhelming in the Dalit Christian community. A Dalit Christian activist Chandra Prasad feels that, "the Indian Church cannot be called Christian if it retains caste and caste related discriminations inherited from Hindu Brahminical social order."[58]

Conclusion

Indian Christians share a two-fold rootedness,[59] one Christian and another Indian. Sometimes Indian Christians are so much rooted in their Indianness, that they have become Hindu-Christians. Hindutva ideology has not only captured the nation of India, it has also rather negatively captured the Church. One example can be the electoral victory of the BJP candidate Pon Radhakrishnan and present Central Minister for Road Transport & Highways, in the Christian dominated (46.85%)[60] Kanyakumari parliamentary constituency. The Christians of Kanyakumari failed to exhibit Christian ideals in the above said election because they rallied in unison along caste lines. The Indian Christians tend to be shallow in their Christianness which can be proved by the atrocities perpetuated by the dominant Caste Christians on their fellow poor Dalit Christians.

The caste system which focus on the colour or *varna* is penetrating into even the Christian youth. Indian Christian youth do take active parts in caste politics. Even Church politics have blended with caste ideologies. South Indian Christian priests and missionaries regularly face various discriminations in North India. The South-North, Aryan-Dravidian, upper caste-lower caste, Dalit-non Dalit divide visually exists in various forms within the Indian Church and Indian Christian society. The Indian Church has to come back to the original Christian commitment where all humans are seen as Children of God and are endowed with dignity and honour. The noble ideals of *Tirukkural*, such as like *pirappokkum ellaa uyirkkum sirappovvaa seydhozhil vaetrumai yaan* – though by birth all lives are of the same, equal nature, only occupational excellence brings glory and stature (*Tirukkural*, 972) should be highlighted by the Indian Christian community at large. The Christian community must reflect the mission of Jesus which was plainly penned in the Nazareth Manifesto centuries back. The Church should focus on justice, equality, holistic wellbeing of all and unity within the Christian community and also in the global human community at large. Not only that,

Indian Christians should be ready to partner with people of other faith to bring about a just society in which none will be discriminated, none will be shamed and none will be ignored nor rejected.

Notes

1 Meenu, "Bodies That Do Not Belong" in www.dalitweb.org/?p=2845 (accessed July 20, 2015).

2 Michael Eric Dyson, *Can You Hear Me Now?* (New York: Basic Civitas Books, 2009), 189.

3 Martin Luther King, Jr., *Where Do We Go from Here: Chaos or Community?* (Boston: Beacon Press, 1968), 48.

4 Ans J. van der Bent (ed.), *Breaking down the Walls: World Council of Churches Statements and Actions on Racism, 1948-1985* (Geneva: WCC, 1986), 53.

5 The word caste comes from the Portuguese word 'casta' signifying breed, race, of same kind.

6 K. M. Panikkar, *Caste & Democracy* (New Delhi: Critical Quest, 2004), 7.

7 V. T. Rajashekar, "Justice, Peace and the Integrity of Creation and the Indian Dalits," in *Radical Justice: An Issue of Justice, Peace and the Integrity of Creation*, ed. Barney Pityana (Geneva: WCC, 1990), 40.

8 Jothirao Phule, "Slavery: In the Civilized British Government under the Cloak of Brahminism," in P. G. Patil (ed.), *Collected Works of Mahatma Phule* (Mumbai: Education Dept., Govt. of Maharashtra, 1991), 1:72.

9 K. K. Pillay, *The Caste System in Tamil Nadu* (Chennai: MTP Publishers, 1979; rep. 2007), 2. The word *varna* as used in the *Rig-Veda* has the literal meaning "outward appearance, exterior, form, figure, shape, colour" besides the figurative "colour, race, kind, sort, character, quality, property."

10 *Jati* is a group of clans, tribes, communities and sub-communities. The term *jati* is translated as caste rather loosely. Under this system, a person is born into a *jati* with ascribed social roles and endogamy and a traditional occupation.

11 Alan Dundes, *Two Tales of Crow and Sparrow: A Freudian Folkloristic Essay on Caste and Untouchability* (Lanham: Rowman & Littlefield Publishers, 1997), 52.

12 Dasyus or "slaves" is a derogatory term used by the Aryans to refer the dark skinned indigenous population of the Indian sub-continent. It is a Sanskrit word found in ancient Indian texts such as the *Rig-Veda* and *Arthasastra*. It usually means "enemy" or "servant." The Dalits and scheduled tribes who do not form part of the Hindu varna social system, are called *avarna*. *Vanara* means forest dweller but is translated as monkey. In Ramayana the *vanaras* are the monkeys who helped Rama. They refer to the people who lived in central India and they favoured Aryan invasion. *Rakshasas* are demonic beings. They are also called as man-eaters. *Rakshasas* were most often depicted as ugly, fierce-looking and enormous creatures and with two fangs protruding down from the top of the mouth as well as sharp, claw-like fingernails. They are shown as being mean, growling like beasts and as insatiable cannibals. The term *Ashura* is translated as "demon," "harmful supernatural force," "slave," "servant" or "barbarian" depending on the context in which the word is used. The word *Naga* in the Sanskrit language means *snake* or *serpent*. Maybe they were a serpent-worshipping group who were later described as *serpents* themselves in ancient Indian literature. In present context Nagas refer to a group of Tribals who inhabit the North Eastern hilly terrains of India. Sanskrit word *mleccha* means "non-Vedic," "barbarian" and is used as a derogatory term in the sense of "impure and/or "inferior" people. *Chandala*

is a Sanskrit word for someone who deals with disposal of corpses, and is traditionally considered to be untouchable.

13 Swami Dharma Theertha, *History of Hindu Imperialism* (Chennai: Dalit Educational Literature Centre, 1992), 178-179.

14 Rajendra Pandey, *Minorities in India: Protection and Welfare* (New Delhi: APH Publishing, 1997), 100.

15 Sebastian Alackapally, "Ambedkar: Vision of Conversion and Mission of Emancipation," in *Tradition and Inovation: Philosophy of Rootedness and Openness*, ed. Saju Chackalackal (Bangalore: ATC, 2011), 336.

16 Kancha Ilaiah, *Post-Hindu India: A Discourse in Dalit-Bahujan, Socio-Spiritual and Scientific Revolution* (New Delhi: SAGE Publications, 2009), 4.

17 J. Maurus, *Living Moments of Wholeness* (Mumbai: St. Paul's, 1994), 26.

18 S. Kappen, *Tradition, Modernity, Counter Culture: An Asian Perspective* (Bangalore: Visthar, 1994), 2.

19 Oliver Mendelsohn and Marika Vicziany, *The Untouchables: Subordination, Poverty and the State in Modern India* (New Delhi: CUP, 2000), 7.

20 Kappen, *Tradition, Modernity, Counter Culture*, 4.

21 Panikkar, *Caste & Democracy*, 4.

22 J. A. David Onesimu, *Dr. Ambedkar's Critique towards Christian Dalit Liberation* (Delhi: ISPCK, 2008), 75.

23 S. Radhakrishnan, *The Foundations of Civilisation: Ideas and Ideals* (Delhi: Orient Paperbacks, 1936; rep. 2010), 78.

24 Rape is the most common crime against women in India. Before 3 February 2013, the definition of rape in Section 375 of the Indian Penal Code excluded marital rape, same sex crimes and considered all sex with a minor below the age of sixteen as rape. After 2 April 2013, to include martial rape and same sex crimes, the definition was revised through the Criminal Law (Amendment) Act 2013, which also increased the legal age of minor to eighteen. For details see Section 375 of the Indian Penal Code.

25 http://www.ndtv.com/india-news/ghar-wapasi-behind-nuns-rape-alleges-bengal-minorities-commission-vice- chairperson-747516 (accessed February 5, 2016).

26 Media was filled with Nirbhaya case; people protested and sought justice in all street corners. Books were written and even the judicial system amended. See Rajesh Talwar, *Courting Injustice: The Nirbhaya Case and the Aftermath* (New Delhi, 2013).

27 Kiran Saxena, "Legitimatising Subjugation of Woman: Role of Religion in India," in *Women Politics and Religion*, ed. Hem Lata Swarup and Sarojini Bisaria (Etawah: Aditya, 1991), 86.

28 See http://timesofindia.indiatimes.com/city/delhi/Nigerian-held-for-raping-girl-from-Nagaland/articles-how/44952994.cms; http://e-pao.net/epSubPageExtractor.asp?src= news_section.Press_Release.Press_Release_ 2011. A_Naga_Girl_from_Manipur_ Sexually_Assaulted_and_A_Boy_Attacked_in_Delhi_ 20111017 (accessed February 5, 2016).

29 See http://indianexpress.com/article/india/india-others/dalit-girl-severly-beaten-as-her-shadow-falls-on-high-caste-muscleman/ (accessed February 5, 2016).

30 See http://www.newindianexpress.com/nation/Rape-Those-Two-Dalit-Girls-UP-Khap-Panchayat-Orders-Villagers/2015/08/20/article2984588.ece (accessed February 5, 2016).

31 See D. N. Jha, *The Myth of the Holy Cow* (New Delhi: Navayana: 2009; rep. 2015).

32 Hindutva, or "Hinduness," a Sanskrit term coined by Vinayak Damodar Savarkar in 1923, is the predominant form of Hindu nationalism in India. Prafull Goradia, a former MP from the BJP cognizes Hindutva in a positive way by relating with the socio-political aspiration of the Indian nationalists. His book, *The Saffron Book* (New Delhi: Contemporary Targett,

2001) deals with Hindutva as an ideology which will fill the vacuum created by the demise of communism, the decline of socialism and the disappearance of Nehruvian secularism in India. He believes that Hindutva will hold the ideological centre stage in contemporary Indian politics.

33 Suchitra Krishnamoorthi, "Dear BJP, I'm a Hindu and I reject Hindutva," in http://www.dailyo.in/politics/hindutva-hinduism-bjp-rss-narendra-modi-congress-sonia-gandhi-rahul-gandhi-anti-national-meat-ban-beef-ban-intolerance-religion/story/1/6209.html (accessed September 15, 2015).

34 Nehemiah Thompson, "Hindutva: A Historical Review" – A Paper Presented in a Seminar on Religious Harmony, Organized by Nesamony Institute of Religion and Society (NIRAS), Nesamony Memmorial Christian College, Marthandam on January 11, 2003.

35 "Five Dalits lynched to death for skinning cow, sacred to Hindus," http://www.asianews.it/news-en/Five-Dalits-lynched-to-death-for-skinning-cow,-sacred-to-Hindus-7052.html (accessed March 10, 2015).

36 S. Anand, "'Holy' Cow and 'Unholy' Dalit," http://www.outlookindia.com/article/holy-cow-and-unholy-dalit/217815 (accessed March 10, 2015).

37 Sadanand Dhume, "A Murder over Beef Exposes Indian Tensions," http://www.wsj.com/articles/a-murder-over-beef-exposes-indian-tensions-1444322291 (accessed March 10, 2015).

38 Nayantara Sahgal has inscribed her protest by writing an open letter titled "The Unmaking of India." In it she says, "… India's culture of diversity and debate is now under vicious assault. Rationalists who question superstition, anyone who questions any aspect of the ugly and dangerous distortion of Hinduism known as Hindutva – whether in the intellectual or artistic sphere, or whether in terms of food habits and lifestyle – are being marginalised, persecuted, or murdered… The Prime Minister remains silent about this reign of terror. We must assume he dare not alienate evil-doers who support his ideology." Cited in "How India's Writers are Fighting Intolerance," in http://www.bbc.com/news/world-asia-india-34513311 (accessed October 15, 2015).

39 Eugene Volokh, "Man murdered by mob in India for allegedly eating forbidden meat," https://www.washingtonpost.com/news/volokh-conspiracy/wp/2015/09/30/a-mob-in-india-just-dragged-a-man-from-his-home-and-beat-him-to-death-for-eating-beef/ (accessed October 15, 2015).

40 "Haryana CM Khattar says remarks on Muslims and beef 'misconstrued'," http://www.hindustantimes.com/india/muslims-have-to-give-up-beef-to-live-in-country-haryana-cm-khattar/story-8T0fngqCyGt81pdkNLzvsL.html (accessed October 17, 2015).

41 "BJP MP Sakshi Maharaj for death to those who slaughter," http://indianexpress.com/article/india/india-news-india/bjp-mp-sakshi-maharaj-for-death-to-those-who-slaughter-cows/ (accessed October 17, 2015).

42 One day beef festival was organized in Chennai to protest Dadri murder on 10-11-15; http://timesofindia.indiatimes.com/india/Beef-festival-in-Chennai-to-protest-Dadri-murder/articleshow/ 49306766.cms (accessed October 15, 2015). Beef fest was celebrated in Kerala to protest against Dadri killing on 6-1015; http://www.ndtv.com/kerala-news/beef-fest-celebrated-in-kerala-college-to-protest-against-dadri-killing-1229496 (accessed October 15, 2015).

43 Kancha Ilaiah, *Buffalo Nationalism: A Critique of Spiritual Fascism* (Kolkata: Samya, 2004).

44 Ibid., xxv.

45 Ibid., 143.

46 Ibid., 143.

47 Ilaiah, *Post-Hindu India*, 7.

48 M. N. Srinivas, "Some Reflections on the Nature of Caste Hierarchy," in *Caste, Hierarchy, and Individualism: Indian Critique of Louis Dumont's Contributions*, ed. R. S. Khare (Delhi: OUP, 2009), 103.

49 Louis Dumont, *Homo Hierarchicus: The Caste System and its Implications* (Delhi: Vikas Publications, 1970), 151.

50 Duncan B. Forrester, *Caste and Christianity: Attitudes and Policies on Caste of Anglo-Saxon Protestant Missions in India* (London and Atlantic Highlands: Curzon Press and Humanities Press, 1980), 99.

51 Jawaharlal Nehru, *The Unity of India* (New York: The John Day Company, 1942), 50-51.

52 K. Wilson, *The Twice Alienated: Culture of Dalit Christians* (Hyderabad: Booklinks Corp., 1982), 21-22.

53 "Do Christians also Practise Caste System, asks SC," in http://timesofindia.indiatimes.com/india/Do-Christians-also-practise-caste-system-asks-SC/articleshow/2218560.cms (accessed August 12, 2015).

54 Megan Sweas, "Caste First, Christ Second, for Some Indian Christians," http://religiondispatches.org/caste-first-christ-second-for-some-indian-christians/ (accessed August 12, 2015).

55 "Caste Identity Within the Church: Twice Alienation," http://www.dalitchristians.com/html/castechurch.htm (accessed August 12, 2015).

56 S. M. Michael, *Dalits' Encounter with Christianity: A Case of Mahars in Maharashtra* (Delhi: ISPCK, 2010), 43.

57 "Dalit Christians in India file complaint with UN against the Vatican," in http://www.ucanews.com/news/dalit-christians-in-india-file-complaint-with-un-against-the-vatican/73861 (accessed August 12, 2015).

58 D. Manohar Chandra Prasad, *The Book of Exodus and Dalit Liberation: With Reference to Minjung Theology* (Bangalore: ATC, 2005), ix.

59 Johnson Puthenpurackal, "Cultural Rootedness and Cultural Openness," in *Culture as Gift and Task: Philosophical Reflections in the Indian Context*, ed. Keith D'Souza (Bangalore: ATC, 2008), 75.

60 http://censusindia.gov.in/Dist_File/datasheet-3330.pdf (accessed February 05, 2016).

9

Humans for Sale
Objectification, Commodification and Reification of Human Beings

Ashley Miranda
Divyadaan, Nashik

Abstract: Human beings are capable of great goodness and yet they are also often guilty of unimaginable cruelty. This cruelty is expressed in the human tendency to reduce fellow human beings, to the status of objects for one's use, pleasure and profit. The impact of the commodification of human beings is invariably felt first in the violence and exploitation of the *body* and is a phenomenon that is more prevalent than we would dare to admit. It touches practically everyone's life. Perhaps we are not directly involved in the worst kinds of human commodification like reducing women and children to mere sex objects, but that does not mean we have done no wrong. The food that we eat, our clothes and the homes we live in are tainted with the blood and sweat of the oppressed, silent, helpless people whose humanity is seriously compromised in very subtle ways. One of the saddest facts about human exploitation is that some of the worst exploiters are people to whom the victims are linked to relationships of care and love: family members, to be precise. Any form of exploitation, whether it involves harm to the body or not, invariably leads to the breaking of the human spirit. This said it must also be acknowledged that the human spirit is amazingly resilient and that while most victims are destroyed some come out of their experiences of abuse and exploitation as amazingly stronger and compassionate persons. Of course this should not put us into a 'denial mode' and lead us to think that the situation of those who are exploited and abused is not as horrific as it is often made out to be. Nothing can justify human exploitation. Even one woman or child exploited is one victim too many!

Keywords: Abuse, Human exploitation, slavery, commodification, objectification, reification.

Introduction: Human Depravity with No Limits

Voltaire has a delightful little story of two giants on a cosmic journey who visit a little mound of mud which they initially think of as uninhabited, but eventually discover to be inhabited by some very tiny microscopic creatures, one of which they find extremely strange and amusing. It turns out that these creatures call themselves humans and think of themselves as the greatest beings in the universe; the ones for whom everything exists, for whom everything was made. The giants are tickled no end; they have never seen so much arrogance, such an exaggerated sense of 'self-importance' and destiny.[1]

We recognize this sense of 'self-importance and destiny' in ourselves; it is the secret of our survival and prosperity. While we acknowledge the fragility of our individual lives as human beings we very rightly feel proud of all that the human race has achieved over the millennia. Ours is a dynamic universe in which every creature is caught up in the relentless vortex of evolution. The human being alone among all these creatures is above this process, not in the sense that he can stop it but in the sense that he is able, to an extent, to influence its speed and give it a direction.

Considering the gigantic proportions of space and time, the human claim to being special is indeed laughable. But this is precisely what the great religions claim; this is precisely the conviction on which human civilization and history is built on. Different religions, seers and philosophers have at different times, down the ages, spoken of man as 'a friend of the Gods', as 'containing within himself a spark of the divine', as 'made in the image and likeness of God', 'as identical with the divine in the core of his being.' It is only recently that questions have been raised about man's specialness, with many thinkers contending that this idea of specialness has caused immense suffering to other creatures and irreparable damage to creation as a whole. Human beings are a part of nature, not superior not inferior, a product of evolution, nothing more nothing less!

Human Person: Citizen of Heaven and Earth but also of Hell!

This paper is rooted in the conviction that the human person is unique among all creatures; a creature among creatures, and yet the greatest of all creatures. Weak, fragile and even insignificant and yet the only creature that can ask the question of the meaning of life and take steps to ensure that this life, however brief, is lived purposefully. The human person is an extraordinary creature, created by God in his image and likeness, a being called by God to a close and intimate relationship with him. The human person is a spiritual being in the fullest sense of the term and yet he is unique in that his spirit is totally and wholly rooted in the flesh. The human person is at one time both a citizen of heaven and a citizen of earth. What this paper wants to contend is that this same human person who so uniquely straddles heaven and earth in that he/she can dissolve the distinction between heaven and earth by the choices he/she makes, is also a being who uniquely straddles earth and hell and can by the choices he/she makes, blur the distinction between earth and hell, not only for himself/herself and his/her fellow creatures but for all of creation as well. It is the very same gift of freedom that makes him/her the greatest of creatures which also exposes him to the risk of being the most depraved and wretched of all creatures, capable of deeds so abominable that he/she could make the devil seem like a boy scout.

Much has been said about the human vocation of love and how the ability and willingness of human beings to go beyond themselves and care for the other in a spirit of genuine self-emptying and generosity enables them to explore the highest potentials of human nature. In the recent years many philosophers have focused on what they consider to be the subtle craving for power that lurks just below the surface in all human interactions. It often masquerades itself as love and this is what makes it particularly vicious.

Among those who have highlighted this aspect of human nature especially in the context of social interaction are Sartre, Schopenhauer, Nietzsche, Foucault and Derrida among others. Sartre is famously reported to have said, "The other is my hell;"[2] which means that human beings spontaneously tend to reduce other humans to the status of objects on which they constantly pass judgments.[3] Schopenhauer held that the body is the expression of the will, which is essentially at war with itself. He went on to add that since desire and will is the very core of the world, human existence as such is violent.[4] Nietzsche, in his *Will to Power* and a number of other works asserts that underlying everything that humans do is a not so subtle desire to dominate. Humans are egoistic through and through. Even the most altruistic action is ultimately, even if unconsciously, directed towards manipulation. Nietzsche sees this *Will to Power* as one that is not only characteristic of every human dynamic but also one that pervades the whole world and all the processes that constitute it.[5] Foucault is famous for his assertion that all human relationships, be they among individuals or within families, or in society as a whole are characterized by power relationships that are often characterized by immobility, irreversibility and stagnation, which must most appropriately be called sates of domination.[6] Derrida holds a view very similar to that of Foucault. He says that all "absolute truth claims" are manifestations of power structures operative in society.[7]

Of course, we must admit that we are not restricted to just two diametrically opposed and mutually exclusive ways of understanding the human being. The narrative that claims that the human person as a loving being by nature need not be contrary to the narrative that views the human person as a being struck by an unquenchable thirst and relentless hunger for power. There could be and there is a third narrative that claims that the human person is both angel and beast, a being who seeks love and seeks to love in an attitude of total self-giving, and yet at the very same time a being who seeks power and control not only over his own life but also over that of his fellow men and all creation.

It is on the second part of this third narrative that we will focus on henceforth. This desire to dominate, to exercise power over self and others is expressed in a number of ways, none more brutal and vicious than the tendency to reduce other humanbeings to the status of commodities, things to be used, as objects possessing monetary value or no value at all. This tendency which is as old as humankind itself is known by a number of names, among which terms such as objectification, commodification, and reification are the most used. This is usually accompanied by a refusal to acknowledge the spiritual or non-material dimension of the human personality and a reduction of a person's identity and value to that of his physical body.

Reducing Human Beings to the Status of Objects

Objectification is the tendency to identify the human person purely and simply with his body. It is reasonable to consider the human body as an object since it belongs to the physical realm, and like any object of the physical realm it can be studied by means of empirical observation. The body is subject to physical laws and so it is indeed legitimate to think of it as an object. But to reduce the whole of the human person to the status of an object is another matter altogether. The body is constitutive of human identity and so understanding ourselves as persons or other persons would require that we carefully take note of the bodily dimension of human existence. Immanuel Kant is among the most prominent philosophers to have reflected on the phenomena of objectification. He argued that human beings have an intrinsic dignity that must be respected. This respect, he believed, is shown in treating every person as an end and never as a means. He held that objectification of a person is contrary to human dignity and is most often expressed in treating other persons as things for our use and casting them aside 'like a lemon sucked dry' as soon as they have exhausted their usefulness.[8] In contemporary discourse the notion of objectification finds prominent place in feminist theory. While many feminist thinkers focus on the propensity on the part of many men to reduce women to the status of mere tools for their purpose, there are a few feminists who point out that women are often equally guilty of thinking of themselves purely as objects with their excessive, almost paranoid obsession about, their appearance.

Martha Nussbaum is credited with coming up with what is perhaps the most systematic analysis of the phenomenon of objectification to date. She says objectification in relationships between human beings has one or more the following features: instrumentality, denial of autonomy, inertness, fungibility, violability, ownership, denial of subjectivity.[9] To my knowledge, some of the deepest insights into the human tendency to objectify self and others are found in the thought of Martin Buber in his discourse on "I-Thou" and "I-it" relationships. Buber holds that in our relentless yearning for immediate gratification we do not stop at seeking to possess more and more; sooner rather than later, this yearning expresses itself in turning fellow human beings into objects of gratification. This is what happens in I-it relationships. They are not characterized by dialogue as any genuine relationship should be, the only one that matters is the 'I' and 'My' personal interests.[10]

Attaching a Price Tag to Human Beings

Commodification of human beings is a related concept that invariably involves objectification. It is a refusal to acknowledge the personhood of human individuals as beings who for that reason possess an intrinsic dignity. As the term suggests commodification makes of human beings commodities to which a price can be attached. Commodification can be of two types: first commodification of oneself, and second commodification of other people. Again we can also speak of commodification that is voluntary and a commodification which seeks to exploit the other. Yet again we can also make a distinction between the commodification of the whole body and the commodification of certain body parts.[11] Not all are agreed that commodification involves a violation of the intrinsic dignity of the person who is commoditized. Some argue that if a human being can capitalize on one's intellectual gifts and so also on one's artistic or kinaesthetic talents, what is wrong with capitalizing on one's physical assets? In a discussion on IAI TV on the theme *Selling Ourselves: The Body as a Commodity*, Catherine Hakim one of the participants uses the term 'erotic capital' to say that every person is perfectly justified in using his or her 'erotic capital' to get ahead in life. In the same discussion a couple of other participants Hallie Rubenhold and Brooke Magnanti argue that using one's body for economic advantage is perfectly legitimate and respectable even; it is only when commodification is imposed on a human being against one's will is it immoral.

Things Become Persons and Persons Become Things

Reification is a term closely linked to both Objectification and Commodification. It refers to the tendency that individuals and societies have of reducing humans to the status of things while at the same time entrusting certain things produced by human beings with an almost human status. The person loses his/her identity in objectification, but eventually human made things give him a new identity, respectability and social status. This term was first used by Marx who held that with reification the process of human abasement set into motion by the industrial revolution reaches its completion.[12] The distinction between being and having made by Marcel,[13] and made popular by John Paul II,[14] immediately comes to mind here. Both Marcel and John Paul II explain that our dignity as humans stems from the fact that we are persons made in the image and likeness of God; unfortunately, today many of us prioritize having over being. We think we are someone because of the clothes we wear, money in our purses, our cars, our properties, our qualifications. We respect others not so much because they are fellow human beings, but because of what they possess, their status and wealth, their physical and material endowments. This is 'reification' – impure and deceptively simple, 'reification' at is subtlest worst! The person is depersonalized, and on the other hand what is basically a thing acquires a 'personal character' that confers dignity on the human who thinks he/she possesses the thing in question. This is a situation in which one who begins as a possessor ends up being possessed and the thing that is possessed becomes the possessor.

Objectification, Commodification and Reification may be pedagogically distinct concepts but in real life these are part of the one sad dynamic of the exploitation and dehumanization of human beings. While this exploitation might originate in the warped spirit of the human person, its effects are experienced, no matter what kind of exploitation, in the body – in its pain and suffering, in its fragmentation, in its crucifixion.

Persons for Sale: Human Brutality at its worst

Human society has made much progress over the years, and we would not be deceiving ourselves if we said that today there is a greater sensitivity and appreciation of the value and dignity of human beings, more access and better safeguards to ensure the defence of basic human rights. However, in sheer numbers and in the level of brutality, we in our contemporary times must consider ourselves unsurpassed in our capacity to be inhuman. Human brutality is practically as old as humankind itself and has had as its loci, as we said on/in the human body.

The Many Faces of Equally Dehumanizing Prostitution

Prostitution is considered to be the most ancient, and some add most important and indispensable profession.[15] Large numbers of women have had to sell themselves, down the ages, for the gratification of men. Rarely, if ever, this 'selling' has been voluntary. In fact, it is often described as the choice made by those who are without choice.[16] Never has it been ennobling even though apparently certain types of prostitutes and 'comfort women' as they were called did apparently enjoy a certain social status. And even more rarely has it been the 'woman' who did the selling of her body. Most often it was others who sold her and others who gained from the money made. When men realized that satisfying their insatiable cravings would require more money than they could dream of having they ingenuously created the institution of the temple prostitute or the *devadasi* – women who were available cheaper if not totally free. Across cultures and time, prostitution has flourished in practically every society, only the working conditions and extent of exploitation has differed. Most often it has been violent and abusive, at other times it has been subtly refined but abusive nevertheless in a very clever way. Debra Kelly lists ten types of prostitutes in history in an article she has written with the same title. They are (1) The *Mut'ah* (a kind of temporary marriage agreement); (2) The *Tawaif* (women in North India who were dancers and musicians; (3) The *Hetaira* (high class courtesans of Ancient Athens who practiced their profession openly on the streets of Athens offering their services to the elite) (4) The *Zonah* (female prostitutes of the Hebrew Bible); (5) The *Ganika* (high class comfort women that served the nobility); (6) The *Auletrides* (women who besides being proficient in many performing arts like singing, dancing, music, and acrobatics perform at private parties and offer sexual services); (7) The *Comfort Women* of World War II (women from Korea and other parts of Asia forced by the Japanese to serve their personnel during the war); (8) The *devadasis* of India (temple prostitutes, sought after in their youth) (9) The *Temple prostitutes of Ancient Greco-Roman Society* (slave women forced to offer their services in order to earn revenue for the temple in which they served) (10) The *Ying Chi* of *Ancient China* (women whose task was to offer 'friendship' and entertain men who served in the army.)[17] From the Indian point of view, it is important to note that notwithstanding our claims to being a civilization that respects women and holds them in high regard[18] prostitution has existed in India since Vedic times. It was so rampant in certain societies and times that some kings had a special officer overseeing the department of harlotry. Vatsyayana the second century author of the *Kamasutra* speaks of nine kinds of prostitutes namely *Kumbhadasi, Paricharika, Kulata, Sawirini, Nati, Shipakarika, Prakashavinashta, Rupajiva* and *Ganika.*[19]

One could ask the question, what has changed as far as prostitution is concerned? The answer would be 'precious little.' Prostitution has become more abusive, more violent, more pervasive and more debasing, if anything. While women still constitute the vast majority of those pushed into or exploited in what today is euphemistically called the 'flesh trade', this commodification has become more universal in its choice of victims now to include men, children and even infants. Another thing that has changed today, at least in some societies is that prostitution has become a legitimate and even respectable business with minimum wages stipulated, health insurance and working hours. Some even claim that this is a life choice they have made freely out of a host of options available with no compulsion whatsoever. Some well-meaning people argue that women have always been property anyway and have never in the past been recognized as individuals having personal rights.[20] In their childhood, they were the property of their father and after marriage they became their husbands' property. There is nothing wrong then if today they freely choose to earn their living by selling their bodies. At least now their bodies are their own, and they get paid for services which were once demanded from them as a matter of right by those who owned them. I personally have my reservations about the validity of these claims that anyone could freely choose prostitution as a career choice.[21] Prostitution, under whatever guise it is practiced – escort services, strip or pole dancers in clubs, massagers in parlours and health clubs, porn stars, item girls or high end call girls is never an expression of free choice and personal emancipation.[22] There is always some abuse and victimization somewhere either in the present or in the past that has led to the erosion of one's sense of self-respect and personal dignity.

When it comes to the dehumanization of human beings or the reduction of not only their bodies but their whole being to the status of objects nothing comes close to the trade and trafficking of women and children for sexual exploitation. It is called the business of the future since it makes something like a close to a hundred billion dollars a year for those who run it.[23] Estimates are that sexual commodification of children earns racketeers something like 20 billion dollars annually.[24] Human beings can be sold and sold and resold unlike things like drugs which can be sold just once. This is what makes this business especially lucrative. More than fifty percent of modern day slavery is in some way connected with sexual exploitation. Studies estimate that there are at least two million children who are in situations of 'sexual slavery for profit' around the world.[25]

Other Forms of Trade in Human Beings

We have focused mainly on prostitution in our expose of the inhumanity of the human exploitation that leads many unscrupulous individuals to sexually brutalize the bodies of vulnerable women and children for their selfish monetary advantage. However, this is not the only kind of commercial sexual exploitation that exists in this world. Other industries linked to that of prostitution and equally brutal are the industries that promote pornography, paedophilia and also relatively respectable industries that run hotels and motels, industries that promote modelling and provide escort services. And this commercial sexual exploitation is part of an even larger phenomenon that goes under the name "Modern Day Slaveries." Before we list them it needs to be said that while some of these forms of exploitation may not have a 'sexual violence' component to begin with, sooner or later the victims find themselves victimized even sexually. Secondly all these forms of slavery make of the body a commodity with a price. And what is ironic is that while billions of dollars change hands in the many transactions that make up these business, only a fraction of these transactions put money into the hands of the victims. The more time the victims are bought and sold as commodities in these businesses the more they are brutalized and the poorer they become. They usually have few or no options at all. For many of them even death often appears as a merciful option. The magnitude of this modern day slavery is both mindboggling and frightening. Estimates show that between 27 million to 36 million people are enslaved in different parts of the world today. India alone has close to 14 million slaves.[26] The money generated is phenomenal. Slavery generates profits of more than 150 billion dollars worldwide annually.[27] While these different forms of slavery exist in practically every corner of the world, we in India find ourselves cornered into admitting that practically all these forms of slavery and that too in its worst forms exist in India. Besides exploitation of human beings for commercial sex work, human beings are also traded and exploited as bonded labourers, in the sector that provides people to do domestic work, in the entertainment and advertising industry, in many begging cartels which use vulnerable women and children to make mindboggling sums of money for the handlers.[28] Besides that there is money to be made in trafficking in human organs and providing babies for adoption. Sadly there are very many people who have no problems about making money and acquiring great wealth through these means that hurt the weakest and most vulnerable. With every passing day we invent new and newer forms of victimization and slavery. The kidnapping of young men and women and even children to serve in guerrilla or religious armies, to be sold in the bride market, and ever increasingly as suicide bombers seems to be becoming ever more popular today.[29]

Conclusion

Human trafficking that expresses itself in exploitation and commodification is closer home than we care to admit. It touches practically everyone's life. Few among us can say 'I am absolutely not guilty of such a crime.' Perhaps we are not directly involved in the worst kinds of human commodification; perhaps we have never intentionally violated the dignity and rights of any person. But that does not mean we have done no wrong. We need only to open our eyes and be more aware of the facts. The 2014 Global Slavery Index, Annual Report, says that 'modern slavery' is used for the production of 122 different goods used in day to day life in at least 58 different countries of the world.[30] The food that we eat, the clothes that we wear, the homes that we live in are often grown, sewn and build by people who have to labour in slave like conditions where they have to work because of a lack of viable alternatives and where they are poorly paid.[31] In the context of human commodification it would not be very much off the mark to say that if we are not in some way part of the solution it is likely we are in more than one way part of the problem. Another significant feature of practically every kind of 'modern day slavery' is that the victims are very often put into the situation they are in by people who are close to them and linked to them in relationships of care and trust: people like mothers and fathers, husbands, and family members. A third equally important point is that while the degradation is apparently directed to the body of the person victimized it is invariably the person as a whole that is harmed; his or her spirit is harmed too. Therefore instead of describing their condition as 'bodies on sale' we would be closer to the truth if we termed it 'persons for sale.' A fourth point to note is that the human being is amazingly resilient. It is true that for the vast majority who are victims of commodification their story does not have a happy ending. But it is also true that there are significant numbers of human beings who come out of this exploitation and abuse as stronger and more compassionate individuals. Their capacity to love and to care seems to be in proportion to their suffering. The more they have suffered and experienced victimization the more they seem to be able to forgive the past and to channelize all the pent up anger and pain within them into courageous initiatives on behalf of those who suffer.[32] This does not mean however that 'human slavery' of any kind can ever be justified. Even one human being exploited is one slave too many. This brings us to a fifth consideration. Human beings tend to normalize extremely painful experiences in order to survive. Victims often begin to think that they are in some way responsible for their own sufferings. Some other victims even develop a sense of attachment to their oppressors. They might even speak positively of them. The 'Stockholm Syndrome'[33] as this is popularly called is a survival strategy that baffles but makes sense nevertheless. On the one side of the coin are victims normalizing their experiences and on the other side is our tendency to do the same. When exposed to stories of human suffering and exploitation we are shocked at first, but we quickly begin to rationalize and say that we can do nothing about it and even get into denial mode concluding that the problem in question is not so widespread and not so terrible after all. A sixth and final fact to note is that victims of 'Human trafficking' often suffer not only the abuse of their unscrupulous 'owners' but also from the 'blindness and self-righteousness' of so called good people. Rehabilitation becomes very difficult for them because many 'good people' make an unreasonable connection between the suffering and the moral worth of the victims. They conclude that those victimized have brought what they have gone through upon themselves. Victims of exploitation receive a lot of pity and charity, but not enough respect. People are afraid to welcome them into their homes, to make them part of their social lives, to trust them, to employ them. Human beings who suffered dehumanization have not forfeited their humanity. When we fail to recognize their intrinsic worth as persons we show ourselves to be essentially not very different from their abusers.

Notes

1 Voltaire, *Candide and other Stories*, trans. Roger Pearson (Oxford: Oxford University Press, 1990), 101-121.

2 Sometimes this quote from *No Exit* is translated as "Hell is other people."

3 Of course, there are other interpretations of these words of Sartre which hold that it is not so much others who objectify us as we ourselves who let ourselves be defined by others' judgements about us thus creating hell for ourselves. See http://rickontheater.blogspot.in/2010/07/most-famous-thing-jean-paul-sartre.html (accessed August 10, 2015).

4 See G. H. McAleer, *Ecstatic Morality and Sexual Politics* (New York: Fordham University Press, 2005), 3.

5 See Travis J. Denneson, "Society and the Individual in Nietzsche's The Will to Power," *The Secular Web*, http://infidels.org/library/modern/travis_denneson/power.html (accessed August 15, 2015).

6 Michael Foucault, *Ethics: Subjectivity and Truth*, Vol. 1, ed. Paul Rainbow (New York: The New Press, 1997), 283.

7 See Marcus Honeysett, "Assumptions behind Derrida's Theory of Deconstruction," *Bethinking*, http://www.bethinking.org/truth/assumptions-behind-derridas-theory-of-deconstruction (accessed August 21, 2015).

8 *The Stanford Encyclopedia of Philosophy*, s.v. "Feminist Perspectives on Objectification," http://plato.stanford.edu/archives/sum2014/entries/feminism-objectification/ (accessed July 17, 2015).

9 Ibid. Fungibility is the treatment of persons as interchangeable with objects. Violability is the refusal to recognize boundaries.

10 Tilina, "The Self in Relationship," http://selfinrelationship.blogspot.in/2011/03/martin-bubers-i-thou-relationships.html (accessed September 20, 2015).

11 Tsuyoshi Awaya, "The Human Body as a New Commodity," http://googleweblight.com/?lite_ url=http://homepage1.nifty.com/awaya/hp/ronbun/r010.html&ei=2fAjhQcs&lc=en-IN&geid=7&s=1&m=421&ts= 1443596081&sig= APONPFmd7lk0oUU1Fxtl3M rnW 8hFU KHtRg (accessed August 12, 2015).

12 See Wade A. Bell Jr., "A. Phenomenological Take on the Problem of Reification," http://ojs.ub.gu.se/ojs/index.php/modernasprak/article/viewFile/3059/2615 (accessed August 15, 2015).

13 Gabriel Marcel, *Being and Having*, trans. Katherine Farrer (Glasgow: The University Press, 1949), 163-164. Marcel holds that as a material reality one could say 'I have a body;' but he is of the view that it would be more accurate to say that 'I am my body' since my body is not disposable as a thing is, and also because the body is part of who I am as a human being.

14 John Paul II, *Evangelium Vitae* (1995), 23 and 98; See also John Paul II, *Redemptionis Donum* (1984), 4.

15 See Elizabeth Abbott, *A History of Celibacy* (New York: Scribner, 2000), 269-270.

16 See Soroptimist White Paper, "Prostitution is Not a Choice," https://www.soroptimist.org/whitepapers/ whitepaperdocs/wpprostitution.pdf (accessed September 21, 2015).

17 See Debra Kelly, "10 types of Prostitutes in History," http://listverse.com/2014/02/11/10-types-of-prostitutes-in-history/ (accessed July 12, 2015).

18 See "Respect for Women," http://www.iloveindia.com/indian-traditions/respect-for-women.html (accessed September 30, 2015).

19 See Manohar Laxman Varadpande, *History of Indian Theatre: Classical Theatre* (New Delhi: Abhinav Publications, 2005), 154.

20 Some claim that even 'religious life' in the Catholic Church flourished in certain times largely because many women saw it as a way out from bondage. They did not want to be owned by any man in marriage so they chose to be owned by Christ, which effectively meant for them freedoms and opportunities that would otherwise be will beyond the reach of their wildest dreams. http://www.ozedweb.com/history/middle_ages_women_in_religion.html (accessed November 15, 2014).

21 Prostitution may be institutionalized and mainstreamed in many societies today but it would be a mistake to label it a profession when in fact it is very plainly 'human rights abuse.' Even reputed bodies like the World Health Organization and Amnesty International have defined it a profession. But most activists working with and for prostitutes think this is a big mistake.

22 It needs to be noted here that there are many groups claiming to represent those engaged in prostitution today which resist the portrayal of the prostitute as a helpless victim who needs to be rescued.. Apparently even the Indian Sex Workers' Manifesto 1997 criticizes the depiction of sex workers as 'powerless…., abused victims…. objects of pity." See Venla Roth (ed.), *Defining Human Trafficking and Identifying its Victims* (Leiden: Martinus Lijhoff Publishers, 2012), 40-41.

23 See International Labour Office, *Profits and Poverty: The Economics of Forced Labour*, http://www.ilo.org/wcmsp5/groups/public/---ed_norm/---declaration/documents/publication/wcms_243391.pdf (accessed August 1, 2015).

24 See "Combatting Child Sex Tourism," United Nations Human Rights, April 10, 2013, http://www.ohchr.org/EN/NewsEvents/Pages/ChildSexTourism.aspx (accessed September 21, 2015).

25 See "Global Sex Trafficking Factsheet," Equality Now, http://www.equalitynow.org/node/1010 (accessed September 30, 2015).

26 Cf. Becca Stanek, "This is what Slavery looks like in the 21st Century," *News Mic*, November 17, 2014, http://mic.com/articles/104458/this-is-what-slavery-looks-like-in-the-21st-century (accessed June 26, 2015); Monique Villa, "They Walk among us: Slavery in the 21st Century takes many forms," *The Globe and the Mail*, October 18, 2013, http://www.theglobeandmail.com/globe-debate/they-walk-among-us-slavery-in-the-21st-century-takes-many-forms/article14924976/ (accessed October 02, 2015).

27 Kristine speaks of 13 billion dollars as annual profits, but most estimates put it at more than ten times that. See "Global Forced Labour generates $ 150 billion a year in Illegal Profits," *The Guardian*, http://www.theguardian.com/global-development/2014/may/20/global-forced-labour-generates-billions-illegal-profits-un (accessed July 18, 2015).

28 See Sadika Hameed, Sandile Hlatshwayo and Evan Tanner et. al, *Human Trafficking in India* (Stanford University and The Asia Foundation), March 12 2010, pdf document, vi.

29 "25 Painfully Disturbing Facts about Human Trafficking," YouTube video, https://www.youtube.com/watch?v=dqCSgCDGNT8 (accessed January 26, 2015).

30 "35.8 million People Held in Modern Slavery," Aljazeera America, November 18 2014, http://america.aljazeera.com/articles/2014/11/18/modern-slavery-millionstrappedtoday.html (accessed September 29, 2015).

31 Noy Thrupkaew, *Human Trafficking is All around You. This is How it Works.* (TED Talks, Vancouverbc, March 2015), 18.55.

32 Cf. Sunitha Krishnan, *The Fight Against Sex Slavery* (TED India, November 2009) 12.42; Rachel Lloyd, *Human Trafficking* (TEDxUChicago, 2012), 19: 23.

33 See Joseph M. Carver, "Love and Stockholm Syndrome: The Mystery of Loving an Abuser," *Counselling Resource*, http://counsellingresource.com/lib/therapy/self-help/stockholm/ (accessed September 30, 2014).

10

A Medieval Perspective on the Body
St. Thomas Aquinas and the Male-Female Difference

Dolreich Pereira
St. Pius X College, Mumbai

Abstract: Was St. Thomas Aquinas a misogynist? This question guides us in seeking to understand his thoughts on sexual difference as stated in Question 92 of the *Summa Theologiae*. Many authors have used the phrase *deficiens et occasionnatum* to assert the misogyny of Thomas Aquinas. However, for Thomas, the deficiency is not to be found on the side of the generation of the product, namely the female, but on the side of the generator, namely the male! We observe some elements of equality and even superiority of the women from the texts cited by him. The creation of Eve clearly requires divine intervention; just like Adam, she was created body and soul directly by God. Gender equality is further suggested by that beautiful image in question 92: Eve was not created from Adam's head that she should dominate him, or from his feet that she should be subordinate to him, but from his side, his rib to mark her equality with him. Aquinas was not a misogynist. He lived in a patriarchal society which was thoroughly misogynistic. But his vision exceeded the precise point of his epoch to predict and announce the liberation of women from certain obligations of another age within which certain people would like to keep them imprisoned. Inasmuch as he was able to transcend the Aristotelian in his thinking, we can consider Thomas Aquinas to be a feminist of his time.

Keywords: Thomas Aquinas, Aristotle, misogynist, Genesis, Creation of woman, male-female difference, gender equality, medieval.

Introduction

This paper is an opportunity to clarify a long-standing debate: Was St. Thomas Aquinas a misogynist, as is presupposed by many people, notwithstanding the fact that many of his assertions have been quoted out of context and passed on from book to book or, nowadays, from blog to blog? That is my aim in seeking to understand his thoughts on sexual difference as stated in Question 92 of the *Summa Theologiae*.[1]

To avoid common simplifications on such a subject, let us acknowledge the complexity of the issue. Indeed, Thomas, like all medieval thinkers, did not consider doing the commentary and exegesis of Sacred Scripture as we do today. He read these texts according to the culture and the social and religious context of his time, particularly in terms of his fundamental project: developing a highly structured theological doctrinal synthesis. To do this, he used the irreplaceable resources provided by its two main thinkers, Aristotle and St. Augustine, from whom he also did not hesitate to keep a healthy distance, guided by his desire to judge everything according to a firm theological point of view that was totally focused on Christian salvation.

It also requires us to stay away from the frequent temptation to judge the mediaeval past in terms of our current concerns. It is indeed due to a lack of sense of history that we come to interpret the ancient authors from the ideas and mores of our time. Thus, pronouncing Thomas misogynist is to forget that he was a man of a specific time, and notwithstanding the culture of his time, he affirmed, at least in essence, the principle of gender equality, as we shall see.

Indeed, while noting that in medieval society women had a better place than the bourgeois society of the 17th and 18th centuries, one must not forget the socio-cultural structures of traditional patriarchal societies. Dominated by the fundamental problem of survival, constantly threatened by numerous causes of mortality, and a life expectancy much lower than ours, these societies gave top priority to procreation. Thus, motherhood seemed the essential purpose of a woman, a requirement which she had to submit, and the ancient authors (Aristotle and the Stoics, for example,) attempted to explain it by biological and anthropological considerations.

Another socio-cultural factor also played a powerful role: the strict hierarchy of feudal society introduced a rigid regime of subordination between social strata, and it reflected within domestic society. This concern for prioritization, and the subordination that is linked to it, was one of the characteristic features of medieval society and justified by religious faith where all beings were considered to be participating in God in varying degrees. In this participatory vision, each being found its place in a kind of grand pyramid, and received divine influx through the mediation of the one who was above. But, and this is essential, the functional subordination of beings towards each other in no way affected or diminished their equal dignity as a person. On this point, Kari Elisabeth Borresen notes an agreement between the thought of Thomas and the prevailing social situation: "For him this state (subordination) is found as a fact that need not be proven or justified because it is entirely rooted in the structure of society and the customs of that time."[2]

On this point, the proposals of Aquinas are mostly a reflection of the culture and ideas of his time, and therefore possess only a contingent character in his mind. Nevertheless, we need to identify clearly what was fundamental for him, and what needs to be updated and adapted to the social context of our times. This, to my mind, will be the best way to manifest the perennial validity of the teaching of the Angelic Doctor.

Woman in the Thinking of Aquinas

To begin with, I would like to examine the manner in which Aquinas considered women. On this point, I differ from another writer, Pierre Camus who has written an interesting article on the myth of the woman in the works of Thomas Aquinas.[3] According to him, "the anthropology of femininity, although outdated, is still likely to take on a symbolic meaning which escapes from the conditions of its emergence..."[4]

The author seeks to uncover the underlying symbolism of womanhood in the thought of Thomas Aquinas. Despite its academic interest, this perspective is not the subject of my investigation. I would like to look at the thinking of Aquinas on women as he developed it at his level of consciousness. For him, the realm of the symbol is, in fact, a mode of knowledge applicable to Sacred Scripture, but not to natural and physical realities which must be directly grasped by the intellect and the senses. Hence, the object of our study is the feminine nature as understood by Thomas through its intellectual documentation.

It is certain that in his day, women were only accorded a secondary role in the generation of offspring. Thomas himself believed that the Holy Scriptures gave evidence to this hierarchy of gender. But in reality, it is his philosophy that provided the intellectual framework for the understanding of the revealed Word; the latter would be interpreted by the former. This process is not new: centuries and cultures have influenced our reading of Revelation which, while remaining unchanged in itself, has provided every era with nourishment to assimilate. So, let us not be surprised if in digging into the thought of Thomas we come to unearth the presence of the true sap of Revelation.

Q.92: On the Production of Women

In the 13th century, the first three chapters of Genesis did not give rise to any exegetical research of the historical-critical type. The two creation stories were designed, not as two different traditions, but as a continuous text teaching a single suite of events. How then are we to understand these stories of the creation of woman presented by Chapters 1 and 2, which have so many remarkable differences?

St. Augustine made a distinction between the creation of the world through his theory of *rationes seminales*[5] narrated in Chapter 1, and the same creation in its concrete reality, reported in Chapter 2. But such is not the thought of Thomas. Indeed, we do not find either a recapitulation or a critique of this view. This is in keeping with the style of Aquinas who would never directly oppose the most learned among the Latin Fathers. But as we shall see, the thought of Thomas is quite clear in several texts. At the beginning of his teaching career, he dealt with theological issues in the Commentary on the Sentences of Peter Lombard and at the end of his career he did the same in the *Summa Theologiae*, sometimes even following the same order; however, the intellectual construction in each case is different. The *Summa* presents a logical and clearer development; it is a personal work and not a commentary. There is an entire section in both books devoted to the creation of woman: *Commentary on Book II of the Sentences*, Distinction 18, Question 1; *Summa Theologiae* Ia, Question 92 in full. In both works, this study is preceded by similar research on the creation of man.[6]

It is instructive and curious to us that the two creation stories in Chapters 1 and 2 of Genesis were written as if they were mixed and placed on the same plane. That is why Thomas, too, invokes in his study the text from one or the other. Where does the soul of Adam come from? Obviously it is a creation of God: as the soul in its generation cannot emanate from the begetter because of its spirituality, hence the soul of the first man can only be created: this is reflected in Genesis 1:27, "God created man in the image of himself."[7] But we also have as well, "God breathed on his face and he took life" (Genesis 2:7). This, for Thomas, is a unique event; it is also the place where he abandons the traditional Augustinian position.

But the first of these quotations ends there. There is no question of the other sex in the rest of the sacred text, while Thomas clearly admits that it is included in the sixth day of creation. But then this is the body of Adam and Eve. As far as the bodies of Adam and Eve are concerned, it is Chapter 2 which is invoked in Question 91, a.1, s.c. and Question 92, a.3, s.c.: God made the body of man from the dust of the earth, the body of the woman from Adam's rib. Then immediately there appears an inflection given to the biblical text which Thomas does not change but interprets in the *sedcontra* of Question 92, article 1, in which he says: "It is not good that man should be alone: let us give him a helpmate for him." That's all because Thomas would not have had the idea of adding anything to the biblical quotation.

But soon after, the body of the article tells us that the helpmate (*adjutorium simile sibi*) is created only for procreation. Indeed, if it had been necessary to fill the loneliness of the first man, it would have been better to have another male to keep him company or even using some industrious friend to play his sports and games. If God created a being dissimilar to Adam, it can only be for this unique feature that only she can do – give man the necessary material for fecundity. But this motivation of God is purely the invention of Thomas. It is not found in Scripture. Clearly, it is his own logical interpretation, inevitable in the context of Aristotelian physics which dominated his perspective. This way of thinking locates women immediately in their generative function. What is it to be a woman, or more precisely what does it mean to be a being that is not a man? It is to do what man cannot accomplish on his own: to procreate and perpetuate the species. In this perspective, one could reach the point of excluding any female being who is not a mother.

The text then proceeds to relate the physical laws of generation according to Aristotle. However, Aquinas advances an important thesis, also taken from Aristotle, to legitimize the existence of the second sex. In higher animals, the genitals are separated in different individuals, their sexual union, far from constant, must occur either naturally, during coitus or in rational beings, by an act of the will. Indeed, the human being is ordered to something other than only reproduction, the bulk of his time is devoted to the noble work for which he is intended, "*quod est intelligere,*" It does not say anywhere that this intellection belongs only to man, and woman is deprived of it. So, even though it is implied, Aquinas suggests an equality of the sexes. He continues to follow the sacred text, recalling from the fact of the sexual act that "they shall be two in one flesh" (Genesis 2:24).

Many authors have used the phrase *deficiens et occasionnatum* to assert the misogyny of Thomas Aquinas. We need to study this more closely. The Latin translation of Aristotle that was used by Thomas Aquinas states that the philosopher said: "*femina est mas occasionatus*" (The female is a misbegotten male). The argument of Aristotle is true from one point of view, but wrong from another, says Thomas. What are these two views? One concerns the "particular nature," that is to say, the one generated by the male, and the other concerns the "universal nature," that is to say, the human species.

From the perspective of particular nature, *femina est aliquid deficiens et occasionatum* (a woman is an accidental and defective thing), said Thomas in a response to the objection: it involves a disability and a failure. To understand the meaning of this statement, let us go back to an old biological error. In procreation, the male was attributed more importance than he actually had. It was believed – and for a long time thereafter – that "the active power contained in the male seed tended to produce a male (*virtus activa quae est in semine maris, intendit producere sibi simile*).[8] And Thomas adds, it is not enough that the male generates something similar to himself, (*sibi simile*), that is to say another male, because the male must possess the perfection of the masculine sex (*perfectum secundum masculinum sexum*) to be a real man, because it creates perfect males, physically or mentally. To speak of the perfection of the masculine sex does not imply in any way, an *imperfection of the other sex*: nature tends to perfection equally in both sexes.

In this hypothesis, one must retain with care that if a female is produced, something was missing, something went wrong; hence the Latin term *deficiens* (deficient). Taking gardening as an analogy, the cause may lie in the seed, or in the state of the soil or weather conditions (viral causes were as yet unknown at that time). If an ATM machine is programmed to dispense currency notes for Rs. 500 but instead dispenses notes of Rs. 1000, we immediately contact the technician because something is not working, something is *deficiens*.

The term *deficiens* must draw our attention to the male generator and to the conditions and circumstances of the generation. This is clearly the case when we read the answer of Thomas to the argument reported above in the Latin text. The deficiency is not to be found on the side of the generation of the product, namely the female, but on the side of the generator, the male. For Thomas, the deficiency is in the male and subsequently carried to the female, who is the product of this generation.

Thomas himself confirms this interpretation when in the *Summa contra Gentiles*, he looks into the question of the gender and age of those who are resurrected. Those who thought that *deficiens* was a term that referred to females, looked with pity towards the poor female as they felt justified to argue that there would be no females after the resurrection, since this great event must repair the *defects* of nature: hunchbacks would be straightened out, the lame would walk and the blind would see! So, if the female is an imperfection, she should disappear after the Resurrection. No, says Thomas: the female sex is also resurrected to bear witness to the perfection and order of nature created by Divine Wisdom.[9] Alas! It has escaped the observation of many people that when Thomas pronounced the word *deficiens*, he uttered it from the point of view of the male.

The initial argument said "*Femina est mas occasionatus*" (the female is an accidental male). How do we understand this term that has been translated by several as "mutilated" or "imperfect"? To understand this, we need only to recall the biological error I mentioned earlier. Before and after Thomas Aquinas, it was thought that, in the generation of humans, the male would produce a male when everything was working normally; it was a male that was created male and it was perfect, that is, a male with all parts intact and perfectly proportioned. When the generating male missed its target, it engendered an imperfect male (either missing a part, or having one too many or poorly proportioned) or it engendered a female. In both cases, the generating male had missed its target. The female was therefore considered a missed or failed male.

The comparison of the archer aiming and missing a target helps to understand this. The adjective "failed" or "missed" does not, in this context, have the same meaning as in the expression "tomboy," which is applied to a girl who looks and dresses like a boy. It is the target that was missed and not the effect produced. This is why we can achieve much more than we intended. The female is not an imperfect male: it is something else. If an apple tree produced an orange among apples, one should not say that it is an imperfect apple. An orange that should have been an apple makes more sense!

After considering the arguments of Aristotle concerning "particular nature," that is the male which generates an offspring, and have agreed with Aristotle, Thomas positions himself from the point of view of "universal nature," that is, from the point of view of the species. Here, the female is not a missed target: it is aimed for or desired, as much as the male, to contribute to the survival of the species.

From the perspective of "particular nature," Thomas used two adjectives: *deficiens* and *occasionatus*; from the point of view of "universal nature," he only retains *occasionatus*. When a male generates an imperfect male or a female, something had been lacking on the side of the male generating or in the conditions of the generation. Hence, the term *deficiens* is used. But when universal nature creates a female, it does not have to seek for that which would not work, because universal nature needs both the sexes. Universal nature would have a problem only if a monster was created.

We therefore cannot say that the female is an accidental or occasional male; the female is not a male. However, neither one nor the other of these adjectives gives us a true understanding of the idea contained in *deficiens*. The significance of this word has been overlooked as if Aquinas had introduced it without any reason. This term requires us to turn towards the side of the male generator; the other term (*occasionatus*) asks us to turn towards the target. Something was missing from one side; accordingly, the target was missed.

We have just examined the answer to the first objection in Q.92, article 1 which informs us in what way the woman is considered "defective" (*deficiens*) and "misbegotten" (*occasionnatum*). The "defectiveness" is derived from the non-resemblance to the human perfect that is the male. However, Catherine Capelle points out that the word *occasionatum* did not exist either in classical Latin, or in the Latin of the early Christian centuries.[10] *Occasio* in classical Latin refers to an "occasion" but with a positive nuance: it is more an "opportunity" than a "hazard."

Among Christians, the word evolved towards a negative connotation: what was before, a "fortuitous opportunity," now became also an "occasion to sin." In the case of the latter, the derived adjective *occasus* now carries a sense of purpose, of death, although the sense of cause and of condition is not excluded. However, the medieval adjective *occasionatum* clearly means "hazard:" the meaning is thus reversed. It is an effect without a known, free and rational cause. According to Capelle, it seems that this word was invented in the Middle Ages to translate the Greek *automatou* (αυτομάτου),[11] literally what happens by itself, and therefore spontaneously by chance without the intervention of a human will.

The meaning of the text is precisely that of a being that is unpredictable about its causes as these, in fact, are of various kinds: they can be psychological in the father and mother, or be attributed to physics or even the weather. But Aquinas adds that even though the birth of the female being is "misbegotten" from a certain (Aristotelian) perspective, there is no denying that it belongs to the order established by God. Thus, there is a kind of opposition in the text: in relation to the particular nature of the father, there is a defect; but "as regards human nature in general, woman is not misbegotten, but is included in nature's intention as directed to the work of generation."[12]

Yet, the purpose of this universal nature depends on God, the author of nature. Also, to create the universe, God must produce not only males but also females.[13] Here, again, we can wonder: (to escape being a misbegotten being), does the woman exist only to produce children? Do we not have here a woman who is tasked with the propagation of the species (*opus generationis*) and who is defined and reduced to this sole function because for everything else, it would be better to have a male colleague who would supposedly be more effective? On this point, we feel that Thomas is very close to Aristotle; he seems to be enclosed (so to speak) in the Hellenistic mentality which was that of the *gynaeceum* (women's quarters). Even though he is sometimes inspired by Sacred Scripture, the precise point of our investigation is still not clear on the horizon.

The story of the creation of woman in Chapter 2 of Genesis shows both the legitimacy and fundamental consequence of this divine act: the woman is produced from man thus affirming the primacy of the male and the equally unfailing connection between the two sexes (see Ia, q.92, a.2). But, as a derived being, the woman is naturally at a lower rank. This primacy of the male is illustrated by Thomas, among other texts, in his Commentary on the Book of Job. Given the inferiority of women, it is normal for parents to prefer the birth of a boy to a girl; thus, in the Book of Job, his seven sons and three daughters are a blessing from God. The relationship between the two groups of children is indeed those of the perfect to the imperfect. Moreover, we are told, the boys bring to their parents more advantages than girls.[14] It is needless to point out how this last assertion arises from a sociological context.

Returning to the text of the *Summa*, question 92, article 1, the answer to the second objection states that as far as political authority is concerned, the woman was subject to man even before the first sin. For already inequalities existed in creation, and in fact it was in the nature of things, we are told, because reason was present more in men than in women. This is a statement that clearly comes from Aristotle, but Genesis is silent on this point.

The third objection is even more serious and leads straight to our next paragraph: God should have foreseen that woman would lead man into sin; so why did he not avoid this disastrous creation? Aquinas' answer to the third objection is not short of irony: if God had to avoid creating anything that causes sin in man, He should have created nothing at all!

Wanting to interpret the sacred text more closely, Aquinas is keen on knowing why woman was created from man's rib. Four reasons for article 2 have been carefully analyzed by Borresen.[15] The first was already present in Pierre Lombard: just as God is the cause and master of the universe (because it comes from God), so too is Adam the first and head of all humanity not excluding the feminine – the principle being that what emanates from its source is less than its source and depends on it for its life. Such is the relationship between man and woman![16] The second and fourth reasons are drawn from Augustine: the fact that woman comes from man creates the intimacy of their union and explains the divine word "he will leave his father and mother and will cling to her." (Genesis 2:24). The third argument comes from Aristotle: in humans the male-female union is not only required for generation, but also for the education of children and all that domestic life entails.[17]

When this doctrine is applied to Christ, it can be seen as both confirmation and exception. In every human birth, the material provided by the mother is derived from Adam. So, is the case with the semen that comes from the father but it is also the carrier of original sin. According to Aquinas, if Christ is the son of Adam from the first point of view, he is not from the second, because the Virgin Mary brings to the new being the matter that is without a doubt derived from Adam. But the male semen to inform this material is replaced by the operation of the Holy Spirit.[18] Moreover, according to the *Compendium Theologiae*, the Virgin Mary really conceived the Son of God; she is really his mother.[19] But for every human being, the soul comes neither from the father nor from the mother. It is created directly by God. No doubt, in animals, according to Thomas, the soul comes from the father, the body, from the mother. But for men it is not the same as we have seen. Thus, he affirms the spirituality of the soul and the direct fatherhood of God.

However, the Commentary of Aquinas on the Gospel according to Matthew gives us a different perspective and we must learn to relativize the somewhat negative contribution made by the texts invoked so far. The genealogy narrated in Chapter 1 of this Gospel mentions only four women, all of them sinful: an incestuous daughter, a prostitute, an idolater, an adulteress. One would expect Aquinas to remark that they were already purified by penance to take on their role in the ancestry of the Saviour. But their sinfulness is passed by without any remark since for Thomas these women have no positive action in generation. They are simply the ground for the positive action of the male, according to Aristotle. This comment is absent from the Commentary on Matthew. Aquinas only gives spiritual reasons for the intervention of sinners and the supposed natural sinfulness of the woman is not invoked at all; it is only the sin of David that is recalled.

We also observe some elements of equality and even superiority of women from the texts cited. Thus, we are reminded by Aquinas that, like that of Adam the creation of Eve clearly requires divine intervention. Creating man from the slime of the earth and his wife from the rib suggests that the impossible is achieved. But what we fail to notice in the images of the biblical text taken literally is that the pre-existing matter from which man is created is inert clay whereas the pre-existing matter from which the women is created is animated, living, sensitive matter, namely the rib. Moreover, we note that Eve is not created by Adam: according to the text, she is not his daughter; just like him, she is created body and soul directly by God.

Gender equality is further suggested by that beautiful image, even if it is medieval, referred to in article 3 of this same question 92: Eve was not created from Adam's head that she should dominate him, nor from his feet that she should be subordinate to him, but from his side, his rib to mark her equality with him.

This equality is confirmed by article 4: Returning to the Aristotelian scheme, we find that matter which generates every human being is the semen of the man and woman. Apart from this natural production, no other source can produce a human body if not God himself as the first cause of the universe. Hence, it is God alone who could produce either man from the slime of the earth or a woman from the rib of man.[20]

So, this question actually unfavourable to women since it is based on an Aristotelian interpretation of Genesis (so to speak), still suggests gender equality on this point: Adam and Eve were both created by God as far as their soul is concerned like other humans. But as far as their bodies are concerned, they are also equal, since neither of them has begotten the other. Furthermore Eve is the equal of Adam because she has been created from his rib.

Conclusion

Despite the social structure which subordinated woman to man, Aquinas had the merit of clearly noting that such subordination was only of a secondary nature, and on this point he did not hesitate to move away from Aristotle. Thanks to a truth of faith, that the vocation of every human being is to live the life of grace, all men like women, are equally images of God at a fundamental level: "The image of God, in its principal signification, namely the intellectual nature, is found both in man and in woman. Hence, after the words, "To the image of God He created him," it is added, "Male and female He created them" (Gen 1:27).[21] Also, when it comes to grace, there is equality between the sexes.[22]

Certainly, in our secularized world, limiting gender equality to the field of grace may seem very simplistic. But for a medieval, that was really the point. The subordination of woman to man appeared to him only as a contingent reality, linked to culture and a way of life, which was not open to the theologian to dispute. Also, the thought of Thomas was open to the possibilities of change, of altering socio-cultural structures, except for what concerned the essentials.

Finally, I have tried to show that the charge made against the author of being a misogynist is incorrect. He was not. He lived in a patriarchal society which was thoroughly misogynistic. But because of his grace and his intellectual acuity, his vision exceeded the viewpoint of his epoch to predict and announce the liberation of women from certain obligations of another age within which certain people would like to keep them imprisoned. Inasmuch as he was able to transcend the Aristotelian in his thinking, we can consider Thomas Aquinas to be a feminist of his time.

Notes

1 *Summa Theologiae* (Hereafter, ST), q.92. The production of the woman (Ia q.92, a.1-4).

2 Kari Elisabeth Borresen, *Subordination et Équivalence: Nature et Rọle de la Femme après Augustin et Thomas d'Aquin* (Oslo: Universitets-forlaget, 1968), 142 (translation mine). The original text in French reads as follows: "Pour lui cet état (de subordination) se constate comme un fait qui n'a pas à être prouvé ou justifié parce qu'il est tout à fait enraciné dans la structure de la société et dans les mœurs de l'époque."

3 Pierre Camus, "Le mythe de la femme chez saint Thomas d'Aquin," *Revue Thomiste* 2, (1976): 243-265.

4 Ibid., 246 (translation mine). The original text in French reads as follows: "l'anthropologie de la féminité, bien que périmée, reste susceptible de revêtir un sens symbolique qui la soustrait aux conditions de son émergence…"

5 The term *rationes seminales* translated variously as germinal or causal principles, primordial reasons, original factors, seminal reasons, virtues, or seed-like principles, is a theological theory on the origin of species. It is the doctrine that God created the world in seed form, with certain potentialities, which then developed or unfolded accordingly over time; what appears to be change is simply the realization of the preexisting potentialities. The theory is a metaphor of the growth of a plant: much like a planted seed that eventually develops into a tree, when God created the world he planted *rationes seminales* from which all life sprung. It is intended to reconcile the belief that God created all things, with the evident fact that new things are constantly developing.

6 *Commentary on the Sentences*, Book II, Distinctions 16 and 17; ST Ia, questions 90 and 91.

7 ST Ia, q.90, a.2, Sed contra.

8 ST, Ia, q.92, a.1, ad 2.

9 "In like fashion, also, the frailty of the feminine sex is not in opposition to the perfection of the risen. For this frailty is not due to a shortcoming of nature, but to an intention of nature. And this very distinction of nature among human beings will point out the perfection of

nature and the divine wisdom as well, which disposes all things in a certain order." *Summa contra Gentiles*, Book IV, Chapter 88.

10 Catherine Capelle, *Thomas d'Aquin féministe?* (Paris: Vrin, 1982), 53.

11 See Aristotle, *De Generatione Animalibus*, Book IV, ch. II. This word *occasionatum* reappears many times in the work of Aquinas and usually with reference to the woman. See, for example, his Commentary on the Gospel according to John (16:21): "*Ad partum enim sequitur duplex gaudium: unum de evasione doloris; aliud, et maius, de ortu prolis: quod quidem maximum est, si proles sit masculini sexus; cum masculus sit quid perfectum, femina vero quid imperfectum et occasionatum*" (After a birth there is a double joy: one, because the pain is past; the other, and greater, is over the birth of the child. This joy is greater if the child is of the male sex, since the male is complete, while the female is incomplete and fortuitous).

12 "*femina non est aliquid occasionatum, sed est de intentione naturae ad opus generationis ordinate.*" ST Ia q.92, art.1, ad primum.

13 *ST*, Ia, q.92, a.1, ad 1.

14 Commentary on the Book of Job, Ch. 42, Lesson 1.

15 Borresen, *Subordination et Équivalence*, 131

16 Commentary on the Book of Sentences, Book II, distinction 18.

17 Aristotle, *Ethics*, VIII, 12, 7; Commentary of Thomas, Lesson XII.

18 "Christ's body was in Adam in respect of a bodily substance, – that is to say, that the corporeal matter of Christ's body was derived from Adam: but it was not there by reason of seminal virtue, because it was not conceived from the seed of man. Thus, it did not contract original sin, as others who are descended from Adam by man's seed." ST IIIa, q.31, a.1, solution 3; also q.32, a.3.

19 "Both Creeds assert that the Son of God was born or was made flesh of the Virgin Mary. The woman of whom any person is born is called his mother, for the reason that she supplies the matter for human conception. Hence, the Blessed Virgin Mary, who provided the matter for the conception of the Son of God, should be called the true mother of the Son of God. As far as the essence of motherhood is concerned, the energy whereby the matter furnished by a woman is formed, does not enter into the question. She who supplied matter to be formed by the Holy Spirit is no less a mother than a woman who supplies matter that is to be formed by the energy latent in male seed. If anyone insists on maintaining that the Blessed Virgin ought not to be called the Mother of God because flesh alone and not divinity was derived from her, as Nestorius contended, he clearly is not aware of what he is saying. A woman is not called a mother for the reason that everything that is in her child is derived from her." *Compendium Theologiae*, ch. 222.

20 *ST*, Ia, q.92, a.4, respondeo.

21 ST, I, q.93, 4, ad 1; also q.93, 6, ad 2.

22 ST, II. II, 177, 2, ad 2.

11

In Search of Woman
Re-making Ourselves

Gayatri Mendanha
Symbiosis School for Liberal Arts, Pune

Abstract: Simone de Beauvoir, in The Second Sex, stated that, "A woman is not born, she is made." Judith Butler speaks of gender as performative. Both these philosophers call readers to recognise the underlying hollowness at the centre of the constructed fact and performativity of gender. Both urge towards transcendence and a re-making differently. In acting authentically, in ontological freedom (Beauvoir) and in subverting and parodying the normative gender binaries (Butler) one could institute alternative ways of being and acting that will have greater liveability for all as its aim. Yet, one cannot escape the gaze of the other and the social policing of behaviour. This paper attempts to grapple with ideas of gender, sex and the body and explores the possibilities and challenges that lie in re-making ourselves differently.

Keywords: Sex, Gender, Embodiment.

Introduction

Simone de Beauvoir writes, in *The Second Sex,* "One wonders if women still exist, if they will always exist, whether or not it is desirable that they should, what place they occupy in this world, what their place should be."[1] Moi entitles her famous book-length essay "What is a woman?" In the asking and answering of these questions we wander in search of "woman" and her "place." One is confronted with definitions and categories that lean towards an essentialist understanding. Another approach is a transcending of definitions that by their very nature, in generalising, exclude and to seek instead, individual lived experiences to better understand ourselves and each other. In this search one cannot escape the weight of history and social structures that forge us even before we are born. If gender is a contingent social construction, can we re-make ourselves and in this re-making, re-create structures themselves differently? Is it possible for us to challenge and dismantle the structures around which we have built ourselves and our identity?

In the first two sections of this paper, I shall engage the reader with the task of re-thinking the ideas of sex and gender that we, as social beings, inherit. I shall explore these realities as both restrictive in their social implications and freeing in their fluidity and possibilities. In the next section, I shall explore a transcending of sex and gender as categories to the reality of the lived body. Finally, from re-thinking, I move to a re-making of ourselves and look at the challenges that it presents to the doer.

Re-thinking Sex

The body with its physical attributes betrays us even before we are born, we are categorized, named and framed, and the weight of history and society fall upon our shoulders. The declaration of the sex of the child assigns a gender to the body. She is now in the discursive realm of sexual and gendered norms, one through which her identity, relationships and behaviour will be moulded. Butler speaks of a medical interpellation which, "shifts an infant from an 'it' to a 'she' or a 'he,' and in that naming, the girl is 'girled' and brought in the domain of language and kingship through the interpellation of gender."[2] In India, through the sex-determination test, the girl-child is "girled." The inescapable reality of the gender roles ascribed to her, in some cases, lead to her murder. We know that her "existence is already decided *by* gender."[3] The body is not a "*tabula rasa*" but already is part of discourses that exist prior to its existence. The fact that the body *is*, that it is visual and tangible, compels labels and definitions, it is spoken about and constituted even before it is born.

Sex is never a mere, mute fact of nature; the body enters into complex social, political and historical discourses in and through which it gains meaning and significance. Hence, different bodies are constituted differently. Born into hierarchical power structures within a hetero-sexual matrix in a patriarchal system, one can either be male or female, upon which masculinity or femininity is inscribed and propagated. Besides, while *some* bodies are recognised as "human," others are relegated to the non-human or sub- human domain. Infants and children born with gender anomalous bodies are administered corrective surgery or their "condition" is veiled.

According to Young in *On Female Body Experience*, the female child learns to use and regard her body and her abilities as instructed to her within a certain cultural and normative context. A girl accepts notions of muscular weakness which leads to a non-mobilisation of her bodily resources. Young thus demonstrates how male and female bodies are constructed differently and that there are manifest differences that are not innate. While we may hold that gender is a cultural construction and there are few innate or natural differences between the differently sexed bodies, would we also hold that the body is neutral? Would we hold that the sex of the body ought to not influence the subject? Would not differently sexed bodies experience the world differently? Gatens states that we cannot escape our sex: "Concerning the neutrality of the body, let me be explicit that there is no neutral body, there are at least two kinds of bodies; the male body and the female body....The subject is always a sexed subject."[4] Experiencing and perceiving the world and ourselves through a female body must mean differently, from that of a male body. Moreover, the body in its sexed appearance is gendered. Gullickson in analysing Moira Gatens' essay titled "A Critique of the Sex/Gender Distinction" writes, "The body, from which we cannot escape, constantly affects us. It is embedded in what it means to be the person we are, and is necessarily bound up in our gender."[5] She further adds, "Everything we do and think is drenched in the cultural meaning of what it means to be sexed."[6]

On the other hand, Moi reminds us that, "the sex of a body is always there, but it is not always the most important fact about that body. The dying body or the body in pain is not necessarily grasped primarily in terms of sexual difference... If, on the other hand, I am trying to get pregnant, this is a project that certainly foregrounds my sexed body."[7] Moi adds, that "In a scene of flirtation or seduction, for example, a woman may want to foreground her body."[8] In these instances when I am directly engaged with the physicality of being a woman, I would want to foreground my sexed body, taking in its pleasures and experiencing its nuances. However, if I am in the work-space or at a conference, I would want to engage intellectually with people and ideas, in ways that do not foreground my sexed body. In yet other spaces the colour of my skin will foreground my sexed body.

Interestingly, even sex, is not a fixed given. One can change one's body through cosmetic surgery and sex-change operations, to make the body 'mean' differently. However, these choices are only presented to those who can afford it; financially and socially.

Re-thinking Gender

While watching the 2005 movie adaptation of C.S. Lewis' *The Lion, The Witch and The Wardrobe*, I was struck by this conversation between Tumnus the faun and Lucy, who are meeting each other for the first time:

Tumnus: "...I-I'm sorry, please allow me to introduce myself...My name...is Tumnus."

Lucy: "Very nice to meet you, Mr Tumnus! I'm Lucy Pevensie."

extends hand to shake

Lucy: "Oh...you-you shake it!"

Tumnus: "....Why?"

Lucy: "I.....I don't know! People do it...when they meet each other..."[9]

Butler's notion of performativity reveals that the heart of our interactions with self and other is a stylized repetition of acts that are not our own, and are not owned by anyone, but in their repetitive doing come to exert so strong an influence, that they may be taken to be natural and essential. Butler implies that often we are not consciously and actively aware of our own actions. We make choices which we think are our own, but underneath each choice are forces that decide for us. When we pause or are compelled to deconstruct our behaviour we discover the abyss and a centre which is not fixed and cannot hold. In this discovery lies our freedom.

According to Butler, gender is "the repeated stylisation of the body, a set of repeated acts within a highly rigid regulatory frame that congeal over time to produce the appearance of substance, of a natural sort of being."[10] As de Beauvoir demonstrates, each of us are confronted with the reality of everyday life as it is enacted out before us: "In truth, to go for a walk with one's eyes open is enough to demonstrate that humanity is divided into two classes of individuals whose clothes, faces, bodies, smiles, gaits, interests, and occupations are manifestly different. Perhaps these differences are superficial; perhaps they are destined to disappear. What is certain is that for the moment they exist with a blinding obviousness."[11]

This performative understanding of gender gives to gender the illusion of essentialism which serves the heterosexual norm. At the heart of the binary gender roles is the preservation of the heterosexual norm. This norm is preserved because it facilitates reproduction and the propagation of a particular kinship system. This rigid framework ensures that performing one's gender wrong will have punishments and social implications. Thus, Moi writes, a woman who refuses to conform can be labelled both *unfeminine* and *unnatural*.[12] Butler demonstrates how the subject, born into a gendered world is compelled to cite her 'femininity,' goaded by the rigid and policing restrictions of society: "... This is a 'girl,' however, who is compelled to 'cite' the norm in order to qualify and remain a viable subject. Femininity is thus not the product of a choice, but the forcible citation of a norm, one whose complex historicity is indissociable from relations of discipline, regulation, punishment."[13]

The individual strives towards cultural survival, and conforms accordingly. In the unconscious repetition of acts, an identity is instituted, which furthers the illusion of gender as natural.

The Lived Body

Having looked at the notions of sex and gender, we move on to the phenomenology of being a woman; the entirety of a woman's experience of herself within her world. Each individual woman constructs herself within the boundaries of her world from which she makes meaning, harbours relationships and forges an identity. Rather than trying to define "woman" under one universal category that implies *sameness*, Moi speaks of "producing a concrete, historical understanding of what it means to be a woman (or a man) in a given society."[14] She agrees with de Beauvoir's understanding of the body as a situation, who writes of the "historically and socially situated understanding of the concrete, material, living and dying body."[15] She explores an ordinary understanding of what a woman is.

In the bid to appeal to a universal sisterhood, to appeal to women to join forces against systems, feminists ignore historical, social and embodied particularities. Butler, reminds us that, "gender is not always constituted coherently or consistently in different historical contexts, and because gender intersects with racial, class, ethnic, sexual and regional modalities of discursively constituted identities."[16] Different bodies are constructed differently; they experience the world and its struggles differently. An upper class, high-caste Indian woman will not identify with a Dalit woman's plight. Being of the same sex cannot be equated with sameness. Even the fact that women share common biological characteristics is not ground enough for a common experience. It is in and through dialogue with individuals and individual experiences that we can arrive at a different meaning of what it means to be a woman in different contexts.

Grosz writes, "There are always only specific types of body, concrete in their determinations, with a particular sex, race, and physiognomy."[17] In gaining insights into our relational understanding with others we will encounter multiple axes such as race, gender, class, sexuality, nation and culture, keeping in mind that none of these axes themselves are fixed or static. This exposes us to the ever fluid social and power structures through which we derive meaning and which are full of multiple significations. Butler writes that the very term woman "becomes a site of permanent openness and resignifiability."[18] Similarly, Moi, who follows de Beauvoir's existentialist approach, writes, "a woman defines herself through the way she lives her embodied situation in the world, or in other words, through the way in which she makes something of what the world makes of her."[19] In this open-ended, ongoing dialogue with self, other and the world, each gives the other signification, one that is open to re-signification.

Re-making Oneself: We are Our Choices

Existentialist theory holds that while we are constrained in facticity by the givens of our body and its relation to its environment, we also possess an ontological freedom to construct ourselves in relation to this facticity. For de Beauvoir, an authentically assumed existence is the realisation that one is inescapably on one's own when it comes to our choices and actions that create who we become. A woman makes sense of her embodied condition in the world and in her freedom constructs her own identity. Although the body is historically and socially situated, that is not all that defines a woman. Women are 'not a fixed reality' but are always in a process of becoming. We can choose to maintain a creative and critical engagement with our environment and its interpretation of our bodies. Moi writes, "To claim that the body is a situation is to acknowledge that the meaning of a woman's body is bound up with the way she uses her freedom."[20] A woman's lived experiences are the choices she makes within her situation.

According to Butler, gender is performative, that is, norms concerning femininity obtain insofar as they are continually re-enacted through corporeal activities. We enact, through imitation and reinterpretation, actions from the past. We all have our own diverse ways of effecting this imitation; nonetheless it is an imitation of a collective history. The acts that we "do" are not our own but are acts that we have been born into. Butler writes that, "The body is not passively scripted with cultural codes, as if it were a lifeless recipient of wholly pre-given cultural relations. But neither do embodied selves pre-exist the cultural conventions which essentially signify bodies."[21]

Our bodies in their situatedness restrict our embodied options. Our individual history and the norms of our society limit our freedom and our choices. Butler writes, "Surely, there are nuanced and individual ways of doing one's gender, but that one does it, and that one does it in accord with certain sanctions and proscriptions, is clearly not a fully individual matter…"[22] Butler underscores that the dominant norms are always the norms of heterosexuality, and gender is policed to maintain it. Butler argues that there is always the "…socially sanctioned ostracizing and violence and the accompanying psychological anguish that awaits those who dare to step over the lines that determine the fundamental meanings of our bodies."[23] Gender as performative has cultural survival as its goal, and we perform acts in the accordance with legal rules and cultural norms. We are aware of the price of nonconformity and the punishments that await those who do not "do" their gender correctly. Butler gives us the following analogy, "Just as a script may be enacted in various ways, and just as the play requires both text and interpretation, so the gendered body acts its part in a culturally restricted corporeal space and enacts interpretations within the confines of already existing directives."[24] There are choices, although regulated and limited. The possibilities that present themselves within the regulatory framework in which we move and act are limited. It is a constrained freedom.

So, the subject is given a choice, to act and imitate in ways that conform or to resist, through non-conformity, the imposed socio-cultural and bodily norms. While being shaped by social practices, I can also engage critically with them, and in engaging with them I act in ways that subvert or radically re-signify the norm. In its acted repetition it gives only an appearance of being "essential" and "natural." A heteronormative society establishes and perpetuates misguided connections between sex, gender, and sexuality. Butler writes that when one frees masculinity and femininity from particular bodily forms, "gender itself becomes a free-floating artifice, with the consequence that man and masculine might just as easily signify a female body as a male one, and woman and feminine a male body as easily as a female one." [25]

This opens up possibilities for us to repeat and do our gender differently. Butler's claim on the penultimate page of *Gender Trouble* is that "[t]he task is not whether to repeat, but how to repeat, or, indeed to repeat and, through a radical proliferation of gender, to *displace* the very gender norms that enable the repetition itself."[26] It is a call to subversive possibility and agency. Its goal is radical and political. Butler gives us the example of drag, through which gender is parodied. It reveals the imitative nature of gender identity and disturbs our naturalised normative gender conceptions which govern our bodies and sexualities. In disrupting essentialist binaries which exclude and oppress, we open up multiple possible identities. Individuals from around the world and across time, have chosen defy the norm and transcend the restrictive boundaries of gender presented to them. Joan of Arc, Jhansi ki Rani, Queen Elizabeth I are all women who challenged the norm. The lives and work of the *bhakta* and *sant* poets of India and of the European medieval saints "followed a trajectory of critique, protest and opting out of the heterosexual system…"[27] In acting, they have instituted alternate ways of being. In entering spaces which were closed to them and in making radical decisions they questioned, critiqued and exposed the normative binaries and gender roles. "Both men and women altered gender categories by trying to strip them of meaning – by walking naked, by growing their hair long, and by rethinking the terms of gender."[28]

Stone writes that, "Butler's own philosophical framework entails that effective subversions can only be carried out collectively. The linguistic instability that enables subversion also ensures that subversions can effectively undermine established meanings only when they are *repeated*, frequently and insistently enough to prevent conservative forces from reinstating tradition."[29] We must keep in mind however, that all our actions are acted out in particular contexts. It is a subversion that must take place from within existing discourse, since that is all there is. In conservative or liberal cultural spaces, different interpretations could produce political effects that are beyond our control. We can never predict in advance the hidden effects and consequences of our actions.

However, although we are presented with choices we often make choices that keep us within what we have come to believe is our own comfort zone. Very rarely will individuals choose to be subversive and disrupt the norm. As Bauer writes, "Put simply, Beauvoir's answer is that *the system works*, to a very significant degree, for both women and men. Not only do both men and women benefit from the lopsided relationship between the sexes, but also, Beauvoir speculates, both may well be *happier* in this arrangement than they would be if things were otherwise." We have been born into and in adopting and constructing ourselves around gender norms have constituted a social identity to which we have become attached. As embodied beings, we are influenced by our own histories and in acting under the gaze of the other we construct our identities in a particular context.

A range of factors condition which particular "agentic possibilities" subjects take up. The reasons for acting subversively, the agentic possibilities and the extent to which subversion is viable depends on the norms within that cultural context, how many other subjects engage in similar subversions and if subversion is necessary to one's survival. Butler writes, "One might wonder what use "opening up possibilities" finally is, but no one who has understood what it is to live in the social world as what is "impossible," illegible, unrealisable, unreal and illegitimate is likely to pose that question."[30] She encourages subversion for those whose lives it would improve, but she also goads individuals who perpetuate the system because *it works for them*, to challenge it precisely because it is a hierarchical, heterosexual system that does not look to the 'liveability' and empowerment of all. It is explorations of agentic possibilities that lie in re-creating who we become and the way we see each other. A system that constrains and regulates our behaviour and that we in aping, perpetuate, makes a mockery of our understanding of freedom.

Conclusion

Butler's ideas of gender as performative enable a perceiving of the gender norms as acting out, through imitation and repetition. She challenges us to foster a critical relation to received gender norms and in doing so to open agentic possibilities of "acting" differently. Simone de Beauvoir in speaking of women as an ongoing process of becoming gives us a freedom beyond the "fixed" givens. Both philosophers emphasize individual agency and goad their readers towards freedom, in opening up other ways of seeing and acting. They present the reader with useful choices and possibilities. In acting in ways that expose and parody the heterosexual matrix, we pull back the mask to discover its hollow constructedness. Our givens are not all; the creation of the acts we perform define who we become and how we influence the structures to which we owe our existence but could refuse to be defined by. Ultimately, it is a matter of choice, a choice influenced by our histories and identities; choices that we enact every day and in acting, institute. The production of embodied subjectivities is a collective, ongoing and always unfinished process.

Notes

1 Simone de Beauvoir, *The Second Sex* (New York: Vintage, 1989), xix.
2 Judith Butler, *Bodies that Matter: On the Discursive Limits of "Sex"* (New York: Routledge, 1993), 7.
3 Ibid., x.
4 Moira Gatens, "A Critique of the Sex/Gender Distinction," in *A Reader in Feminist Knowledge*, ed. Sneja Gunew (London: Routledge, 1991), 145.
5 Anna Gullickson, "The Significance of Sexed Bodies: An Analysis of Moira Gatens' A Critique of the Sex/Gender Distinction," *Undergraduate Review* 12, no. 7 (2000): 4.
6 Ibid., 4.
7 Toril Moi, "'I am a Woman': The Body as Background in the Second Sex," *Paroles Gelées* 17, no. 2 (1999): 11.
8 Ibid., 12.
9 Quote by Lucy, http://www.narniafans.com/forum/archive/index.php/t-5324.html (accessed October 13, 2015).
10 Judith Butler, *Gender Trouble: Feminism and the Subversion of Identity* (New York: Routledge, 1999), 43-44.
11 de Beauvoir, *The Second Sex*, xx–xi.
12 Toril Moi, "Feminist, Female, Feminine," in *The Feminist Reader: Essays in Gender and the Politics of Literary Criticism*, ed. Catherine Belsey and Jane Moore (New York: Basil Blackwell, 1989), 123.
13 Butler, *Bodies that Matter*, 232.
14 Toril Moi, "What is a Woman?," in *What is a Woman and Other Essays* (Oxford: Oxford University Press, 1999), 5.
15 Ibid., x.
16 Butler, *Gender Trouble*, 6.
17 Elizabeth Grosz, *Volatile Bodies: Toward a Corporeal Feminism* (Australia: Allen & Unwin, 1994), 19.
18 Judith Butler, "Contingent Foundations: Feminism and the Question of Postmodernism" in *Feminist Theorize the Political*, ed. Judith Butler and J. Scott (London: Routledge, 1992), 16.
19 Moi, "What is a Woman?," 73.
20 Moi as cited in Iris Marion Young's *On Female Body Experience: "Throwing Like a Girl" and Other Essays* (New York: Oxford University Press, 2005), 16.
21 Judith Butler, "Performative Acts and Gender Constitution: An Essay in Phenomenology and Feminist Theory," *Theatre Journal* 40, no. 4 (December 1988): 526.
22 Ibid., 409.
23 Butler as cited in Nancy Bauer, "Beauvoir on the Allure of Self-Objectification," in *Feminist Metaphysics: Explorations in the Ontology of Sex, Gender and the Self*, ed. Charlotte Witt (Netherlands: Springer, 2011).
24 Butler, "Performative Acts and Gender Constitution," 526.
25 Butler, *Gender Trouble*, 10.
26 Ibid., 189.

27 Ruth Vanita, "Thinking beyond Gender in India," in *Feminism in India*, ed. Maitrayee Chaudhuri (New Delhi: Kali for Women and Women Unlimited, 2004), 74.

28 Ibid., 75.

29 Alison Stone, "Towards a Genealogical Feminism: A Reading of Judith Butler's Political Thought," *Contemporary Political Theory* 4, no. 1 (2005); http://www.palgrave-journals.com/cpt/journal/v4/n1/full/9300135a.html (accessed October 13, 2015).

30 Butler, *Gender Trouble*, viii.

12

Body, Gender and Sexuality in Family

A. Pushparajan
Madurai Kamaraj University, Madurai

Abstract: Of the numerous challenges that the family is thrown open to today, a more fundamental challenge is coming from a misplaced emphasis on the role of the body (merely as objects), the misconception of the gender role and a misperceived understanding of sexuality. With this assumption, the paper first proceeds to indicate the misplaced emphasis on the role of the human body by undertaking a scrutiny of premarital relationship in the first part and bringing out the misperceived understanding of the gender role as well as sexuality, by critically analysing the extramarital relationship in the second part. The third and the final Part of the paper tries to give a wholesome solution by making a detailed analysis of human nature, in the light of Gandhian insights, and thereby presents an integral approach to the understanding of the body, gender and sexuality and thereby re-establishing a stronger base for family life.

Keywords: marriage, sexuality, gender, family, body, human nature, Gandhi.

Introduction

Today there is so much of stress, hurt, anger and infidelity among the married couple that many of them think of a break up as a quick solution. They don't seem to make a positive effort to struggle with the problems of marriage. The divorce rate in many western countries[1] has reached around 50%, while in Indian cities the number of divorce-cases is increasing daily.[2] Demands for same sex-unions are snowballing. Co-habitation or live-in relationships are on the increase. Outsourcing of new parenthood like surrogate motherhood seems to be picking up. Single parenthood is getting preferred to the usual method.

These trends are probably reactions to the suppressive practices found in the traditional system of the family. As against the scornful approach to the body in the past, the body may be glorified today. As opposed to gender discrimination and gender inequality, constructed purely on biological differences and indoctrinated by patriarchal culture, people may emphasize their gender autonomy today. As a reaction to the excessive taboos on sex in the past, today's laxity may have arisen, which is expressed in pre-marital and extra marital relations. But the net result is that the very foundation of family is shaken. The first cell of human civilization has begun to decay and to degenerate.

What is needed is a middle path wherein the role of the body, gender and sexuality are accepted in due proportion and integrated with one another in a holistic framework, such that the body is neither ignored nor glorified but is understood as an integral part of the individual's personality. Gender is constructed neither purely upon biological difference nor upon merely one's own construction, but is treated with due recognition, respect and complementarity. Sexuality is neither despised nor hyped but is allowed to play its necessary role within the family set up.

This paper is precisely an attempt at presenting such a mid-path and reinstating a strong foundation to the family. First, a scrutiny of the premarital and extra-marital relationship is undertaken in the first two parts so as to untangle the misplaced emphasis on the body and the misconceived roles of gender and sexuality. The third and final part of this paper, after pin pointing the basic flaw in those practices will suggest the remedy, taking cues from M. K. Gandhi's analysis of human nature.

Body in Premarital Relationship

In the traditional method of 'arranged marriage', the young man is allowed to see his prospective life-partner in the presence of experienced people who are all interested in his welfare. They all discuss the various indications for suitability. Above all the first impression of the boy or the girl will be given priority in the choice. It is ultimately the 'faith' that counts in the choice.

As against this, it is becoming common among many families in major cities to allow youngsters to decide the suitability of one's life partner by dating. Dating is said to be a form of mutually agreed upon social activity by which the couple meet for companionship, beyond the level of friendship, with a view to assessing each other's suitability as a partner in marriage. Notwithstanding the many benefits the new method may have, several questions crop up.

After all, one meets only a handful of people in one's life. Considering the number of people residing in a city it is only from handful of persons one comes across that one is supposed to choose from. How could one be sure of one's choice as the most suitable? If at all one is able to test one's emotional compatibility during dating, it applies to the emotion expressed at that time only. But 'times' are not the same always. Accordingly one's moods are also changing, besides the changes in the bodily conditions and in one's perceptions. Unless the couples manifest great maturity, and are ready to make compromises, and negotiate with the new circumstances of life, their marriage is bound to fail. After all, one's life is the way one makes it to be. Really it is 'faith' in one another that plays a crucial role in actual married life, as in the traditional method.

A major problem in dating is in relation to the way the body is considered by the couple. If they were involved in sexual sharing while already dating, both of them would know that it was a lapse, and even morally evil. Now, after the marriage each is daunted with the thought: 'what guarantee is there that the other would not be falling into similar lapses with those others whom the other had already dated?' Thus both are unhappy. As a result they may even eventually get separated, divorced and re-married.[3]

If the couple had agreed to save the physical union until they were married, they might just indulge in some 'beginnings' of love making, at the physical level, surely with the hope that after marriage, when they would be able to be with each other all day and all night, their love would grow to the maximum point. But all these romantic fantasies will really vanish within a few days or months after marriage, when they would realize that they are not getting what they expected out of marriage, certainly not in bed and not in the routine of daily living. Thus, premarital misconceptions about the 'bodily' aspects as established by some scientific studies end up in post-marital disillusionment, even trigger a 'need' for extramarital relations.[4]

But these so called 'needs' are nothing but an obsession with a consumerist lifestyle in family life, bee-searching of bodies after bodies which is bound to incur violence of all kinds, and finally the mutual destruction of the family. The wise words of Pope Francis, stated although in a different context, are applicable to our context here. "When people become self-centred and self-enclosed, their greed increases. The emptier a person's heart is, the more he or she needs things to buy, own and consume (even others' body)."[5]

In a word, all these problems are ultimately traceable to the misplaced emphasis on the body, and fancying that all about marriage was related to body and bodily pleasure.

Gender and Sexuality in Marriage

It is true that in the traditional family set up, 'gender' has been seen more as based upon biological sex, been ascribed as 'weaker roles', and they have been confined to the four walls of the kitchen. The gender differentiation and even discrimination constructed by patriarchal society and indoctrinated by culture and taught/practiced in the family has led to a lot of gender injustice and gender inequality. True. However, the trend is changing at least in urban settings. It has become a common practice among the couples in big cities to go in for full time employment outside their home. Indian husbands in general are still not comfortable with a strong, independent and modern woman. They want their wife to be an earning partner but not a high-powered career woman. They only expect that their women will have to fulfil their role of home-maker efficiently. On the contrary the working wife would rightly expect her husband to lend a helping hand in her daily chores at home. If her expectations are not met then they are bound to undergo a lot of tension at home, besides the stress at work-place. Thus, they are easily led to think that their marriage is a failure.[6]

It is not unlikely that one of the partners may work all night, six nights a week. Obviously it is difficult to get and to give emotional and psychological support to one another. In such a case it is not a surprising thing if either/both of the couple may engage themselves in infidelity, cheating or adultery. It might all start with the boss already married to a woman, taking his subordinate woman to lunch or a drink. These acts in the beginning may not prove to be unfaithful. But if such companionship is deliberately sought out because something is missing in their respective marriages, then surely it is a sign of infidelity. People among the so called elitist circles seem to even encourage sexual infidelity provided that it does not disrupt their marriage or publicly embarrass them.

Even from practical standpoint, the extra marital relationship is certainly questionable. It is bound to have serious repercussions on their marital relations once the couples begin to indulge in comparisons and contrasts. The spouse cannot be emotionally the same to the original partner with whom wedding vows were exchanged. What about one's commitment to the other even in illness, misfortune or old age? A number of other questions also arises: Is marriage all about the sexual gratification or emotional fulfilment only? Can persons be treated in the same way as we deal with material commodities? Could a partner be merely 'used and thrown away' after one's gratification? What about the human dignity of such persons who are simply used, even with consent? What about the children's attitude to such parents, when they come to know about their parents' relations outside the family. Will not such relations make a severe impact upon their children's development?

Human Nature

From the foregoing it is hopefully evident that the role of the body, gender and sexuality either in the traditional set up or in the postmodern set up cannot be overemphasized in one way or another. The real solution lies in treating these components 'holistically' and 'integrally.' First let me pinpoint a basic flaw in the one-sided approach to body/gender/sexuality. Next, let me suggest the integral approach as the right alternative to sustaining the sanctity of marriage and the stability of the family. In both these steps, it is Gandhian insights that are of great help to the exercise.

The Basic Flaw in the One-sided Approach

Obviously 'family' is the first cell of human society, which starts with marriage between two heterosexual persons, leading into a relationship of parents and children, extending into a wider relationship of kith and kin, embracing them all in an emotional and psychological binding, lasting for generations. One may also define family as that primary institution in which common life & mutual aid is assured among the members with an inbuilt moral responsibility governing members in moral relationships. Home is the first school in which parents and grandparents are the first teachers and the family is the first text book for the child to learn the culture of his people. To put it in the words of Pope John Paul II: "The family constitutes the fundamental "cell" of human society" and civilization.[7]

The nucleus of the family is the intimate union of father and mother, which depends upon sexual union, too. Human sex must actually compress both union (of flesh) and communion (of hearts and souls); it is by no means a passing fling in the night or a loss of self-discipline that results in regrets. Couples, who alone can practice restraints, respecting each other's body and gender as sacred mysteries, not treating them as objects, can make a meaningful family. "In short," says Christopher West, "as sex goes, so go marriage and the family. As marriage and the family go, so goes the world."[8] To put it differently, the bodies of the two opposite genders along with proper use of their sexuality is essential for sustaining family life.

But the present day scenario depicts a sad story because many families seem to take premarital relationship and extramarital relationship as normal. Hence, we have to first consider these aberrations in the foregoing sections. Now it is time for us to probe the fundamental flaw in these approaches. The basic argument of the advocates of the one sided importance to body and gender, allowing free sex either in the premarital or extra-marital relationship may be formulated in the form of a syllogism:

All that is 'natural' needs to be fulfilled, not suppressed, and much less repressed.

The bodily instincts like sex are 'natural' drives.

So, bodily instincts like sex need to be fulfilled, not suppressed nor repressed. In the process, one's body and gender need to be overstressed.

The argument seems to be convincing, and it is of the *Barbara* type. But scarcely do people see that the 'middle term' of this syllogism is ambiguous.

It was to his credit that a great spiritualist thinker like M. K. Gandhi was perceptive enough to unravel the ambiguity, though in a different context. Already in 1926, he made the following remark: "No word seems to be more abused today than the word 'natural'. For instance a correspondent writes, 'as eating, drinking are natural to man, even so is anger. Another seems to argue: 'The sexual function is considered as natural as the other functions of the body. Were it not so, God would not have endowed it to man."[9]

But Gandhi's retort consists of many steps:

1. Indeed, if we were to put the human in the same category as the brute, many things could be proved to come under the description 'natural.' But if they belong to two different species, then "not everything that is natural to the brute is natural to man." On the contrary there are certain features of human life which are distinguishing marks of the human species alone. One example is the notion of 'progress,' which takes place in humans alone, not beasts.
2. It is not one's duty to develop all the functions to perfection, but it is one's duty to develop all the God-ward faculties to perfection and to suppress completely those of a contrary tendency. Even as one is having the same type of animals drives of hunger and sex, one can retire into the innermost depths of one's deeper self and establish an utmost harmony within even in the midst of conflictual tendencies in him. It is humans alone who have this unique capacity to rise above as the most disciplined being, by sublimating themselves. In his innermost being a man could experience that he is not the body but the *Atman*, and that he may use the body only with a view to expressing the *Atman*, only with a view to self-realization. It is from that experience that the human evolves the ethics of subduing desire, anger, ignorance, malice and other passions, puts forth his best effort to achieve the end and finally attains complete success. Only when his efforts reach that consummation can he be said to have fulfilled himself, to have acted according to his nature.
3. Being endowed with discrimination and reason humans could use reason to worship God and to know Him, and regard the attainment of that knowledge as the *summum bonum* of life. The desire to worship God is inconceivable in the brute, while the humans can voluntarily worship even Satan. It must therefore be, and is, human nature to know and find God. When one worships Satan, one acts contrary to one's nature. While to the one whose end and aim is the realization of God, even the functions of eating and drinking can be natural only within certain limits. For having knowledge of God as his end, he will not eat or drink for the sake of enjoyment, but solely

> for sustaining the body. Restraint and renunciation will, therefore, always be his watchwords even in respect to these functions.

Further, having been blessed with choice or free will to accept and reject, humans cannot but distinguish between good and evil, virtue and vice. These mean, in other words, nothing but things to be accepted and things to be rejected, hence bad or sinful. We have within us both good and bad desires. It is our duty to cultivate the former and to suppress or eradicate the latter, and if we fail therein we should remain brutes though born men. Birth as a human being is therefore declared by all religions as a rare privilege – a state of probation. So, it is up to us to successfully come out of this probationary period and establish our true identity as Soul domineering beings rather than brute domineering.[10]

Gandhi had to face many objections already during his life time. A medical correspondent wrote to Gandhi that man is animal first and human afterwards. "Think of the savages and their ancestors when there was no art, no literature, and no science", he wrote. "Man is not made in the image of God; but it is God who is made in the image of man. The question of virtue and vice has nothing to do with God. Your moral code is not debased if you regarded the ape as your remote cousin. Eating, drinking and sexual gratification are absolutely natural to man. Your soul force is figment of imagination."[11]

To such an objection Gandhi replied thus:

A species is recognized and differentiated from the rest by its special characteristics. It would be wrong to say that a horse is animal first and horse after. He shares something in common with other animals, but he cannot shed his horseliness and yet remain an animal. If he were to lose his special virtue of being horse, he would lose his general status as animal too. Similarly, if a man were to lose his status as man, the use of his reason etc., he would lose, with the loss of his status as man, his status also as animal.

As regards the savage too, Gandhi claimed that his nature was fundamentally different from the brute because the brute will always remain brute, whereas the savage had in him the capacity for developing to the fullest height attainable. That some of us do not recognize that status of ours (as image of God), makes no difference, except that then we do not get the benefit of the status, even as a lion brought up in the company of sheep, may not know his own status and therefore does not receive its benefits; but it belongs to him, nevertheless, and, the moment he realizes it, he begins to exercise his dominion over the sheep. But no sheep masquerading as a lion can ever attain the leonine status.[12]

In short, the human is human only when our animal appetites (body and sexuality) or rational faculty (gender and sexuality) are guided by the differentiating principle within, never by allowing them to function on their own under the pretext of being 'natural.'

The 'Integral' Approach

The foregoing considerations will be much more convincing if one understands the unique definition of human nature, proffered by Gandhi. As against the Western philosophers who base themselves basically on the Aristotelian definition of human nature as 'Rational Animal,' Gandhi asserts the following:

'R' is an ambiguous faculty in this that it can either support the S or A. If you are keen on listening to the dictates of the Indwelling spirit, and thereby make your R subservient to your Spirit in you, then the 'A' becomes such a docile dog to your higher goals of life. It is then that the divine spark within you goes on shining more and more effulgent. This is precisely the meaning of being a man of God. But, the same R can support A and stifle listening to the S. To put it in the words of Gandhi "Reason is a poor thing in the midst of temptations. ... Reason *appears* to be on the side of those who indulge in drink and free love. The fact is that reason is blurred on such occasions. It follows the instinct. Do not lawyers engaged on opposite sides make reason appear to be on their side?"[13]

'R' is also the most precarious faculty, too. When R begins to support the A in us, we will stoop down lower than animals. For instance, in the case of palate appetite, if you had followed simply the animal appetite, you may become a glutton. That is all. But when your R begins to support the appetite, you may find new ways like the 'vomitorium' of the Romans, and degenerate the human culture itself. Likewise animals follow the sexual urge only in season. But if a human pursues sexuality, with the support of R, then he may tend to convert even every minute into a season, if only one could withstand the physical strain and drain.

If your R is allowed to support the 'A' in you beyond limits, then there is also the risk of making your S dormant and inactive, and making 'A' the all dominant principle of your existence; you may get lurched in 'animality' and even justify your 'animality-based' actions to such an extent that you may finally reach a stage where your 'S' is smothered and its dictates are stifled. The soul at that stage may have fallen to such an abyss that it will never be able to see God. Although its nature was destined to see God yet by your over-emphasis of body or gender or sexuality, you have practically made it impossible to see God. In a sense it is a stage of self-condemnation or self-negation.

In the light of the remark last mentioned, a Biblical verse which was unintelligible to me for many years began to make sense to me, now. Jesus is reported to have declared: "All sins will be forgiven except the sin against the Spirit" (Mk. 3.28). Granted that Jesus is the most compassionate Lord and that He is destined to be the Saviour of all humanity, I thought, how he could declare a sort of exception to his saving mission. Why should he declare one sin is beyond the purview of his saving action? Such questions would vanish the moment you understand that the so called sin against the Spirit is not a specific sin one commits through an act, but a stage of self-condemnation or self-negation that one lands up in, on account of the life style which was never attuned to Spirit within. Once you have landed up in an abyss of self-negation and self-condemnation, obviously no Saviour can have a role to play at all.

In sum, what is required, then, is that the third principle 'S' must always reign supreme in one's life, so that one's animal appetites (A) and rational faculties (R) are subordinate to the dictates of the Spirit-within-us. It is only by allowing the inner Spirit to govern our whole life, all our thoughts, all our words and all our actions that we would attain the fullest truth of our being. In other words, you must always be attuned to the indwelling Spirit in such a way that you are alive to the dictates of your Inner voice and that you abide by them alone even in the minutest actions/words/thoughts. When the 'S' is made the dominant principle in you, then your 'R' and 'A' automatically become subservient to that higher principle.[14]

This definitional statement of Gandhi regarding human nature may be corroborated by the words of Pope Francis: "We become *fully human* when we become *more than human*, when we let God bring us beyond ourselves in order to attain the fullest truth of our being."[15]

Now, applying the whole analysis to the family context, first and foremost it becomes clear that marriage is not all about the body. Family life is not constituted simply by union of two bodies. Rather it is the communion of two persons. It is their spiritual union that is basically at work in a successful marriage. Their bodily union is indeed a sacrament; signifying and contributing to their spiritual union. As Pope John Paul II observes: the human "is a person in the unity of his body and his spirit. The body can never be reduced to mere matter: it is a *spiritualized body*, just as the human spirit is so closely united to the body that one can be described as an *embodied spirit*."[16] Yes, to look at the personhood of somebody, we need to *see* their body only, and it is as important as their spirit is. There is no other way. When I introduce somebody as so and so, I don't say 'This is Mr. Andrew's body" as if his personhood is different and separate, but only say "This is Mr. Andrews," indicating to his body. "The body, in fact, and only the body, is capable of making visible of what is invisible, leading us to fathom the mystery of human person."[17]

Of course, there is a certain ambiguity about the human body. A body can be used to embrace a child to show one's love and concern for the child. Or the same body can be used to strike the same child in anger. A body can be used to toil to support a family or be allowed to be drunk, lying down on the road. A body can be used to worship God or to worship Satan. What is needed is a responsible choice to use the body. In Gandhian terms, every use of the body needs to be guided and directed by the 'S', the supreme principle. In the Christian perspective, our bodies are created to image God and to demonstrate His love. So, also in marriage embracing a body can be used to image the Trinitarian love of God, or *in the exact same action*, to stain two souls in an act of extramarital lust and spit in the face of God's beautiful plan.[18] Likewise a violent misuse of the body within marriage or the misuse of woman merely as a productive machine of children or simply for unpaid labour in the household work is also not in order. The difference lies in the intent, in the act of will. *It is not the action that defiles the intent, but the intent that defiles the soul* and guides the action. So, there is the need to respect the body, gender, and sexuality, to revere it and hold it in high dignity and treat it with great responsibility, subordinating it always to the dictates of the indwelling spirit, never manipulating it or using and throwing it according to one's whims and fancies.

Conclusion

If the foregoing analysis of human nature is definitional in its content, then, merely 'body' or 'gender' or 'sexuality' cannot be given that much importance as the contemporary scenario seems to do. Nor can they be suppressed or ignored or misused as the traditional system of family has done. There is an urgency to see that they are truly guided and governed by the Spirit-component in us. Especially in a family context, the human body and gender are mysteries to be unravelled day after day, and that human sexuality implies a communion of souls much more than simply a sensual pleasure. If one sincerely foregrounds these components of the body, gender, and sexuality in a sacred and holistic framework in which 'S' reigns supreme, many of the family problems will be solved. Then, the prospects of a peaceful and prosperous family are bound to loom large and bright!

Notes

1 Sweden 54.9, Belarus 52.9, Finland 51.2, Luxembourg 47.4, Denmark 46.7, Belgium 44, Austria 43.4, Czech Republic 43.3, Russia 43.3, United Kingdom 42.6, Norway 40.4, Germany 39.4, France 38.3; http://www.2equal1.com/country-europe/european-divorce-statistics./ (accessed October 25, 2015).

2 In our country the situation is not that bad partly because the traditional view regarding the sacredness of marriage still prevails in society. However, reported by T C S Raja Chockalingam, Additional Principal Family Court Judge, Chennai, in a symposium, about 5-10 cases are filed for divorce every day in the major cities from Delhi to Chennai. http://ibnlive.in.com/news/divorce-rates-are-skyrocketing-in-indian-cities-too/297338-60-120.html (accessed August 8, 2014).

3 Brian Richard Boylan, *Infidelity* (Englewood Cliffs: Prentice-Hall International, 1971), 18-21.

4 Brian Richard Boylan, *Infidelity* (Englewood Cliffs: Prentice-Hall International, 1971), 18-21.

5 Pope Francis, *Encyclical Laudato Si'* (2014), 204.

6 http://ibnlive.in.com/news/divorce-rates-are-skyrocketing-in-indian-cities-too/297338-60-120.html (accessed June 30, 2014).

7 Pope John Paul II, *Letter to Families* (1994), 4.

8 Christopher West, as quoted in <Katie Kimball @ Kitchen Stewardship> Mar 16, 2011, (accessed June 7, 2015).

9 M. K. Gandhi, *Young India*, (June 24, 1926); *In Search of the Supreme*, Vol. I (Ahmedabad: Navajivan Publishing House, 1961), 132.

10 M. K. Gandhi, *Young India*, (June 24, 1926); *In Search*, Vol. I, 132-134. Here, Gandhi sounds almost like Ludwig Wittgenstein. In his *Philosophical Investigations*, Wittgenstein remarks that "A dog cannot be hypocrite, but neither can he be sincere." If one unpacks some of the meaning of this cryptic statement, 'a dog cannot be a hypocrite' would mean he cannot falsify himself, or act in an inauthentic manner. The reason is that he lacks the ability to do this. But he also lacks the ability consciously to 'become' himself. Because, he lacks the freedom to *choose* to behave as a dog, he lacks the freedom to choose not to. His fidelity to his own being is therefore a fact rather than a value. A dog cannot commit suicide, but neither can he become a martyr. See Terry Eagleton, *The Body as Language, Outline of a New Left Theology* (London: Sheed and Ward, 1970), 1.

11 M. K. Gandhi, "More Animal than Human" in *Young India* (July 8, 1926), *In Search*, Vol. 1, 135.

12 M. K. Gandhi, *Young India* (July 8, 1926), *In search*, Vol. 1, 136-139.

13 M. K. Gandhi, *Harijan*, Dec. 23, 1939, p. 386. *In search of the Supreme*, *Vol. 1*, p. 141.

14 This does not mean that the 'A' and 'R' will lose their importance. But, it only means that they will have their identity as well as their role only in relation to the 'S' within self. In other words body will have to be taken care of; mind or gender will have to be asserted; sexuality will have to be expressed, but within the frame work of the governance of 'S.'

15 Pope Francis, *Apostolic Exhortation Evnagaelium Gaudium* (2014), 8.

16 Pope John Paul II, *Letter to Families Gratissimam Sane* (1994), 19.

17 Pope John Paul II, *Theology of the Body*, "Man Enters the World as a Subject of Truth and Love." In his General Audience of 20 February 1980, 19:4.

18 Katie Kimball, "Theology of the Body, Part One: An Education in Being Human," http://www.kitchenstewardship.com/2011/03/16/theology-of-the-body-part-one-an-education-in-being-human/ (accessed March 16, 2011).

Part 3

Approaches of Science and Technology

13

Is the Body Merely Bodily?

Reflections on the Human Body as a Symbol in Bio and Medical Sciences

S. Stephen Jayard

Jnana-Deepa Vidyapeeth, Pune

Abstract: The recent researches and the discoveries in the fields of Bio and Medical Sciences reveal the amazingly complex structures and intricate functions of the human body. Even a cursive look at them makes us realize that the whole body is not just the sum total of its parts and its functions can neither be fully explained in terms of mechanical rules nor can they be reduced to certain fundamental phenomena. This paper seeks to make a modest attempt to show that the body is no more seen as 'a mere physical structure of tissues, cells and molecules,' but it is 'an organic system,' where each and every part is marvellously inter-linked with one another, clearly revealing that the body cannot be seen in isolation of a "phenomenon," what may be differently called as the 'spirit,' 'soul,' 'self,' 'personhood,' 'coordinating agent' and so on. In the first part, the paper briefly analyses the issue of 'Reductionism' in Biology and the Medical Sciences to show that the contemporary neuro and life sciences clearly reveal the untenability of reductionism, at least, in those sciences. In the second part two interesting and intriguing notions of 'placebo' and 'nocebo' effects are briefly discussed. It is mysterious to see how the positive and confident thinking (in mind) of the patient can create positive physical changes (in body), while the negative one creates negative effects. With these analyses the paper aims to bring out clearly that the human body is not just 'bodily,' but also an essential combination of both 'bodily' and 'something more' – of course, to define clearly what that 'something more' means, is a million dollar question, because, for millennia it has kept humanity busy, and probably it will ever keep humanity exploring and guessing about the actual picture of that 'something more'!

Keywords: human body, life, reductionism, bio and neuro sciences, mind-body relationship and placebo-nocebo effects.

Introduction

If at all there is one discipline among the natural and secular fields, apart from the theological and religious ones, that can recognize and be convinced of the sacredness and the intrinsic dignity of the human body, it is the disciplines of Medicine and Biology. The doctors and the researchers in these disciplines have very many chances to witness the amazingly complex and unbelievably intricate structures of our human body. Even a cursive look at the nature and the functions of the whole body and its parts makes them realize that the whole body is not just the sum total of its parts and its functions cannot be fully explained in terms of mechanical rules. More and more researches in the fields of bio and neuro sciences reveal more stimulating facts about our body.

This paper seeks to make a modest attempt to show that the body is no more seen as 'a mere physical structure of 'tissues, cells and molecules,' but it is 'an organic system,' where each and every part is marvellously inter-linked with one another, clearly revealing that the body cannot be seen in isolation of an element, what may be differently called as 'spirit,' 'soul,' 'self,' 'personhood' and so on. In short, the body is not merely bodily, but 'body plus something' and that in turn implies that humans are no more seen as merely physical beings, but psychosomatic (*Psyche* = spirit; *soma* = body) beings.

In order to highlight this fact, the paper, in the first part, takes up the issue of 'Reductionism,' a tendency that has permeated several disciplines like Mathematics, Philosophy of Mind, Biology, Metaphysics etc., holding that, among many other insights, 'the whole is just the sum of its components' and that 'many theories in a discipline can comfortably be reduced to just one or a few theories'. The paper argues that the number of those who apply such a 'reductionist approach' seems to be declining, at least in Biology, as the new discoveries and researches in the fields of neuro and life sciences clearly reveal the untenability of reductionism in those sciences. In the second part the paper highlights the two notions of 'placebo' and 'nocebo' effects, which are intimately related to the familiar debate over the mind-body relationship. Studies in the recent decades make us aware of the great power of mind over body. There are sincere and serious case-studies to show that with the power of the mind, even terminal illnesses have been completely cured or greatly abated in their seriousness. The paper, thus, aims to highlight clearly that the human body is not just 'bodily,' but an essential combination of both 'bodily' and 'something more' – of course, to define clearly what that 'something more' means is a million dollar question, which has kept humanity busy over the millennia, and probably it will ever keep humanity exploring and guessing about the actual picture of that 'something more.'

Reductionism: Irreducible?

Reductionism in general means that the nature of complex things can be understood by reducing them to the functions and interactions of their parts that are simpler and more fundamental things. Reductionism also means that all 'special sciences' (biology, psychology, economics etc) are reducible to the basic physical science (physics). Thus, the fundamentals of Chemistry are based on Physics, while molecular biology can be reduced to Chemistry; similarly sociology is based on psychology. The tendency for reductionism is not new both in the natural sciences and humanities. In the ancient Greek Philosophy Thales, a reductionist philosopher began this approach in the 6th century BC, at Miletus in Asia Minor. In his search for the *Arche,* the fundamental stuff reality, he reduced reality to water, the basic substance. Following him many other philosophers upheld different stuff to be the *Arche*. Descartes was the first one, in the modern times, to introduce the idea of reductionism in Part V of his *Discourses* of 1637; he showed that the world was like a machine and all its functions and nature can be clearly understood in terms of the working of its parts. In the past two centuries, this analytical approach to the natural world has increased with the aim of controlling and conquering nature.

Reductionism is sometimes seen as the identification of the reducing elements with the reduced elements, or even as the elimination of the reduced elements with the preference to the reducing elements. It seeks to a reduce theory or a phenomenon to some other (often simpler and more fundamental) theory or phenomenon. For instance, Mathematics looks for the possibility of reducing any mathematical theorem to logic or set theory, while Bio sciences attempt to reduce biological entities like cells to compilations of physico-chemical elements like atoms and molecules; Philosophy of Mind moves towards reducing consciousness to the physical phenomena of the functions of the neurons in the brain, while Metaphysics aims to reduce all sciences to physics. The main purpose of reductionism in the 20th century is to unify all sciences. The efforts for arriving at the "Theory of Everything" (TOE), is one such example, though it has not been achieved even after several decades of serious efforts. There are advantages of making things simpler and more comprehensive. But the question is whether it is possible, or even desirable, in all the fields.[1]

Reductionism in Bio-Medical Sciences

Reductionism in Biology is convinced that every single process in nature can scientifically be analysed and comprehended in terms of its constituent parts.

The whole picture is completely knowable by looking at the individual parts. For instance, the brain is nothing but the result of complex and interacting physical processes and therefore all human experiences of consciousness, intelligence and emotional states are understandable in terms of its neurons. In biology ontological reductionism holds that each system is made up of molecules and their interactions and argues for a hierarchy of chemical, biological and physical properties. Methodological reductionism proposes that biological systems are most fruitfully investigated at the lowest possible level, and epistemic reductionism suggests that knowledge of a higher domain can always be reduced to a lower more basic level.

The clinical practice is basically reductionist, which is manifested in four practices of medicine namely, i) the focus on a singular factor, ii) stress on homeostasis, iii) inexact modification, iv) additive treatments. *The focus on a singular factor*: the human body is taken to be the collection of individual parts and one single part is responsible for the observed behaviour. As a car mechanic changes a particular part in rectifying the problem, the physician isolates that one single part in treating a disease. For example, in treating cancer, the focus is on the tumour, and in treating gastrointestinal bleeding, it is the bleeding vessel or ulcer. *Emphasis on homeostasis*: For several decades it has been believed that our body which has stability and constancy in the face of stress and illness is taken to be a failure in homeostatic mechanism. So, treatment means correcting the deviation by replacing the affected parts. The stability that is considered here is the static stability, not dynamic stability, as we see below. *Inexact risk modification*: Diseases cannot always exactly be predicted, so medical science focuses on risk factors. Usually the one-dimensional 'one-rise factor to one-disease' is given importance. For example, hypertension is seen as a risk factor for coronary heart disease. *Additive treatments*: Reductionism treats multiple issues in a piecemeal manner. For example, in coronary artery disease, each known risk factor is dealt with individually; in co-existence of multiple diseases, like hypothyroidism, diabetes and coronary artery disease, each one is treated individually.

Opposing Views to Reductionism

Emergentism advocates that complex systems and patterns are the emergent properties out of simple interactions among their multiple parts. It argues that the emergent properties of complex systems show that they cannot be reduced to the parts; for instance, evolutionary psychology and socio-biology are held untenable because complex systems are essentially irreducible and only a holistic approach will give us their real picture. Stuart Kauffman argues the same way to show that complex systems lay a limit to reductionism.[2] According to Holism, the complex systems are intrinsically irreducible and since the whole is more than the sum of its constituents, only a holistic approach can understand them properly. This outlook is also not new, as even Aristotle in his 'Metaphysics' proposed that the whole is more than sum total of its parts. In biology it can be interpreted as disease is more than the sum of disordered parts and interactions among them. Similarly, vitalism argues that the laws of physics and chemistry alone will not be sufficient to the processes of life and unlike physico-chemical forces life-principle is self-determining.

Potential Problems with the Reductionist Approach

Reductionism can increase mistrust – Since the specialization increases more and more at the molecular and sub-molecular levels, it goes beyond the grasp of a common person. Even for the specialists as they tend to know go deeper in their own specified little area of research, they lose confidence with regard to other domains. Reductionism runs the risk of oversimplification – The full motivation to reduce the complex phenomenon into more basic components may lead someone to overlook certain significant details that would go against the process of reductionism. Reductionist explanations can land us in confusions about cause and effect – for instance, disordered pathway – is it the cause or result of a malignancy? Which came first? Thus, reductionism may not help us in getting to the roots of the problem. One-to-one evidence based reductionism forgets the complex factors: The design, the trials in the lab, treatments and guidelines to invest in research for new drugs – all are determined by evidence obtained at the clinics. But very often oversimplification takes place, as the researchers tend to categorize patients into subdivision, in order to suit the general categories they have created. But, in fact, each patient is unique and it is not even ethical to squeeze an individual into a category without paying attention to their individual circumstances. It is very difficult to go by one-to-one evidence based; rather many complex factors have to be taken into account, like "the availability or lack of alternative treatments."[3] The media can also be carried away by the reductionist approach. Often the media make big news, like 'a wonder drug is now available,' or 'AIDS cure round the corner,' or 'Immortality almost at hand,' etc. These may mislead people to think that it is just a single-step to reach the cure or the treatment. But they don't elaborate on how each individual is unique and is to be taken as a whole.

System Biology: A Check to Reductionism in Biology

Today's world of science moves on from biology to system biology;[4] the former focuses on the components of a system, the latter focuses on the interactions among the components. The more and more we know about the functions of genes we get increasingly baffled. Since the success of human genome project in 2000, scientists are bewildered to fathom how genes interact to collectively create a system-wide behaviour. The genetic information is contained not only in the genes of the 100 trillion cells in the human body, but also in their interactions between them and between their products. So, we cannot oversimplify that all the emergent-traits can be explained by their components. For instance, complex diseases like cancer, asthma and atherosclerosis cannot be easily explained by a single genetic mutation. Thus, 'system biology' approaches an issue with its holistic and composite characteristics. It extensively uses several mathematical theories and computational models to understand the issues. The fundamental conviction of this approach is that the forest is more than the individual trees it contains. The person, not the disease affecting him/her, is the focus here; since we lack sufficient tools to deal with complex situations and therefore basic question like 'how do a person's sleeping patterns, diet, hobbies, living conditions, comorbidities, stressors and so on add to his/her heart problems?, remains largely untouched.

System biology focuses on dynamic stability, not static stability as in the case of the reductionist approach (which sees the system as a mere collection of static components). Chaotic behaviour of complex heart rate variability is a case to show that there is dynamic stability in our system. Failure to consider such cases in the homeostasis model may lead to ineffective and damaging treatments. In dealing with risk factors, System biology is cautious not to equate one risk factor to one disease, because a disease can have a complex network of risk factors. Therefore it aims at developing more multidimensional analytical methods so that the predictive ability gets increased and holistic. Correcting the additive treatment of the reductionist approach, system biology does not neglect the complex interplay between disease and treatment; so system biology looks for nonlinear treatments, rather than additive ones. There are circumstances whereby complex interplay between parts creates a given behaviour we cannot predict, or explain all behaviours only in terms of its parts.

Further, system biology makes us realize that cells and molecules respond in reference to their context, time and space. It focuses on these three factors in order to study the system-wide behaviour: the context that considers all the components taking part in the process, the time, which considers the changing characteristics of each component and the space that allows the topographic relationships between and among the parts. When we fail to consider all these three aspects we are in danger of losing rich information about the system.

Placebo and Nocebo Effects: Challenges to Reductionism

Placebo comes from the Latin, meaning 'I please.' As in our ordinary experiences all that please us need not be true, moral, good and healthy, placebo is actually a farce medical treatment to create some good effects in the patient. A placebo has been defined as "a substance or procedure... that is objectively without specific activity for the condition being treated."[5] The placebo treatments would include inert tablets, vehicle infusions, sham surgery etc. Lots of researches are done with placebo treatment to understand the neurobiological mechanisms in responding to pain, immune-suppression, Parkinson's disease and depression. These treatments can make an impact even on physiological changes on the brain and its chemical activity, in the heart rate, blood pressure etc. Such treatments help us to figure out what really goes on in the brain in dealing with pain, suffering and illness. Some authors argue that there is no actual placebo effect, because the inert substance given does not cause any effect, so instead, it is better to call it 'meaning response' as the brain associates with the placebo effect. Placebo is very useful in some specific cases where the usual medications cannot be used. For instance, in treating burn patients who have respiratory problems, they cannot often be given opioid (morphine) or its derivatives, as they can increase the respiratory problem and in such cases the placebos are useful.

Placebo effect is related with expectations. Children are more easily impacted by the placebo s than adults. It is the expectation of the patient to feel better that makes him/her feel better. According to Irving Kirsch, "the belief that one has received an active treatment can produce subjective changes thought to be produced by the real treatment."[6] People with Alzheimer's disease lose the capacity to be influenced by the placebos and the probable explanation is that they have lost the prefrontal cortex and therefore cannot have expectations.[7] Conditioning also can take place; that is, if a placebo is given along with the actual treatment simultaneously for quite some time, the placebo is identified with the actual treatment. Due to such expectancy and conditioning, whatever can change that expectancy can increase the extent of the placebo effect also. Even the colour and the size of the pills can change the placebo effect; more than tablets, capsules have better effect; some have shown even cultural background also can have positive effect.[8] Motivation also positively affects the placebo effect and this varies from culture to culture. Recent researches reveal that a placebo can reduce pain-related neural activity in the spinal cord, affirming that placebo can affect parts even beyond the brain.[9]

Various parts of brain are significantly affected by the placebo effect. For instance, placebo relief is associated with the release of dopamine in the brain; placebos reducing depression affect many of the same areas that are activated by antidepressants with the addition of the prefrontal cortex; similarly placebo-caffeinated coffee causes an increase in bilateral dopamine release in the thalamus.[10] Pain is reduced by placebos, and this phenomenon is called 'placebo analgesia'; it is done either by initiating the release of endorphins, which are naturally produced by brain to reduce pain, or by changing the patient's perception of pain whereby pain is seen as a just discomfort and tingling.[11]

Placebos work positively in the cases of several conditions like pain, swelling, depression, anxiety, asthma, epilepsy, erectile dysfunction, panic disorders, irritable bowel syndrome, pain disorders, Parkinson's disease, lower urinary tract symptoms, gastric and duodenal ulcers, heart failure, itch, benign prostate enlargement, osteoarthritis, sexual dysfunction in women and many other such cases.

There is also 'nocebo effect' (nocebo in Latin means, "I will harm), which is just the opposite of placebo effect: Some ill-effects on health can be caused by mere suggestions or belief that they are going to happen, even without any actual and physical intake or applying of any substance or medicines. The notion of placebo effect was quite well-known by the beginning of the 20th century, whereas the notion of nocebo effect became popular only by 1990s. Both nocebo and placebo effects are presumably originated from or created by a state of mind; they have a psychological rather than a physiological cause. They are very much related with the patient's expectations, conditioning, fear and other emotional complexes. It is really amazing that the patient's health can be affected, positively or negatively, even by the uniform worn by the medical professionals treating them, the kind of words that they hear from others, even the type of room that they are placed in for recovery.[12]

Conclusion

By way of concluding the paper, I would like to highlight these factors that fill us with awe and wonder: a) the very notion of life; b) the relationship between mind and body (consciousness and brain); and c) the significance and the dignity of the body. What is life or living? No simple and straightforward answer seems to be available in any one discipline. Perhaps different disciplines – scientific, philosophical and religious ones – can come together to undertake this great task of exploring this, but even then the real grasp of the notion of life seems to be evading. Dictionaries may roughly understand life as "the condition that distinguishes animals and plants from inorganic matter, including the capacity for growth, reproduction, functional activity, and continual change preceding death" or it may also refer to "the existence of an individual human being or animal."[13] We cannot locate life in a living creature: is life in the bones or genes, cells or chromosomes, brain or blood? No answer seems to be satisfactory! The ability to move, to eat, to procreate – are usually taken to be the signs of life; but recently a sperm that has been frozen for several years have been used to impregnate a woman; and all these years, those usual signs of life are obviously missing, but still the element called 'life' must have been sticking to the sperm and that is why it is able to produce another life. Therefore the intriguing question, "what is life?" seems to stay unanswered forever.

Similarly the issue of the relationship between brain and consciousness: Consciousness is obviously much related with the brain, but it cannot be reduced to the brain. There is, for instance, a big debate going on about understanding the relationship between religious belief and the evolution of the brain. Several authors try to explain how at a certain level of evolution the brain begins to support religious consciousness. Kapogiannis and Jordan Grafman argue that the brain, developed for other higher functions, has slowly given rise to our capacity for religious experiences, while Andrew Newberg, is convinced that the brain may be a tool in recognizing religious experiences and receptive to them, but this fact need not automatically lead us to conclude that the brain creates those experiences.[14] As long as we have to use our brains in our investigations into the nature and functions of the brain there will be some residue that we cannot fully understand about the brain. Further, as long as we take a 'conscious' effort to study the intricacies of our 'consciousness' we can never master in our understanding what that consciousness means!

Finally, all these facts and arguments reveal that we need to realize that our body is no more merely 'bodily'; it is not just the accumulation of flesh and bones. A person's dignity is non-negotiable and because a person is expressed in and through the body, the body is sacred, inviolable. The body reveals the person: When someone hits us, we ask 'Why do you hit me?' rather than asking 'Why do you hit my hand or leg or whatever?' Further, this dignity of the body begins right at the time of conception; embryology by and large affirms that the human person begins right at the time of fertilization, where the male and female cells, the sperm and egg, come together: "fertilization marks the beginning of the life of the new individual human being."[15] Christian bioethics also affirms the same conviction that at the moment of fusion of these two cells we have the beginning of the human being.

Notes

1 Being aware of the shortcomings and dangers of reductionism helps us not to be carried away by the sway of, what Daniel Dennett called, 'greedy reductionism,' in his popular work, Darwin's Dangerous Idea, which tempts us to reduce every explanation in every field of science to cellular biology and particle physics. He cautions that even if the lowest level of explanation exists it is not always the best tool to understand it. Once in a while we need to stand away and see things in a holistic manner, as the distance enables us to see a larger picture.

2 Stuart Kauffman, "Beyond Reductionism: Reinventing the Sacred." https://en.wikipedia.org/wiki/Reductionism (accessed May 2, 2015).

3 Mark J. Beresford. "Medical Reductionism: Lessons from the Great Philosophers," ***Quarterly Journal of Medicine 103, no. 9 (1998):*** 721-724. See http://qjmed.oxfordjournals.org/content/103/9/721#sec-2 (accessed May 2, 2015).

4 For this section I mainly rely on Andrew C. Ahn, Muneesh Tewari, Chi-Sang Poon, and Russell S. Phillips, "The Limits of Reductionism in Medicine: Could Systems Biology Offer an Alternative?" *PLoS Medicine Journal* 5 (2006). See: http://www.ncbi.nlm.nih.gov/pmc/articles/PMC1459480/ (accessed April 17, 2015).

5 C. J. McDonald et alia, "How Much of the Placebo 'Effect' Is Really Statistical Regression?," *Statistics in Medicine 2*, no. 4 (1983): 417-427.

6 I. *Kirsch,* "Response Expectancy as a Determinant of Experience and Behavior," *American Psychologist* 40, no. 11 (1985): 1189-1202.

7 See F. Benedetti et alia, "Loss of Expectation-Related Mechanisms in Alzheimer's Disease Makes Analgesic Therapies Less Effective," *Journal of Pain* 121, no. 1-2 (2006): 133-144.

8 Cf. A. J. *de Craen et alia,* "Effect of colour of drugs: systematic review of perceived effect of drugs and of their effectiveness," *British Medical Journal* 313, no. 7072 (1996): 1624-1626; L. W. Buckalew and S. Ross, "Relationship of Perceptual Characteristics to Efficacy of Placebos," *Psychological Reports Journal* 49, no. 3 (1981): 955-961; B. Dolinska, "Empirical Investigation into Placebo Effectiveness," *Irish Journal of Psychological Medicine* 16, no. 2 (1999): 57-58.

9 See F. Eippert et alia, "Direct Evidence for Spinal Cord Involvement in Placebo Analgesia," *Science* 326, no. 5951 (2009): 404.

10 Cf. R. de la Fuente-Fernández et alia, "Expectation and Dopamine Release: Mechanism of the Placebo Effect in Parkinson's Disease," *Science* 293, no. 5532 (2001): 1164-1166; H. S. Mayberg et alia, "The Functional Neuroanatomy of the Placebo Effect," *American Journal of Psychiatry* 159, no. 5 (2002): 728737; A. F. Leuchter et alia, "Changes in Brain Function of Depressed Subjects During Treatment with Placebo," *American Journal of Psychiatry 159,* no. 1 (2002): 122-129.

11 See Norman, Head First (New York: E. P. Dutton, 1989), 229-231.

12 Nocebo and Placebo effects involve an ethical issue also: if a doctor is morally expected to inform the patients about the true state of affairs about health, how can he or she hide or modify the facts to create placebo effects? If so, it may be unethical to use placebo, but on the other hand, as David Newman argues, it will also be equally unethical not to use something that actually helps healing the patients. He calls this 'placebo paradox' and he suggests that as long the one who is administering placebo is honest, open and sincerely believes in the real power of healing one can administer without any qualms of conscience. (See: David H. Newman, Hippocrates' Shadow (2008): 134-59. See https://en.wikipedia.org/wiki/Placebo (accessed May 17, 2015).

13 https://www.google.ca/webhp?sourceid=chrome-instant&ion=1&espv=2&ie=UTF-8#q=what%20is%20life%3F (accessed March 3, 2015).

14 See Dimitrios Kapogiannis et alia "Religion and the Brain: A Debate," in *Cerebrum 2010: Emerging Ideas in Brain Science*, ed. Dan Gordon (Washington DC: Dana Press, 2010).

15 S. Gilbert, *Developmental Biology*, 5th edition (Sunderland: Sinnaure Associates, 1997), 60.

14

Redesigning the Human Body in Science and Technology

Noel D'Costa

Patriarchal Seminary of Rachol, Goa

Abstract: The body indicates and characterizes the identity of the person. The capability of the person is known by the performance of the body. The technologies by being tangential to the bodies provided human beings with comfort, health and entertainment. The body in concomitant with the understanding of the reality outside gives meaning to the person's life. Blooming technologies threaten the basic concepts of the body as given, able to perform, tangential to technology and that which gives meaning to our lives. These technologies with the application of interdisciplinary sciences have made it possible for inanimate matter to transform into life giving animate matter. The line that demarcated technology and biology is blurred. This new technological biological transformation, projected to take place in next to no time opens up a Pandora's box to contemplate upon a new way of understanding human body. This paper tends to reflect on the certain shifts which are envisioned in near future in the understanding of the body. The notions of the body as given to perform by being tangential to the technology, which gives meaning to our life will shift to body as crafted through enhancement to be become instrument, which will alienate us from our lives. These shifts pose us with the question of how far can we go to change the structure and the function of the body.

Keywords: enhancement, technology, instrumentalization, posthumans, alienation, neuroenhancement, anti-meliorist, crafted.

Introduction

The promises and possibilities of altering the structure and functioning of the body are multifarious. Apart from the earlier unassuming means of medicine and education or child-rearing for the growth of a person, the use of science and technology for the better functioning of the body have gradually increased. The use of drugs by athletes to boost the stamina, students to improve their mental capabilities, innumerable people to heighten their sexual performance, to overcome depression, to change the structure of the face through cosmetic surgery, etc., have been taking place in society in the last decade.

The advancement in science and technology in the present decade has been phenomenal. The convergence of various forms of technologies like biotechnology, neuro-technology, information technology, nanotechnology, and the associated sciences has made it possible to look at the body not as a given but that which can be designed from the womb never to see the tomb. The question of redesigning the body through science, engineering, and technology becomes pertinent in the second half of the 21st century. The innumerable forms of technologies to redesign the human body are no more distant fantasies but there are some forms of technology that do exist and there are others under development for implementation in the immediate future.

The escalated use of technology to design bodies invites us to reflect on the fundamental questions. The central question of the debate is whether to accept or reject science and technology which are able to emancipate and enhance the human body. How far "the new technologies should be used in order to improve human capacities or traits in healthy individuals or designed or modified without becoming someone different even "someone else"? "What makes a use 'good,' or even just 'acceptable'?"[1] As Christian philosophers, how can we respond to this debate? The response to these questions is concurring to the metanarrative an individual holds regarding "what we are and what we should become and of what constitutes the greater good."[2] We shall have a passing glimpse of the technologies that exist, are possible and have promised to design the body.

Designing the body: How?

The literature regarding the possibilities or the promises of designing the body or altering the functioning of the body is colossal. Though the earlier non-technological approaches like sleep, training, nutrition, etc. were employed to augment the body and it's functioning, the progression in medical science and technology has surged the rise in the innovation possible in designing the body. There are certain designs and alterations of the body that have already taken place, whereas there are others envisaged in the near future.

In the case of altering the functioning of the brain through Psychopharmacology, there are certain alterations of brain for enhanced mood like Prozac or enhanced concentration like Ritalin or prolonged wakefulness like Provigil available whereas research for drugs for appetite suppressants are in progress. The alteration of the functioning of the body through drugs to enhance male sexual functioning through the growth hormone Viagra or the performance of the athlete through erythropoietin or muscle mass through steroids is also possible. Modifications for facial appearance through Cosmetic surgery are widely practiced.[3]

The real surge came through the interdisciplinary approach in designing the body. The possibilities and promises are mind blowing. The developments in genetic, chemical, surgical, robotic sciences, synthetic biology, genomics, nanobots, informatics and bioengineering have provided a plethora of means to design the body. They promise to deliver on stimulating ideas like 'Singularity'[4] in the near future.

The breaking of the complicated encrypted code through human genome mapping has made available to the Geneticists means to connect strands of DNA with human characteristics. These strands of DNA are now open to manipulation through engineering techniques. The Geneticist alters the genetic make-up of selected cells in the body through Gene therapy to promote regeneration. The identification and location of the genes which are responsible for intelligence, aging, prone to disease, etc. and techniques for selecting and altering the genes foresee a clever, aged and healthier body. There are already preimplantation genetic diagnosis taking place that enables embryos to be selected for particular genetic traits like Huntington's disease and cystic fibrosis. Human germline therapy is in the infancy state with number of experiments conducted on mice.

The ability to manipulate matter at the minutest level through Nanotechnology has provided the means to design the body at its very core. The discovery and use of microscopic robots called nanobots into the human body can do far more than the insertion, deletion, or transposition of the chemical letters of the DNA.[5] They will be able to eliminate bad cholesterol from our arteries or fix the malfunctioning of our memories or provide insulin to diabetic bodies. They will be able to destroy tumours or rebuild cell walls.

Apart from the medical use, the transformation of the human body envisaged from biology to technology is beyond our present intellectual capacity. The use of Cybernetics which alters the mental or physical function of the body by embedding engineering and electronic system within the body is actively pursued.[6] Ray Kurzweil envisioned that the pace of change of our human-created technology is accelerating and its powers are expanding at an exponential pace.[7] He visualised that we are coming at a point called Singularity.

There have been various means and strategies used to enhance the cognitive functions of the individual. We have seen earlier the pharmacological means like stimulants or drugs and non-technological means like exercise, meditation and mnemonics. The use of technology to boost the functioning of the brain is a recent addition. The application of Transcranial Magnetic Stimulation (TMS), Transcranial Direct Current Stimulation (tDCS), Brain-computer Interface (BCI), Deep Brain Stimulation (DBS) and Electroencephalography (EEG) has heightened the functioning of the brain. The computer interfaces on the brain measures and analyses neural signals and converts them into output. They are registered by electrodes in the scalp. They can be used for medical purposes especially in research and clinical as well as non-medical especially in enhancement. The promise of having an internet connection between the brain and the machine can change the way we work, drive and relax. Neuroscience is expected to get at the root of consciousness, emotions, and addictions.[8]

We have seen various ways in which the body can be designed to enhance capabilities like bodily appearance (cosmetic surgery), athletic performance (doping in sports), genetic make-up (genetic enhancement) or brain functions (neuroenhancement).[9] There is a movement of from the designing the body to restore normal human capacity (due to disabled or dysfunctional elements to enhance the human performance) to enhance to do superhuman feats. The human body is moving to a point where humans can reduplicate and then improve what nature has already accomplished through science and technology. The ability to turn matter to organic bodies or read and interpret genomes and modify them and create genetic diversity, adding to the considerable sum that nature has already produced is the promise to be fulfilled shortly.[10]

The promise of the capabilities of the newly designed or redesigned bodies brings us back to the social, ethical and legal implications. Though the promises are for the future and seem to be speculative and exaggerated, they are seemingly appropriate to be realistic to become a topic of serious debate. There have been deliberations at different fronts on these issues. We shall pithily analyse the debate between the proponents and the opponents of designing bodies for enhancement.

Conservatives versus Trans-humanists

The deliberations with regard to the use of science and technology for designing the body have been going on for some time. The Conservatives in the debate like Francis Fukuyama, Leon Kass, Jürgen Habermas, Charles Krauthammer and others reject the idea of enhancement, whereas the Trans-humanists like Nick Bostrom, Ray Kurzweil, John Harris and others support enhancement. Some of them do take intermediate and nuanced positions.

The Conservatives argue that "human nature is sacred and delicate and that it should not be tinkered with, particularly since the consequences of modifying the human form are unpredictable."[11] Leon Kass puts forth three objections with regards to health,[12] equality, and liberty.[13] The Trans-humanists point out that enhancement can cure diseases, radically increase human lifespan, improvise human mental and physical capacities, enrich people's overall quality of life,[14] eradicate needless suffering, "space colonization and the possibility of creating super intelligent machines, along with other potential developments that could profoundly alter the human condition."[15] They argue that each individual has a right to decide to design his or her own life as well as the moral obligation[16] to enhance with available technologies. They claim that enhancement can be justified morally, medically and humanely.

Kirsten Brukamp elaborates the arguments of Leon Kass with regards to health by highlighting the "medical risks, the lack of evidence-based medicine, and financial challenges to health care systems, human nature, virtue ethics, liberty, justice and the social value."[17] Dimitris Repantis gives a list of evidence of the risks and benefits of antidepressants, anti-dementia drugs and psychostimulants currently used for pharmacological cognitive enhancement and concludes that there is a substantial lack of evidence both for the effectiveness and for the long term safety of the enhanced body through drugs.[18]

Fukuyama, a Conservative, brings to light numerous apprehensions. Though Fukuyama's concerns are manifold, his main point of the argument is about the possibility of creating a superior "breed children who are more intelligent, more healthy, more 'normal'"[19] thereby undermining the worth or dignity of normal, unmodified "people who are poor and lacking in education would still fail to take advantage of it."[20] Nick Bostrom retorts that cognitive enhancement has been taking place from centuries through non-biomedical means. The use of science and technology to enhance should not be viewed now as a radical idea.[21] There are others who argue that the earlier means of science were quite elementary, whereas now the technology had taken over to design the body at an exponential proportion, which is a matter of concern. Greta Wagner questions the fairness in the society due to cognitive enhancements. She points out that since society is competitive, fairness becomes the purpose for a certain degree of institutional intervention.[22]

Leon Kass' objection of liberty is questioned by Wrye Sententia. Liberty for her is "every person's fundamental right to think independently, to use the full spectrum of his or her mind, and to have autonomy over his or her own brain chemistry."[23] She argues with the principle of harm that "as long as they do not subsequently engage in behaviour that harms others,"[24] individuals should not be prohibited from using mind-enhancing drugs and technologies. She concludes that the designing of the body may increase a society's overall efficiency and achievements.

Another important argument against human enhancement is about the issue of self-worth, the inborn or natural capabilities and physiognomies of human beings, and the nature and intrinsic value of human achievements. Michael J. Sandel points out that "our capacity to act freely, for ourselves, by our own efforts, and to consider ourselves responsible – worthy of praise or blame – for the things we do and for the way we are"[25] are hampered.

The argument that designing the human body is for the betterment of the human being is often proposed by the Transhumanists. They see "human nature as incomplete, human biology as limiting, and human technology as the pathway to a new form of humanity."[26] The 'Humanity'[27] website in their homepage support the ethical use of technology to expand human capacities to "enable everyone to enjoy better minds, better bodies and better lives. In other words, we want people to be better[28] than well."[29] Kyle Oskvig reflects on the evolved Aristotelian ethics to conclude that the "exercise of physical strength has intrinsic moral value."[30] Michael Hauskeller questions the conclusions from the term better and argues that the term 'better' is "highly context-dependent for whether some neuroenhancement is desirable for people depends on what they are getting better at, what end the improvement serves, and who benefits from it."[31] Other critics see the process of betterment through technology as a kind of mass death or a wilful annihilation of humanity.

Other points of the debate include 'informed-consent procedure'[32] or the consumerist pursuit for enhancement, whereby the craving for "changing the genetic make-up of our children, of inserting artificial implants into our bodies, or of 'uploading' our brains into a new virtual form"[33] for self-improvement cannot be ruled out. Ramez Naam in his book *More Than Human* sums up the arguments in favour of enhancement as "the pragmatic benefits of enhancement, the inevitable failure of any attempts to regulate enhancement, respect for individual autonomy and freedom of choice, and the fact that the desire to enhance is an inherent part of human nature that cannot be suppressed."[34]

The debate on designing the body has highlighted various individual, societal and moral implications. There is a certain categorization and clarification on the different issues deliberated related to the designing of the body like "safety, efficacy, risk-benefit-ratio, autonomy, cognitive liberty, identity, authenticity, pressure to perform, fairness, justice, human nature, medicalization of human life"[35] and the proper role of government. The issues discussed lead us to reflect profoundly on our response to these emerging technologies to design a body.

Designer Body: Challenges Ahead

The conceptualisation of the designer body is unfathomable. The possibility of the imagination is dependent upon the familiarity with the technology mentioned earlier. Though the technology is described in fiction novels, the pace at which the development of technology is taking place makes it seemingly plausible. How can the issues arising from the designer body be adequately discussed?

What are the challenges to the fundamental concepts related to human life? We shall discuss few of these challenges to the common-sense understanding of human body.

Body: Given to Be Crafted

The common understanding about the origin of the body is 'given.' It is given or gifted by God or a supernatural power. The gift of God has to be accepted with gratitude. There are potential capabilities in the body. The structure of the body can be altered through physical exercise and diet regimens. If one wants to increase its capabilities, he/she has to train, practice and pray to God or divine being(s) for enhancement in the makeup of the body. It is only the disciplined effort and the all-powerful God who can provide the desired body.

The technological designed bodies are no more given but that which can be planned, designed and executed in the laboratory or clinic. It will be the result of human venture rather than previously understood concept of creation or evolution. It involves improving the human abilities and capabilities like enhancing our intellect, health and life span through various technologies. It is possible to design organs and through stem cells cosmetically alter our bodies. One can undergo human growth hormone (HGH) treatment to increase their height or plastic surgery to correct the orientation of the facial appearance. Nicholas Agar writes that "the idea that humans could be radically enhanced is not new; but the notion that it's something that we could arrange for ourselves certainly is."[36]

The new designer body invites us to reflect on the Christian understanding of God creating humans in His own image and likeness. The application of science and technology to enhance the looks and productivity of the body challenges the conventional notion of the body as a 'given.' It involves human competencies beyond their normal human nature. The technologically designed bodies from the womb will transcend the way we look at the human nature. The problem lies in whether the body would be embedded in nature or would transcend nature. If the body is 'given', then it is embedded in nature whereas if it is 'crafted', then it can transcend nature. Steve fuller would say that humanity is about the "matching of 'function to form' (biology) and 'message to medium' (technology)."[37] Arthur Caplan argues against the 'anti-meliorists'[38] to claim that the new enhancement technologies are merely the logical next step in an ongoing process of using new knowledge to improve ourselves.[39] It means that even though when the body is crafted it does not transcend nature but it is improvised nature. The point of contention is how far the improvised designed body can be considered as an improvised nature or still in the image and likeness of God

Body: Performance to Enhancement

The evaluation of the human body is done based on how it performs. It is acknowledged that the human body has inherent potentials to boost its performance. The capacity to elevate the performance of the body is dependent on how a person is able to activate his brain, accelerate his muscle or engage in concomitance with the system. Though there are limits to the performance, these limits are set by the optimum level performed earlier by any 'body.' There have been instruments or means to improve the performance. If you want to speak louder, then microphones are made available to amplify the sound or if you have a problem of vision, then spectacles are available. There are various mechanical tools used inside the body to stabilise the performance of the body for medical reasons.

The performance of the body through the insertion from the application of science is incredible. The body will be able to perform astonishing physical and intellectual feats never imagined earlier. The technological enhancement will be able to functionally alter the capabilities, abilities, emotions and other characteristics. The change in performance of the body will not happen because of the application or addition of an instrument but the change will be inherent in the body. There is a shift taking place from the 'performance of the body' to the 'enhanced body.' The question is no more whether the body can perform a particular feat, but whether humans can design a body that can perform that particular feat.

The problem of the 'enhanced body' lies in cases of competitive situations. The designing of the brain to increase the cognitive functions that aims at an increase in mental performance in competitive situations will give an edge for those who have an access to these technologies.[40] There are even possibilities of manipulating the brain of the other person. The principle of harm to others through an 'enhanced body' is another serious drawback in its acceptance. The main problem of the 'enhanced body,' lies in the inability to "know exactly how to make better humans."[41]

Body: Tangential to Instrumentalization

Tangential refers to something which barely touches a matter. The developments in science through its application have provided technology to the body. The body had used these technologies in the past by merely touching it or slightly connecting to it. Television, computers or mobiles are some examples through which the body touches the technology. The technology has offered the body with better health, safety, comfort and entertainment. The bodies were tangential with the technology to carry on the human practices.

The new envisaged designed bodies are no more 'tangential' to technologies but 'instrumental.' The body is made instrument to accomplish a certain task. There was instrumentalization of the body earlier too, but on a small scale. The companies instrumentalized people to buy certain products through the advertisement or the ideology of capitalism by obscuring reason to create a desire for having more and more possessions.

The instrumentalization of new technological bodies will be in-built and intertwined. Technology can be implanted inside a body to achieve certain results. Frodeman is worried about the use of nanotechnology through which "extremely small surveillance devices placed within one's body would be used by authorities as social control mechanisms."[42] Carl Elliott warns that the commercialization of the bodies through inbuilt technologies amounts to unprecedented market access to the body and mind.[43] The instrumentalization of the body will not take place through the ideology or allurement, but by the powerful 'valids' over the body of the consumer of technology, the 'invalids.'

Body: Meaning to Alienation

Our existence makes sense when we give meaning to our lives. Meaning is something which gives significance, importance or value to the person's life. If the subjective dimension claims that the meaning is relative to the subject, then the objective aspect contends that meaning is independent of the subject. Meaning is what fits together with the reality. "A meaningful life is a life upon which a pattern has been imposed that relates not merely to what goes on inside the person's head, but which involves also, in serious ways, the person having an effect upon the world."[44]

The philosophical discussion on meaning has been diverse. Aristotle would find meaning in the human function or Aquinas in the beatific vision or Kant in the highest good. There have been deliberations to come out with a principle that can confer meaning to life. Nevertheless, there are certain concepts like the presence of the divine, divinely ordered universe, relationship with the divine, afterlife, ideas of what is right or wrong, which gives meaning to our lives.

Enhanced bodies alienate us from experiences that give meaning to our lives. There are certain potentialities and experiences that make us human beings. When it is a matter of choice, "significant human value directs us to prefer the more modest achievements of unenhanced humans to the superior performances of radically enhanced posthumans."[45] The process of choosing unenhanced humans takes place because the performance of humans gives meaning to the choice.

Nicolas Agar states that humans who undergo radical cognitive enhancement are likely to go through a form of self-alienation. He writes about two types of alienation due to enhanced bodies. He claims that Cognitive enhancement can disrupt the proper relationship between us and the experiences and commitments that make us who we are and alienation affects our relations with our children.[46] Ronald Cole-Turner goes a little further to envisage that future biomedical technology might offer powerful tools to increase or diminish the storing of memories or modify our psychological mood, moral predispositions, our attachment or bond to other human beings (e.g., our spouse), and our level of self-esteem."[47] This can lead to complete self-alienation.

Conclusion

The given bodies define our performance. It gives us meaning and guides us to what extent we can use the technologies envisaged. Though there are yearnings to be healthier, to know better, feel happier and live longer, the means provided to achieve these through the present advancing technology are a matter of concern. The present technologies "can boost our mental powers and physical constitutions to levels far beyond those previously attained by humans."[48]

Humans along with their bodies are moving to a technological level which is unconceivable. The development and shaping of these new technologies will eventually bring changes to the previously understood concepts, culture and expectations. The pitch of demand will shift from diet, drugs and therapies to bio-chemical, genetic, robotic, informatics and neuro enhancement not only for medical purpose but mental and physical enhancement.[49] The disputes earlier with regard to the use of science and technology, which were "over specific methods, facts, or effects," will shift on meaning, values and beliefs.[50] The acceptability of the new technology to design the body will depend upon "the context in which they are sought, the aims they are heading at, and the consequences."[51]

Christian philosophers have a mission to reflect upon these new developments envisaged in science and technology. The meaning making concepts of the body as given to perform by being tangential to the technology will move to alienation of the body as crafted through enhancement to be instrumentalized. These prospects invite us to reflect on the understanding of the body through a continual transformation through technology, which can go far beyond toward something completely new. The process of reflection should not cloud our minds only with the consequences but incorporate the advantageous possibilities of how far we can go to design the structure and functioning of the body.

Notes

1 Leon R. Kass, "Ageless Bodies, Happy Souls: Biotechnology and the Pursuit of Perfection," *The New Atlantis* 1, no. 1 (2003): 13.

2 Stephen Lilley, *Transhumanism and Society: The Social Debate over Human Enhancement* (London: Springer, 2013), 3.

3 Paul Miller and James Wilsdon, eds., *Better Humans? The Politics of Human Enhancement and Life Extension* (London: Demos, 2006), 7.

4 Ray Kurzweil describes singularity as "a future period during which the pace of technological change will be so rapid, its impact so deep, that human life will be irreversibly transformed... this epoch will transform the concepts that we rely on to give meaning to our lives, from our business models to the cycle of human life, including death itself... Within several decades information-based technologies will encompass all human knowledge and proficiency, ultimately including the pattern-recognition powers, problem-solving skills, and emotional and moral intelligence of the human brain itself... the changes [these technological developments] bring about will appear to rupture the fabric of human history." He says that the mind will be "about one billion times more powerful than all human intelligence today." This mind will be human and non-biological. The neurons will be replaced by electronic circuits that are both computationally more efficient and entirely immune from disease. This will lead to gradual merger of human with machine." Ray Kurzweil, *The Singularity is Near: When Humans Transcend Biology* (London: Penguin Books, 2005), 7-9.

5 Nicholas Agar, *Humanity's End: Why We Should Reject Radical Enhancement* (Cambridge: MIT Press, 2010), 6.

6 Miller and Wilsdon, eds., *Better Humans?*, 7.

7 Kurzweil, *The Singularity is Near*, 24.

8 Lilley, *Transhumanism and Society*, 5.

9 Elisabeth Hildt and Andreas G. Franke, eds., *Cognitive Enhancement: An Interdisciplinary Perspective* (Dordrecht: Springer, 2013), 2.

10 George Church and Ed Regis, *Regenesis: How Synthetic Biology Will Reinvent Nature and Ourselves* (New York: Basic Books, 2012), 12.

11 Nayef R.. F. Al-Rodhan, ed. *The Politics of Emerging Strategic Technologies: Implications for Geopolitics, Human Enhancement and Human Destiny* (Hampshire: Palgrave Macmillan, 2011), 194.

12 Leon Kass argues about safety. He points out that "Athletes who take steroids will later suffer premature heart disease. College students who take Ecstasy will damage dopamine receptors in their basal ganglia and suffer early Parkinson's disease." He concludes that "no biological agent used for purposes of self-perfection will be entirely safe: anything powerful enough to enhance system A is likely to be powerful enough to harm system B." Kass, "Ageless Bodies, Happy Souls," 15.

13 It focusses on the issues of freedom and coercion especially when the use of biotechnical power exercised by some people upon other people, whether for social control like for example, pacification of a classroom or for their own putative improvement or genetic selection of the sex or sexual orientation of a child-to-be. See Kass, "Ageless Bodies, Happy Souls," 16.

14 Al-Rodhan, ed., *The Politics of Emerging Strategic Technologies*, 198.

15 Nick Bostrom, "Transhumanist Values," *Journal of Philosophical Research* 30 (2005): 3.

16 The moral obligation is based in the fact that technologies offer unique opportunity to alleviate human suffering.

17 Hildt and Franke, eds., *Cognitive Enhancement*, 11.

18 Ibid., 10.

19 Francis Fukuyama, *Our Posthuman Future: Consequences of the Biotechnology Revolution* (New York: Farrar, Straus and Giroux, 2002), 159. Straus and Giroux, 2002.

20 Ibid.

21 Julian Savulescu, Ruud ter Muelen, and Guy Kahane, eds., *Enhancing Human Capabilities* (Oxford: Wiley-Blackwell, 2011).

22 Hildt and Franke, eds., *Cognitive Enhancement*, 12.

23 Wrye Sententia, "Neuroethical Considerations: Cognitive Liberty and Converging Technologies for Improving Human Cognition," *Annals of the New York Academy of Sciences* 1013 (2004): 223.
24 Ibid., 227.
25 Michael J. Sandel, *The Case against Perfection: Ethics in the Age of Genetic Engineering* (Cambridge: Harvard University Press, 2007), 25.
26 Ronald Cole-Turner, ed. *Transhumanism and Transcendence: Christian Hope in an Age of Technological Enhancement* (Washington: Georgetown University Press, 2011), 10.
27 It is an international non-profit membership organization claiming over 4000 members worldwide, which advocates the ethical use of technology to expand human capacities. It was earlier known as "World Transhumanist Association (WTA)."
28 By the use of the word 'better,' they "envision the possibility of broadening human potential by overcoming aging, cognitive shortcomings, involuntary suffering, and our confinement to planet Earth."
29 Natasha Vita-More, Ben Goertzel, and David Wood, "Humanity+", Humanity+, Inc. http://humanityplus.org/ (accessed September 28, 2015).
30 Kyle Oskvig, "Harder, Faster, Stronger - Better: Aristotle's Ethics and Physical Human Enhancement," *Journal of Evolution and Technology* 23, no. 1 (2013): 30.
31 Hildt and Franke, eds., *Cognitive Enhancement*, 11.
32 Frederic Gilbert questions the implementation of nanotechnology in brain devices for enhancement in healthy subjects with regards to the ethics of an adequate informed-consent procedure for invasive nano-bionic brain interventions for neuroenhancement. (Hildt and Franke, *Cognitive Enhancement: An Interdisciplinary Perspective*, 11).
33 Miller and Wilsdon, eds., *Better Humans?*, 14.
34 Al-Rodhan, ed., *The Politics of Emerging Strategic Technologies*, 200.
35 Hildt and Franke, eds., *Cognitive Enhancement*, 2.
36 Agar, *Humanity's End*, 3.
37 Steve Fuller, *Preparing for Life in Humanity 2.0* (New York: Palgrave Macmillan, 2013), 40.
38 The anti-meliorist hold that there is a distinct essence of humanity that cannot be touched or changed or manipulated.
39 Miller and Wilsdon, eds., *Better Humans?*, 15.
40 Hildt and Franke, eds., *Cognitive Enhancement*, 6.
41 Michael Hauskeller, *Better Humans?: Understanding the Enhancement Project* (Durham: Acumen, 2013), 2.
42 Lilley, *Transhumanism and Society*, 6.
43 Ibid., 8.
44 Berit Brogaard and Barry Smith, "On Luck Responsibility and the Meaning of Life, " *Philosophical Papers* 34, no. 3 (November 2005). http://philpapers.org/archive/BROOLR.pdf (accessed September 28, 2015).
45 Agar, *Humanity's End*, 180.
46 Ibid., 179-180.
47 Cole-Turner, ed., *The Politics of Emerging Strategic Technologies*, 8.
48 Agar, *Humanity's End*, 5.
49 Miller and Wilsdon, eds., *Better Humans?*, 15.
50 Lilley, *Transhumanism and Society*, 3.
51 Hildt and Franke, eds., *Cognitive Enhancement*, 5.

15

Body in the Media
Organs without Body

Francis Arackal
Amity University, Gurgaon

Abstract: The body has been understood as a gift, traditionally. Generally a gift is given and accepted and not demanded. Sure, gift once received one may do with it what one likes. In the case of the body-gift usually the tendency is to nurture it for its well-being. One may well not be happy with the shape and size of the gift. The dissatisfaction about the body-gift is caused partly by the images that are being bombarded through various media. As a result the body shape ideals are formed both in men and women, nowadays from a very early age. Children in many countries (more so in developed ones) consume media for three to four hours daily on average. The so-called perfect body image standards set by the media are almost impossible to live up to. This can cause low self-esteem in many, leading to depression and ending up in psychological disorders. Contemporary media's – especially advertisements – presentation of the body almost amounts to "organs without body." Faciality has become obsolete and a unified vision of the body has disappeared. Some individuals (celebrities) and organizations have come forward to counter the unrealistic body-image and beauty standards propagated by the media. Ultimately, one needs to develop (or help develop) from childhood a positive body image. For, in fact all are born beautiful because of the substantial beauty flowing from the very beingness of everything.

Keywords: body, body-image, beauty, faciality, media.

Introduction

The body is the physical frame of a person. The roots or genes of this frame – for instance, shortness, tallness, thinness, and fatness – are largely inherited. The body goes through various stages of development: from infant to child to adolescent to adult. The stage from infant to child is the most important in so far as this stage determines how the body shapes up in the future. In third world countries malnourishment, undernourishment is common, which is a factor which gravely affects the future looks of the body.

On the other hand, some bodies are subjected to forced undernourishment in order to conform to a certain body image received mainly from the media, which percolates easily in the society at large. "Body image is how someone thinks and feels about his or her physical self. It is an important part of self-esteem, which is how you feel about yourself. If you have high self-esteem, you feel really good about yourself. If you have low self-esteem, you probably do not feel good about your body or looks."[1]

In our contemporary world the media has become the all-pervasive, omnipotent, omnipresent entity. Hence, the supposedly perfect body image has been flashed everywhere: magazines, newspapers, television, videogames, laptops, tablets, phablets, smart phones and even smart watches. Both the digital natives and the digital immigrants are glued to some form of screen throughout the day. For instance, US kids spend approximately seven and half hours a day using computers, television, video games, and other media. Many of these children keep shuffling among many forms of media at a time.

Researchers have been curious to know how this constant use of media affects people. One very important focus in this research has been to find out if the media influence how children feel about their bodies. Many studies till date have shown that the media do have some bad effects on young people's body image. The studies conclude that it happens through the following ways: 1) People accept ideas about beauty that they see in the media; 2) They compare themselves to these ideas; 3) They try to change themselves to fit these ideas or they work hard to keep certain weight to look good.[2] Body image is not a simple issue. The media have an effect and in this paper we would like to delve deeper into 'Body Image and the Media.'

Brief History of the Concept of Body

The limited scope of this paper does not allow us to present a detailed study. Therefore, we shall focus on the views of a few prominent thinkers. Throughout the history of humankind philosophers and anthropologists have been attempting to formulate a clear concept of the body. In his work devoted to the social construction of the body Anthony Synnott outlines major philosophic schools and their views on the subject.[3] There have been many theories of the concept of the body; many of them date back to the ancient philosophers.

Plato believed that physical bodies are not true substances rather they are ephemeral, and imperfect copies of the eternal Forms. Plato considered the body as a prison for the soul. The body was considered less important and therefore to be shunned in favour of the soul. The soul strives to leave the body in which it is imprisoned. Aristotle rejected Platonic body-soul dualism and spoke of the union of body and soul, the latter being the form of the body. St. Paul envisioned the body primarily as a spiritual creation. St. Augustine followed the Platonic version of the concept of the body. He sees the body as a manipulative force leading to sinful, irrational acts. St. Thomas Aquinas corrected the Platonic dualistic view of the body and presented an integral vision of the human being composed of body and soul. For Aquinas both body and soul was equal in importance. The human being is not something that has a body; it is a body, a living body of a particular kind. Rene Descartes described the body as a physical substance, that is, a machine that functions similar to a clock.

With the Renaissance the attitudes to the body underwent significant transformation. The topic of beauty and perfection of the human body was given much attention. Charles Darwin, Karl Marx, and Frederick Nietzsche contributed much to this discussion. Darwin said that the body is the constant locus of human evolution and "a person per se is equal to an animal from a biological point of view, just more developed. Marx challenged Darwin's position, by arguing that it is capitalism that made proletariat into animals, a working machine. Freud believed in the unity of body and mind."[4]

One of Freud's contemporaries, Otto Rank, in his book *The Double*, states that it is in the shadow that the human being sees for the first time his or her own body. According to Wegenstein, "the body is at the same time mirror or screen for the images from the outside and the perceptive centre; the body is 'what takes shape at the centre of perception'"[5]

According to Henry Bergson's notion of the body, the body (and not soul) provides equilibrium, and is therefore the complementary pole to the mind, without which orientation toward the action would never be possible.[6]

Both Psychoanalysis and Phenomenology "try to separate the subject of the body (the world as perceived through one's body) from the objectified body (the body as it is perceived by the world) – a distinction between the subject of perception and the socially constructed body, between the psychoanalytical *I* and the *Me*."[7]

In more recent times, social scientists such as Mary Douglas and Michel Foucault have begun to pay more attention to the body. For, they consider that the body is a social phenomenon and the perception of the physical body inevitably depends on the social body. In contemporary times the body is no more regarded as divinely given, but something that can be artificially constructed by plastic surgeons and doctors.

The Concept of Beauty

It is through the body, the visible physical form, that beauty is shown forth/ manifested. That body is beautiful which is pleasing to the senses or mind aesthetically. According to the Oxford Dictionary, 'Beauty' is defined as, 'A combination of qualities such as shape, colour or form, that pleases the aesthetic senses, especially sight and intellect' or 'Denoting something intended to make someone more attractive.' Beauty has traditionally been counted as one of the ultimate values along with truth, goodness, and justice. It is said that the ancient Greeks were obsessed with the human body and how they could represent it – as a thing of beauty and the bearer of meaning. According to a recent BBC video our contemporary idea of the perfect body is largely unchanged from that of the ancient Greeks.[8] Plato's account in the *Symposium* and Plotinus's in the *Enneads* connect beauty to a response of love and desire, but locate beauty itself in the realm of the Forms, and the beauty of particular objects in their participation in the Form. Indeed, Plotinus's account in one of its moments makes beauty a matter of what we might term 'formedness:' having the definite shape characteristic of the kind of thing the object is.[9] Though Plato and Aristotle disagree on what beauty is as on so much else, they both regard it as objective in the sense that it does not depend on the response of the beholder.[10] The classical conception treats beauty as a matter of having definite proportions or relations among parts.

St. Thomas Aquinas follows the Greek classical conception of beauty. And integral to St. Thomas' holistic vision of a human person is his view of beauty. According to him three elements are important to term an object beautiful: Proportion, Integrity and Splendour. Of course, in Thomas' metaphysical understanding of beauty he speaks about its transcendental nature: that is every being is beautiful in itself for every being possesses substantial beauty – a beauty flowing from its very existence.

Body Shape Ideals

"The 'body image' construct tends to comprise a mixture of self-perception, ideas and feelings about one's physical attributes. It is linked to self-esteem and to the individual's emotional stability."[11] Surveys conducted in the 1990s in the US indicated that both men's and women's body image perceptions have become more negative over time.[12] While research has shown that women tend to regard themselves as bigger than they really are, for men the opposite is true. Men tend to perceive themselves as underweight and as thinner than they actually are and report a desire to be larger.[13] According to Henwood, Gill and McLean, "Patterns of consumption, life-style choices and media representation of men now often focus upon men's appearance and the male body. ... Media advertising routinely depicts in positive ways youthful toned muscular male bodies or focuses on style in men's clothing and physical appearance."[14] It has been suggested that men seek to embrace physical strength, hardness and power to reinforce the traditional masculine ideal – and at the same time to distinguish itself from ideas about feminity.[15] There is a perception that most of today's males are preoccupied with abdominal stomach muscles (the six-pack abs) in order to hold on to the traditional masculine ideal.

Body Shape Ideals among Men

There are definite ideas about the shape of male body: handsome men are supposed to be tall and have slim waists and hips; they are muscular especially on their chests, arms, and shoulders. It is said that boys who are underweight are ashamed of their bodies. Many of them take to excessive exercises in the hope of toning up their muscles. They may end up using too much time working out, neglecting school and friends. Even boys who work out too much think their muscles are not big enough. They may start taking powders and pills that promise to build muscle. They seem to be affected by what psychologists call the "Adonis Complex."[16]

Body Shape Ideals among Women

It is generally believed that women tend to think a lot about their bodies. A survey conducted in 2001 by *Top Santé* among 3000 women with an average age of 38 found: the great majority (85%) was unhappy with their shape and nine in ten (90%) said their appearance depressed them.[17] Seven out of ten (73%) reportedly thought about their size and shape every day and eight in ten (80%) felt that their lives would be considerably enhanced if they felt totally happy with their body.[18] What would make them happier are physical attributes such as flatter stomach, firmer buttocks and breasts and shapelier legs.

To attain such attributes many young women deprive themselves of nutrition to the extent that they risk serious illness and even death.[19] Epidemiological research has indicated that women's preoccupation with food and body shape is widespread.[20] Smoking, drug abuse, over-exercise, cosmetic surgery and self-harm may well also be part of the profound subjective dissatisfaction with their body image that is evident and prevalent among young women in particular.[21] It is true that men too to carry out extreme weight control tactics but it has long been established that it is women who tend to exhibit more dissatisfaction with their bodies.

The core of body image dissatisfaction has been located within a discrepancy between the perceived self and ideal self. Perceived self is normally in terms of weight and the distribution of fat, which has an effect on one's personality. "The ideal self-image may be considered as either an 'internal ideal' or a 'societal ideal' resulting from the dictates of the surrounding cultural and societal environment as to what constitutes the perfect body."[22]

Media Exposure and Body Image Ideals

Surely, body images would exist without the media. It is natural for societies to develop certain body image standards. Even in the absence of media we would still compare our bodies to those around us. However, contemporary media play a powerful role in setting and influencing certain body image standards. It is no exaggeration to say that the media pressure people to live up to them. One way media influence body image ideals is by presenting role models – persons who set examples for others to copy. The role models can of course be positive or negative. When it comes to body image, a role model is someone who presents himself/herself in a certain way through dresses and looks. "A positive body image role model is someone who sets an example of self-acceptance. He or she encourages others to feel good about their appearance."[23] A model or an actress with a healthy weight could be a positive role model. "A negative body image role model is someone who sets an example of unhealthy behaviour or attitudes about appearance."[24] An excessively thin model or actress is a negative body image role model for young girls. Similarly a body builder who uses steroids is a negative role model for young men.

The media's use of role models is usually subtle and unconscious. Role models used in advertisements are prime examples: companies that produce beauty products choose attractive people to act in their commercials. The company isn't exactly promising that if the audience use their products they will automatically become beautiful/handsome or fit. Reasonable people would not expect, for instance, a deodorant to make them more handsome or attractive. But an implied, subconscious message has already gotten to them and it sets them thinking. The implied message is that physical beauty is important to being successful, happy, and loved. "Beauty sells" is a persuasive technique used by the advertising industry. At the same time it must be added that any deliberate appeals to thinness in messages attempting to 'sell' the thin ideal among young women may meet with resistance. In a study of a campaign designed to promote exercise and fitness among teenage girls, messages were used that appealed to health ('Fitness Today: For a Healthier Tomorrow'), activity ('Fitness Today: For a More Active Tomorrow') and slimness ('Fitness Today, For a Slimmer Tomorrow').[25]

However, not all media messages about body image are subtle. For example, a commercial for Jenny Craig weight loss products, actress Sara Rue talked about her 50-pound (22.7 kg) weight loss. She said, "When you feel good – really good – you can go anywhere, do anything… This is me, 50 pounds gone. Now I can do anything. And for me, that's worth everything. You can do it too."[26] This is an explicit message that thinness leads to freedom and happiness. While there is an element of truth in this message, thinness does not automatically lead to happiness; a thin person can be just as depressed or lonely as anyone else.

Media Causation and Body Image Perceptions

One important factor in relation to potential influences of media body image representations is the extent to which girls make comparisons between themselves and role models featured in glossy magazines. Most advertisements in this context, especially ones of skin care, personal care and apparel products, have models who endorse the product. The advertisements use them as they have the desired skin tone, hair and body structure that has defined the advertising realm's requirement for beauty. This, in turn, has enforced stereotypes within the society with a biased view of beauty. Girls reported making comparisons between themselves and models seen in teen magazines and their initial dieting experiences were triggered by diets found in these magazines.[27] The images of under-weight women make other women who are differently sized, feel insecure and unhappy with their self-image; print advertisements that are extensively enhanced by means of airbrushing and Photoshop, have also contributed to the lowering of self-esteem among women.[28] It has seen a prevalent trend in body surveillance, internalisation, and body shame and appearance control beliefs among the consumers who have been constantly exposed to the beauty stereotypes. According to Wykes and Gunter, "the discovery that perceptions of media effects upon body image can vary depending upon whether such effects are attributed to the influence of self or others."[29] The 'third-person effect' says that "people perceive stronger media effects upon others than upon themselves, where socially undesirable or negative effects are concerned."[30] Applying this to body image perception it is noted that "individuals with higher self-esteem are less likely than those with low self-esteem to compare their own body image with others, and to do so unfavourably."[31]

Impossible Standards

For those people whose ideas of body image are defined by media, especially the visual one, there is a big problem. They need to realize that the images they see in the media aren't real. In many cases it's almost impossible for a real human being to come anywhere close to the 'beautiful' images in the media. From the inception of photography, various techniques have been employed to make people look better in pictures than real life. By using special lights, makeup, and camera angles, photography specialists could make people look younger, slimmer, beautiful, and handsome than they actually are. Contemporary use of advanced computer software has much enhanced the possibility of doing all these to the extent that most people would not even notice the manipulations done. In fact it has become standard procedure for publications and advertising agencies to use digital photographic technology to make models and actors look flawless.[32] News media may be an exception; most news magazines have rules against altering images.

It is not that image makeovers in the media have gone unnoticed by authorities and individuals concerned. In July 2011 the United Kingdom banned cosmetics company L'Oréal's advertisements featuring actress Julia Roberts and supermodel Christy Turlington. The ads for antiaging foundation products, made by L'Oréal's Maybelline and Lancôme brands, were modified by the use of Photoshop and airbrushed to an extent that Britain's Advertising Standards Agency (ASA) considered the ads misleading. In its January 2010 issue, *OK*! Magazine altered a photo of celebrity Kourtney Kardashian that was taken a week after she had given birth. The altered image made it appear that she had already lost all the weight from her pregnancy. The magazine then claimed to provide tips from Kardashian on how to quickly lose pregnancy weight. Kardashian explained that most of the magazine's facts were wrong. She said they "doctored and photoshopped my body to make it look like I have already lost all weight, which I have not."[33]

The Dove 'Real Beauty Campaign' and Perceptions of Beauty

In 2004 Unilever, the maker of Dove personal care products launched an advertising strategy titled 'the Dove Campaign for Real Beauty. The campaign took on a whole new tangent that gave an alternate view of beauty. The brand took steps to reinforce in women – older women and young girls – with the notion that beauty is not completely what the media has portrayed it to be. In its promotional advertisements, the campaign had advertisements that showed how women in the real world, as opposed to the models in advertisements, looked like. It incorporated a variety of media that included TV commercials, magazines, billboard advertisements, talk shows, and a worldwide conversation through the internet. The hope was that the perceptions of beauty that are being disseminated by advertisements could be countered by the Real Beauty Campaign. Advertisers could consider the different body types, rather than only the thin body that has been so far propagated. As part of the campaign, Dove made a pledge to use real women – not models – in their advertisements. Accordingly, women in the Dove campaign ads showed off their curvy bodies, freckles, and natural-looking faces. The company also promised not to edit photographs to change the women's appearances. Such an advertising campaign, it was thought, could also counter the existing stereotypes of beauty. The company went on to sponsor two worldwide studies about body image and self-esteem among women and girls.

The Dove Real Beauty Campaign has been instrumental in creating a new perception of what beauty is. But not everybody believes the company's efforts are completely sincere; the campaign was criticized for several reasons. It is possible that in attempting to counter stereotypes, there might be the formation of new ones. The Dove campaign ads appeared to send the messages that all women are beautiful just the way they are – but they should buy Dove's skin-firming cream. Besides, the 'real' in real women has not been completely redefined. The women who appear in the 'real women' advertisements have been polished to suit the aesthetics of the ads. According to Dove's casting calls the specification for the women to be presented in the advertisements read: no tattoos, no scars, flawless skin, beautiful hair, and bodies that fall nicely between 'not too curvy' and 'not too athletic.' Along these lines, Dove seems to be propagating a positive body image with traditional beauty standards.

Organs without Body

As in almost every other field the digital age has transformed the discussions on the body. The digital image, or better, the logic of new media has literally opened up the body, de-materializing its corporeal layers into fragments of information. 'A body-in-pieces'[34] that appears to be fully autonomous, having left behind its holistic body notion, has been born out of this new configuration. "Over the last two decades, the discourse around and about the body, as represented in popular science, in the arts, in theory and cultural studies, and even in the realm of advertisement and fashion has gotten increasingly *under the skin*.[35] One of the important results of this process of getting under the skin has been the fragmentation of the body: the presentation of a body-in-pieces. It is said that the body at the turn of the 21 century "has become an organ without a body or into an organ instead of a body."[36] In this scenario the face, which has always 'over-coded' other body parts, has now ceased to be the most representative signifier of human appearance; under the skin every organ has an (inter) face. Faces are becoming obsolete. For instance, "Words usually reserved for your face are now possible all over your body," reads an advertisement for the body wash Oil of Olay. What we see in the advertisement is not a beautiful woman with a beautiful face, but an "even-toned" body with a "smooth texture" that is supposed to look "radiant and resilient". These new characteristics are shown in a healthy looking body (mostly legs and arms), indicating a fit body.[37] Thus, "potentially, every organ may stand in for the whole body. ...any body part pushes toward the surface, and becomes able to 'overcode' the rest of the body."[38] This certainly is the latest reality with regard to the body as it is presented in contemporary media.

A Positive Body Image

But from the point of view of the self-perception of one's own body one needs to go beyond. 'Catch them young' also applies to building a healthy body image. Children and teens should be encouraged to accept their sizes, shapes, and appearances. They should also be made aware that it is natural for their bodies to change and sometimes gain weight as they grow. They could also be encouraged to eat healthy food, exercise, and avoid diets. Media awareness/ media education programme, which tells them which information in the media is true and reliable and which is not should be made part of the academic curriculum. Through such programmes children could be made aware that not everything shown in the media is real. Bodies come in all shapes and sizes. Understanding that helps children, teens, and adults to have a more positive body image.

Children, teens, and adults all over the world are exposed to a constant bombardment of unrealistic images and implied messages about body image from a range of media, especially advertisements. Data after data from surveys reveal that the pressure to look young and slim is greater than ever before. On the other hand there are individuals (some celebrities) and groups which are challenging the unrealistic beauty standards set by the media. For instance, the popular TV show *Glee*[39] shows high school characters of various ethnicities and sizes in positive roles. Several episodes of this show have focused on messages of self-acceptance and positive body image. Some TV and movie studios are starting to turn down actresses who have had plastic surgery in favour of women with more natural appearance. For instance, when the Walt Disney Company was inviting people to act as extras in *Pirates of the Caribbean* movie in 2010, the Company specifically screened out women who had breast enhancement surgery.[40]

Conclusion

Perhaps from the time of the existence of the first human beings on earth body image perceptions have existed. Various media over the centuries have only accentuated such perceptions according to the prevalent societal and cultural standards. For instance, ideal standards of beauty for women have changed dramatically over time: from ancient Egypt, ancient Greece, Han dynasty in China, European Renaissance, Victorian England, Roaring Twenties (Europe and the US), Golden Age of Hollywood, Swinging Sixties, Supermodel Era of 1980s, Heroin Chic of 1990s to Postmodern beauty. The contemporary selfie culture has only intensified the postmodern consciousness about one's body-image. To attain the ideal of postmodern beauty women have been turning to plastic surgery of almost any organ. In tandem (presuming that media mirrors the society) the mainstream media too – especially advertisements, which are the financial backbone today of any media for that matter – have been stuck with organs without a body. Faciality[41] (the a priori of the human encounter), as understood by Emmanuel Levinas, no longer exists in today's media. In media terms we are living in a post-facial era.

Notes

1 Celeste Conway, *Body Image and the Media* (Minnesota: ABDO Publishing Company, 2013), 7-8.
2 Ibid., 10-11.
3 https://blogs.stockton.edu/postcolonialstudies/body-in-the-context-of-postcolonial-studies/body-as-a-concept-historical-development/ (accessed July 05, 2015).
4 https://blogs.stockton.edu/postcolonialstudies/body-in-the-context-of-postcolonial-studies/body-as-a-concept-historical-development/ (accessed July 05, 2015).
5 Bernadette Wegenstein, *Getting Under the Skin: The Body and Media Theory* (Cambridge: The MIT Press), 28-29.
6 Ibid., 29.
7 Ibid.
8 http://www.bbc.com/culture/story/20150605-is-this-the-ideal-body shown on 6 & 7 June 2015 (accessed July 05, 2015).
9 http://www.plato.stanford.edu/entries/beauty (accessed July 05, 2015).
10 Further, objective beauty means beauty is a universal aesthetical ideal derived from reality external to the mind and validated by the mind via reason; it need not involve collective assent or disinterest. In the course of history (especially in the media) the objectivity of beauty was lost sight of. See Barry Vacker, *Beauty and Beast* (of Advertising) (Advances in Consumer Research, Vol. 20, 1993).
11 T. F. Cash and M. L. Szymanski, "The Development and Validation of the Body-Image Ideals Questionnaire," *Journal of Personality Assessment* 50, no. 2 (1995): 290-301.
12 Maggie Wykes and Barrie Gunter, *The Media & Body Image* (London: Sage, 2005), 2.
13 Ibid., 5.
14 K. Henwood, R. Gill and C. Mclean, "The Changing Man," *The Psychologist* 15, no. 4 (2002): 183.
15 Wykes and Gunter, *The Media & Body Image*, 5.
16 In Greek mythology, there was a beautiful young man named Adonis. Goddesses fought over him because of his dazzling looks. Adonis knew that he was a prize. Some boys and men today want to look perfect. They think about their bodies most of the time.
17 Wykes and Gunter, *The Media & Body Image*, 3.
18 "Why do most women hate their bodies?" Daily Mail, 9 August 2001, http://www.dailymail.co.uk/news/article-65453/Why-women-hate-bodies.html (accessed April 22, 2016).
19 Brazilian model Ana Carolina Reston died from anorexia in 2006. See Conway, *Body Image and the Media*, 33.
20 Wykes and Gunter, *The Media & Body Image*, 1.
21 Ibid., 1.
22 Ibid., 4.
23 Barb Palser, *Selling Ourselves* (North Mankato: Compass Point Books, 2012), 17.
24 Ibid., 17.
25 Wykes and Gunter, *The Media & Body Image*, 151.
26 As cited in Palser, *Selling Ourselves*, 18-19.
27 Wykes and Gunter, *The Media & Body Image*, 150.
28 Research has shown that when overweight women look at photographs of models, their self-esteem declines. Other research has shown that viewing magazine photos of women with thin, idealized bodies can improve body image for some women, but only for a short time.
29 Wykes and Gunter, *The Media & Body Image*, 152.
30 Ibid., 152.

31 Wykes and Gunter, *The Media & Body Image*, 152.
32 Almost all magazines admit to altering images to make them more idealistic. This can set an impossible standard of beauty for the magazine's readers.
33 Palser, *Selling Ourselves*, 38. Many images in the media and advertising have been retouched, but some companies are criticized for overly editing an image so that it is not realistic.
34 Wegenstein, *Getting Under the Skin*, 78.
35 Ibid., 79.
36 Ibid., 80.
37 Ibid., 89.
38 Ibid., 80.
39 Glee is an American musical comedy-drama that was aired on the Fox network from May 2009 to March 2015. The cast of Glee offers diversity in race and body type.
40 More examples of positive action on body image are found in Palser, *Selling Ourselves*, 67-71.
41 It is a term put forward by philosopher Emmanuel Levinas (1906-1995) meaning face is the primordial organ of human communication.

Part 4

Spiritual Dimensions

16

The Body of the Earthlings in *Laudato Si'*
A Philosophical Appreciation

Kuruvilla Pandikattu
Jnana-Deepa Vidyapeeth, Pune

Abstract: Based on the explicit goal of Pope Francis's *Laudato Si,'* "not to amass information or satisfy curiosity, but rather to become painfully aware, to dare to turn what is happening to the world into our own personal suffering and thus discover what each of us can do about it," this chapter seeks to study the concept of the human person in this document. Going beyond the objectification of human beings in a throw away culture, the article looks at the "precious and precarious" nature of the human body and pleads for a "re-membering" of the earthlings. This this article looks on the human body based on *Laudato Si'* as contributing to the ecological connectedness with the whole universe.

Keywords: *Laudato Si',* Pope Francis, Philosophy of body, human ecology, human body, earthlings.

Introduction

How is the body to be understood and appreciated in our encounter with earth and ecological concerns? With the aim of appreciating the body in Pope Francis' second encyclical, *Laudato Si',* we first study one trend in contemporary science that makes body almost useless. Then we go situate the basic thesis of *Laudato Si'* as taking a stand against the objectification of the body and maintaining a throw-away culture. Then we study specifically the understanding of the body in the document. This leads us to enlarge our vision of ourselves as bodily beings 're-membering' the earthlings in this earth. Finally we raise some philosophical queries.

On the whole our approach is phenomenological. It seeks to understand the rich notion of the body from *Laudato Si'* and contrast it with that of some of the contemporary views.

Making Nature Useless

"What if we become completely independent of nature?" asks Jesse H. Ausubel, Director of the Program for the Human Environment at The Rockefeller University. He holds that soon the natural resources may not be needed, making nature useless, or "nearly so, at least in a traditional market sense."[1]

Suppose businesses keep lifting their efficiency and dematerialize more and more. Suppose we use not scarce but the most common elements in the crust such as magnesium, aluminium, and notably silicon, which makes not just chips but stone and glass. And instead of weaving ourselves ever more tightly into the biosphere, suppose we decouple not only from energy and materials but from the biosphere itself.

Our ancestors were completely immersed in the biological system. Later, agricultural humans controlled some of the biological system, to augment productivity and consequently number. Technological humans could largely cut ties with the biosphere and construct an internal world, writes Ausubel.[2]

In fact, Ausubel wonders whether nature really matters. He elaborates: "High incomes, great longevity, and large population concentrations have been achieved in every class of environment on the Earth. We manufacture computers in hot, dry Phoenix and cool, wet Portland. We perform heart surgery in humid Houston and snowy Cleveland. Year round we grow flowers in the Netherlands and vegetables in Belgium. ... We have insulated travel, communications, energy generation, food availability, and almost all major social functions from all but the most extreme environmental conditions of temperature and wind, light and dark, moisture, tides, and seasons."[3]

So, he asserts that our common goal is to render ourselves independent of nature. "For all the poetry about Nature, we have basically retreated into walled cities, autarchic except for the input of energy or negentropy. Most of this no longer arrives by chlorophyll. Indeed, some is now furnished by uranium, and most, indeed nearly all, could be, as we get better at manufacturing hydrogen to carry energy around."[4] The profound importance of nuclear power is its capacity to decouple us from the biosphere.

In practice, the trend toward the megalopolis is creating zones of great density, leaving the possibility of creating very low density patches. Meanwhile, we will continue the shift, toward landless and vertical agriculture. Eventually, the microbes will do the work of most of the food production, from whom we can never decouple.

Cities will function essentially as closed systems where most materials, including water, will be recycled. From the point of view of the materials balance, the main factor that must be accounted for is the materials locked into the system and the losses in the recycling process. "We will never dematerialize completely but we can stop grinding up new crust," he admits.

A highly efficient hydrogen economy, landless agriculture, industrial ecosystems in which waste virtually disappears during this silicon century – these can enable large, prosperous human populations to co-exist with the whales and the lions and the eagles and all that underlie them. The primeval forest can tranquilly regrow for the amusement of naturalists.

He quotes The 1952 Paley Commission Report that started the think-tank Resources for the Future approvingly: "The growth of demand is at the core of the materials problem we face."[5] We may still worry for a few decades about exhausting primary resources and overloading the environment, as we pass the peak use of just about everything except information. We will keep doubling our use of information every ten years, and that will liberate the rest. And within another 60 years we may smile, because our actual achievement will have been to achieve conservation by establishing an enduring trajectory of making Nature useless" (Ausubel 2015).

Is it legitimate to dream to uproot ourselves totally from nature? Perhaps when we make nature useless, we may be making ourselves obsolete! Such a position is found in the encyclical of Pope Francis which we shall try to explore now.

Beyond Objectification and Throwaway Culture

On Thursday June 18, 2015, Pope Francis released his encyclical *Laudato Si'*: "On care for our common home." The encyclical addresses humanity's responsibility to protect and conscientiously cultivate the earth. Ultimately, the Holy Father advocates an *integral ecology* as the best response to the environmental crisis. This response, illuminated by the Christian faith, is *integral* because it addresses not only the environmental issues of today, but also various economic, social, cultural and moral ones. In fact, three major themes emerge in the encyclical: human ecology, the objectification of creation, and today's "throwaway culture."[6]

Human Ecology

Drawing on the teachings of the two previous popes, Benedict XVI and St. John Paul II, Pope Francis uses the concept of "human ecology" to denote the interconnectedness of the natural environment and human culture. For example, when humanity respects itself, the earth rejoices, but when humanity degrades itself, the earth suffers, too.[7] The Holy Father uses the biblical story of Cain and Abel to illustrate this point. After Cain kills his brother Abel,

God cries, "What have you done! Listen: Your brother's blood cries out to me from the soil! Therefore you shall be banned from the soil…If you till the soil, it shall no longer give you its produce" (Gen 4:10-12a). Pope Francis says, "Disregard for the duty to cultivate and maintain a proper relationship with my neighbour, for whose care and custody I am responsible, ruins my relationship with my own self, with others, with God, and with the earth" (LS, 70). Because, the "book of nature is one and indivisible," including men and women, all creatures on the earth and the earth itself, "[t]here can be no renewal of our relationship with nature without a renewal of humanity itself" (LS 6, 118). An authentic human ecology recognizes that human beings are an integral part of the environment which we are trying to protect and promote.[8] We need to respect "our unique place as human beings in this world and our relationship to our surroundings" (LS, 15).

The Objectification of Creation

Another theme in *Laudato Si'* is the objectification of creation, which Pope Francis treats as a grave issue. He notes that creatures are not "merely… potential 'resources' to be exploited…they have value in themselves" (LS, 33). In other words, creation is not just an object to be used. The objectification of creation leads to mass consumerism on the part of humanity, damaging the earth and her resources as well as doing harm to the poor and to future generations. Consumerism is a result of "no longer speak[ing] the language of fraternity and beauty in our relationship with the world," of ceasing to relate to the world as a subject and instead choosing to manipulate and possess it as an object (LS, 11).

Objectification and consumerism can also take place in the human realm. There can be a consumeristic approach to persons when we stop relating to each other with love and respect, and instead seek to possess each other. Possession and domination of a person mirrors the possession and domination of the earth that Pope Francis seeks to challenge in this encyclical.

At its root, the sin of possession – and indeed all sin – results from humanity's assuming the place and actions of God. The Pope writes that "our presuming to take the place of God and refusing to acknowledge our creaturely limitations…distorted our mandate to 'have dominion' over the earth (cf. Gen 1:28), to 'till it and keep it' (Gen 2:15)" (LS, 66). Pope Francis calls for us instead to relate to the earth in a brotherly and sisterly way. He includes the text of St. Francis of Assisi's hymn, which speaks of "Brother Sun" and "Sister Moon." Our fellow human beings are truly our brothers and sisters of one Father; we should accompany them through life, relate to them as fellow children of God, and refuse to treat them in a consumeristic way, as objects.[9]

The "Throwaway Culture"

Lastly, Pope Francis criticizes the "throwaway culture," which is fuelled by a vicious cycle of using and trashing precious environmental resources (LS, 16, 20-22, 43). His criticism also extends to a culture that throws away *people*.[10] He notes that "it is clearly inconsistent to combat trafficking in endangered species while remaining completely indifferent to human trafficking, unconcerned about the poor, or undertaking to destroy another human being deemed unwanted" (LS, 91). And in his first apostolic exhortation *Evangelii Gaudium*, the Pope described a "throwaway" culture as one wherein "human beings are themselves considered consumer goods to be used and then discarded" (EG, 53).

There are many victims of the "throwaway" mentality – the unborn, the elderly, the poor, the disabled, the lonely, and the orphan. Abandoned spouses and children also suffer from the effects of a culture where divorce and separation are prevalent. Francis' plea to reduce waste should resound also as a plea to reduce the harms incurred by divorce and by treating marriage as a temporary arrangement, a theme the Pope has addressed before. The Pope has also previously spoken strongly about protecting children, whom he considers the "first victims" of the harms of divorce and separation. And he has affirmed that children's lives are never mistakes and thus can never be thrown away; "every marginalized, abandoned child…is a cry that goes up to God."[11] A renewed respect for marriage as an inviolable sacrament, and a commitment to caring for separated and divorced couples and their children, can help reverse the discarding of people.

The Preciousness of the Body in Laudato Si'

The Pope writes in accessible prose, with characteristic bluntness and creativity. He remarks, "The earth, our home, is beginning to look more and more like an immense pile of filth" (LS, 21). With great clarity, he rebukes the cultural trends that contradict the design of the Creator for the human body and connects this with ecology. He says, "The acceptance of our bodies as God's gift is vital for welcoming and accepting the entire world as a gift from the Father and our common home, whereas thinking that we enjoy absolute power over our own bodies turns, often subtly, into thinking that we enjoy absolute power over creation" (LS, 155)

The Pope's words are also poetic. He states that "The entire material universe speaks of God's love, his boundless affection for us. Soil, water, mountains: everything is, as it were, a caress of God" (LS, 84). He exclaims with awe, "How wonderful is the certainty that each human life is not adrift in the midst of hopeless chaos, in a world ruled by pure chance or endlessly recurring cycles" (LS, 65).

The Holy Father sees the environmental problem as part of a much larger, more serious problem: Our failure to consistently recognize the truth that everyone and everything is interconnected. He explains, "When we fail to acknowledge as part of reality the worth of a poor person, a human embryo, a person with disabilities – to offer just a few examples – it becomes difficult to hear the cry of nature itself; everything is connected."

He recalls that we are born of the dust and receive life and refreshment from the water of the earth. Thus, our body, the earth and the water are deeply appreciated. "Christianity does not reject matter. Rather, bodiliness is considered in all its value in the liturgical act, whereby the human body is disclosed in its inner nature as a temple of the Holy Spirit and is united with the Lord Jesus, who himself took a body for the world's salvation" (LS, 235).[12]

He admits that Christians have not always appropriated and developed the spiritual treasures bestowed by God upon the Church, where the life of the spirit is not dissociated from the body or from nature or from worldly realities, but lived in and with them, in communion with all that surrounds us (LS, 216).

He takes the example of Jesus to illustrate this point. His appearance was not that of an ascetic set apart from the world, or of an enemy to the pleasant things of life. Of himself he said: "The Son of Man came eating and drinking and they say, 'Look, a glutton and a drunkard!'" (Mt 11:19). He was far removed from philosophies which despised the body, matter and the things of the world. Such unhealthy dualisms, nonetheless, left a mark on certain Christian thinkers in the course of history and disfigured the Gospel. Jesus worked with his hands, in daily contact with the matter created by God, to which he gave form by his craftsmanship. It is striking that most of his life was dedicated to this task in a simple life which awakened no admiration at all: "Is not this the carpenter, the son of Mary?" (Mk 6:3). In this way he sanctified human labour and endowed it with a special significance for our development.

So, in clear terms he affirms: "Learning to accept our body, to care for it and to respect its fullest meaning, is an essential element of any genuine human ecology. Also, valuing one's own body in its femininity or masculinity is necessary if I am going to be able to recognize myself in an encounter with someone who is different" (LS, 155).

'Re-Membering' the Earthlings

The encyclical is a plea towards "whole-making" or "re-membering" ourselves in the earth. In other words it speaks of an "integral ecology,"[13] that looks at human beings as an integral part of the earth and cosmos.

The Pope cleverly extrapolates Paul VI's phrase "integral development," which appeared in the 1967 encyclical *On the Progress of Peoples*. The concept was the brain child of the French Dominican economist, prophet and missionary to fishermen of North-western France, Louis-Joseph Lebret (1897-

1966). Paul VI, citing Lebret's work in a footnote, explains it this way: "In order to be authentic, development must be complete; integral that is, it has to promote the good of every person and the whole person" (LS, 14). This is an important back-drop for an understanding of the Pope Francis's "integral ecology."[14]

In a kind of lament, he tells us in the opening paragraphs, "We have forgotten that we ourselves are dust of the Earth; our very bodies are made up of her elements, we breathe her air and we receive life and refreshment from her waters" (LS, 2). In the fourth chapter devoted in its entirety to "Integral Ecology," he reminds us once again: "Nature cannot be regarded as something separate from ourselves or as a mere setting in which we live. We are part of nature, included in it and thus in constant interaction with it" (LS, 139). Here the pontiff is elaborating one of Thomas Berry's "Principles of a Functional Cosmology," namely, "Earth is primary, and the human is derivative."[15]

Philosophical Reflections

Is our body a replaceable entity? Platonic and advaita philosophy will answer it affirmatively, but not contemporary phenomenology. Phenomenology of the body and perception philosophically made viable by Maurice Merleau-Ponty[16] and Gabriel Marcel[17] fits in with an integral or holistic anthropology, which goes against a dualistic and fragmented approach to the human person.

Similarly, the encyclical proposes a new anthropology based on relationship, interrelatedness, connectedness, synthesis, and whole as more than sum of parts, dynamic, evolving, dialogical, inclusive, partnered, appreciative, principled and born out of inner conviction.[18]

As philosophers we need to realise that this phenomenological approach goes against some of the contemporary trends in philosophy of science, cognitive theory and artificial intelligence where the body is seen almost as superfluous and replaceable, through robots, cyborg or fyborg, of The Matrix type.

The news that an Italian scientist wants to replace the full body of a Russian next year is a case in this direction.[19] The implication is human beings are basically the brain, which can be replaced by another body. If this is so, then the brain can be further replaced by a powerful computer, making brain uploading a possibility.

Conclusion

Basically what is at stake is our self-understanding, coupled with the dignity of the human body and that of the person. Can we consider the body as an interchangeable appendix to our brain, making our body as well as the material nature, almost interchangeable or useless? That would be a tremendous challenge to the Christian understanding of the human person, based on God taking on flesh and the resurrection of the body, the anthropology emphasised by *Laudato Si'*.

Moving away from such theoretical considerations, the call of the encyclical is clearly articulated by Pope Francis in the first chapter. He holds: "Our goal is not to amass information or satisfy curiosity, but rather to become painfully aware, to dare to turn what is happening to the world into our own personal suffering and thus discover what each of us can do about it" (LS, 19).

Notes

1 Jesse Ausubel, "We Must Make Nature Worthless," *Real Clear Science*, September 19, 2015, http://www.realclearscience.com/articles/2015/09/19/we_must_make_nature_worthless_109384.html (accessed June 5, 2016).
2 Ibid.
3 Ibid.
4 Ibid.
5 Ibid.
6 Juliana Vossenberg is the Summer 2015 intern for the Secretariat of Laity, Marriage, Family Life, and Youth at the United States Conference of Catholic Bishops. http://www.foryourmarriage.org/reading-laudato-si-in-light-of-sexuality-marriage-and-family-life/ (accessed October 10, 2015); see also Kuruvilla Pandikattu, *Light of Truth*, 2015.
7 Juliana Vossenberg, "Reading Laudato Si in Light of Sexuality, Marriage, and Family Life," *For Your Marriage*, http://www.foryourmarriage.org/reading-laudato-si-in-light-of-sexuality-marriage-and-family-life/ (accessed June 5, 2016).
8 Ibid.
9 Ibid.
10 Ibid.
11 Ibid.
12 Here, Pope Francis is quoting John Paul II Apostolic Letter *Orientale Lumen.*
13 See http://globalsistersreport.org/column/capital-e-earth/environment/laudato-si%E2%80%99-encyclical-re-membering-27271 (accessed October 10, 2015).
14 Margaret Galiardi, "Laudato Si': An Encyclical of Re-Membering," *Global Sisters Report*, last modified June 24, 2015, http://globalsistersreport.org/column/capital-e-earth/environment/laudato-si%E2%80%99-encyclical-re-membering-27271 (accessed June 5, 2016).
15 Ibid.
16 Mary Rose Barral, *The Body in Interpersonal Relations: Merleau-Ponty* (Lanham: University Press of America, 1984).
17 R. Bradley DeFord, *Gabriel Marcel and a Christian Theology of the Body*, PhD Dissertation (Chicago: University of Chicago, 1986).
18 Kuruvilla Pandikattu, "The Indian Paradox: Scientifically Foreword, Religiously Inward and Economically Backward," in *Religion, Society and Economy*, ed. A. Vonach and K. Pandikattu (Frankfurt: P. Lang, 2003).
19 It may be mentioned that the Italian doctor Sergio Canavero has drawn criticism from the medical community for his idea. See http://www.independent.co.uk/news/science/head-transplant-russian-man-to-become-first-to-undergo-pioneering-and-controversial-surgery-10162639.html (accessed October 10, 2015).

17

Fasting and Feasting
Differing Philosophies of the Body

George Karuvelil
Jnana-Deepa Vidyapeeth, Pune

Abstract: This article, while underscoring differing philosophies of the body, focuses on an important spiritual practice related to a particular version of the philosophy of the body, namely fasting and ascetic practices. By pointing out this particular spiritual approach as a common feature in all the religious and spiritual traditions, this article works out a mystical view of the body.

Keywords: fasting, abstinence, spiritual benefit, mystical view, trans-natural, experience.

Introduction

An important dimension of philosophizing on the body is its relation to practices like fasting and feasting undertaken by religious believers of all hues. I focus on fasting, not because it is the most important, but because it is the least understood in our times. Let me illustrate two completely different ways of looking at it so as to situate the discussion. The first instance is from my personal experience. Following a particular interpretation of the post-conciliar theology, there was this companion of mine in theology who could find no meaning even in a minimal fasting like the one done on the Ash Wednesday in the Catholic Church. That this was not a rare aberration became clear to me when years later, a seminarian, under the influence of a professor, decided to go for meal to a hotel on an Ash Wednesday.

Contrast these with the case of Siddhichandra, a Jain monk of the Tapa Gaccha Order who lived and debated about Jain beliefs and practices in the Mughal court in the early modern period (late sixteenth, early seventeenth century). The emperor engages him in extended debates about the futility of fasting, abstinence from sex, and other bodily austerities. Failing to persuade him, the emperor Jahangir is said to have ordered him to forgo his austerities, which Suddhichandra flatly refused. The outcome, we are told, is that Suddhichandra was exiled not only from the royal court, but also forbidden from wandering in the kingdom; he and other monks were to go into the forests since forest alone is "an appropriate residence for ascetics."[1] Here we have the case of a man who engages in bodily austerities even when he has to pay a heavy price for it.

Obviously both these camps are operating with different philosophies of the body. Many in the first camp tend to see fasting as an uncalled for ascetic practice that has no room in our enlightened times. Others would reason: What is the point of fasting? Isn't eating in moderation better so that I have strength to work and to serve, they ask. Many would go a step further and say that fasting is a part of that history of the Church which saw body and its desires and inimical to the spirit; therefore, the earlier we get rid of such practices, the better. The other camp seems to illustrate what the first camp loath the most namely, seeing the body and its instinctual desires as an enemy to be conquered. The Jain practice of Santhara or voluntary death by renunciation of food made headlines recently when the Rajasthan High Court banned the practice, which was subsequently overturned by the Supreme Court. It is appropriate, therefore, to focus on the philosophies of the body that are at work in fasting and feasting. What are we to make of these different philosophies of the body?

The paper will have three unequal parts. First we shall see that fasting remained a pervasive feature in the ancient and the medieval world, recommended by practically all religions, physicians and philosophers for its immense spiritual and physical benefits. Faced with the ubiquity of fasting and its unquestionable benefits raises the question as to how the modern world came to look down upon this practice. I shall briefly attempt to answer this question in the second part. Then in the third part, I shall outline a mystical view of the body.

A Ubiquitous Practice

Let us begin with clarifying the distinction between fast, abstinence, and starvation. Fasting is limiting or giving up on the intake of food; abstinence means to give up a particular kind of food or drink or some form of amusement. Fasting leads to hunger and abstinence makes us aware of our craving and inordinate attachment. Both may be undertaken for reasons of physical health and spiritual well-being. A patient for example, needs to abstain from certain foods for medical reasons. There is also the distinction between fasting and starving: fasting is when the body supports itself on its reserves; starving is when deprivation continues to a point beyond where the body can support itself on its reserves.[2]

Fasting is a common practice found in practically all religious traditions, whether Muslims, Hindus, Buddhists or others, so much so that it is hard to come across any spiritual tradition that does not advocate some form of fasting and abstinence. Fasting played a key role in the spiritual journeys of Moses, Jesus, Buddha, and Muhammad. Besides the spiritual traditions, philosophers like Plato and Socrates recommended fasting for increasing mental and physical effectiveness.[3] It is also recommended by physicians, ancient and modern. Hippocrates (4th cent BCE), the forefather of Western medicine recommended it for treating a varied range of illnesses. So, did Paracelsus (16th cent), and Avicenna advocated fasting. Such is also the case with the Caraka (c. 8th cent BC), of the ancient Indian system of ayurveda.

Let me illustrate the benefits of fasting with one man's testimony. Paul Martin was the air traffic controller in Alaska in the 1950s. The work was so demanding that he hardly had time for rest or even weekly holidays. As a result he was becoming irritable, overweight, constantly tired, and feeling much older than his 34 years. Finally, he decided to take a break. He went into a health resort in California where he undertook a fast for 14 days under the direction of a physician. He says he drank as much water as needed, but ate nothing for fourteen days. About the fifth day he developed a sore throat, back ache, and his teeth began to hurt. The doctor explained that this was normal as the body was cleansing itself of toxic substances. By about the tenth day these symptoms eased. On the 14th day he broke his fast, again under medical supervision, in a gradual fashion. The benefits he received from this fast, he says, were "increased energy, calmness, improved concentration, and a feeling of well-being." "My energy", he says, "was greater than it had been since I was 20. I fell asleep immediately at night, slept soundly and awoke refreshed and alert."[4] He went back to work and the pressure of the work continued to be high, but in the midst of such pressure he could remain calm and composed.

That is the testimony of one person. These days there are a number of books and articles that deal with the health benefits of fasting. Some of the proven health benefits include elimination of toxins from the body, elimination of food allergy sources, defeating sinus and mucus problems, normalizing blood pressure, keeping the arteries young, maintaining healthy cholesterol levels, assisting in curing mental and emotional disorders, and above all, in increased levels of energy.

Besides such health benefits, there are also many spiritual benefits to fasting. These benefits include deliverance from sinful or unhealthy habits, preparation for receiving special revelations from God, and speedily answered prayers.[5] It was commonly understood in the ancient world that in times of crisis and great need, prayer was to be accompanied by fasting. Scot McKnight, a well-known Anabaptist turned Anglican theologian, makes this central to the Christian understanding of fasting. He considers the instrumental view of fasting that is undertaken with a view of producing results as wrongheaded. "If one wants to see the full Christian understanding of fasting, one must begin with A, the grievous sacred moment. That sacred moment generates a response (B), in this case fasting. Only then, only when the sacred moment is given its full power does the response of fasting generate results (C) – and then not always, if truth be told." (2009 p. xix) By "grievous sacred moments" he means an awareness of sin, death, fear, an impending disaster, and so on, which fill the pages of the Bible. Fasting in the Bible is a response to such sacred moments of life. For example, when the disciples of Jesus failed to cast out demons from a child, Jesus tells them that this kind can be cast out only by prayer and fasting. The Zulus (an ancient South African tribe) have a saying that highlights the insight that fasting is a preparation for receiving revelations from God: "The continually stuffed body cannot see secret things." Small wonder that we see Moses and Daniel in the Old Testament fasting in preparation for receiving divine revelation (Ex. 34:28, Dt. 9:9; Dan. 9:3, 10:2ff). Jesus himself is portrayed as fasting for forty days before his ministry.

Understanding the Present

Awareness that fasting was so highly valued in the ancient and the medieval world, within Christianity and outside, raises the question as to how there is so little appreciation of this practice in the modern world. McKnight rightly points out that our attitude to fasting depends on our attitude to our own bodies. He draws our attention to the fact that Christianity, having imbibed the Platonic dualism of spirit and matter, has had an uneasy relationship to the body at least from the time of St. Augustine. A dualistic view sees ourselves as spirits that are imprisoned in the bodies, body becomes the enemy to be conquered and body becomes a "monster to be conquered" as McKnight puts it. Fasting, then, is a means of conquering the body. This explains why the philosophy of yoga, based on Samkhya metaphysics, which is as dualistic as any philosophy we can get, has a very positive attitude to fasting. So, is the Jain practice of Santhara; it is a means of cleansing the spirit.[6]

Is the contemporary indifference, if not aversion, to fasting a reaction to the dualism of the past? The picture is more complex than that. There are some specific historical factors at work. The first is the anti-ritualistic strand of the Protestant Reformation. Based on their principle of *sola fidei* (faith alone) for salvation, they saw the Catholic practices, including fasting, as wholly unnecessary and as idolatrous attempts to become meritorious before

God (McKnight). When this notion of assured salvation is taken together with dualism, it would seem to lead to a position where what happens to the body has no consequences for the spirit. If neither fasting nor feasting matters, why bother to fast? One might as well indulge the body without any negative impact on the spirit. Then there is the much discussed modern disenchantment of the world that sought to banish gods and the spirits from the world, preparing the way for a kind of materialist monism.

We are far from the heydays of modern thinking today. There is an increased awareness of the holistic character of the human person. How are we to conceive our body in the changed context? It is in this context that I want to introduce the idea of a mystical understanding of the universe.

Body: A Mystical View

It is hard to find a flawless definition of mysticism. Some think of it as a Religion beyond religions; others consider it necessarily tied to religions. The former is a kind of essentialist view that can be traced to the Upanishadic leanings of Walter Stace and whose prominent contemporary spokesperson is Rober K. Forman. The latter is a reaction to the essentialist view and may be called the empiricist view. The main spokesperson of this view that denies any essential core to mysticism is Steven Katz. Closely analysing the texts of mystics from different religious traditions, Katz argues that all of them are different as the beliefs and practices of their respective religious traditions necessarily influence their experiences.

I seek to bypass the partisan polemics of both the groups by focussing on experiences that are universally acknowledged as mystical but do not fall into any particular religious category, i.e., nature mysticism. Narrating a couple of instances of such experiences and analysing them, I shall draw out its implications for understanding the human person and the practice of fasting. Let us begin with some instances. A frequently quoted example is the following line of William Blake:

> To see a World in a Grain of Sand
> And a Heaven in a Wild Flower,
> Hold Infinity in the palm of your hand
> And Eternity in an hour.

The next example is also a well-known passage, taken from the life of Bede Griffiths:

> One day during my last term at school I walked out alone in the evening and heard the birds singing in that full chorus of song, which can only be heard at that time of the year at dawn or at sunset. I remember now the shock of surprise with which the sound broke on my ears. It seemed that I had never heard the birds singing

> before and I wondered whether they sang like this all the year round and never noticed it. As I walked on I came upon some hawthorn trees in full bloom and again I thought that I had never seen such a sight or experienced such sweetness before. If I had been brought suddenly among the trees of the Garden of Paradise and heard a choir of angels singing I could not have been more surprised I came thus to where the sun was setting over the playing fields. A lark rose suddenly from the ground beside the tree where I was standing and poured out its song above my head, and then sank still singing to rest. Everything then grew still as the sunset faded and the veil of dusk began to cover the earth. I remember now the feeling of awe which came over me. I felt inclined to kneel on the ground, as though I had been standing in the presence of angel...[7]

There are a number of significant things that can be said about this kind of experience. However, for our present purpose I want to focus only on one feature that I shall call (for want of a better word) the twofold character of such experiences. By this I mean a sharp distinction between the locus of experience and the "object" of experience. Both the above citations make the distinction clear. Where the poet ordinarily sees the same grain of sand and wild flower as the rest of us, what he sees on this occasion is different; he sees a 'world' in a grain of sand, a 'heaven' in a wild flower. Similarly Griffith's experience is not an experience of the birds and the trees as he experiences them in his ordinary state of consciousness ("sensory intellectual consciousness", as Stace terms it) but something completely different. It is this fact that brought a sense of surprise and awe to Griffiths. Both are experience that took place *in and through nature* but *not experiences of nature.* Nature becomes the gateway to an experience that has a trans-natural character; nature, so to say, is merely the locus of a trans-natural experience.

My use of "trans-natural" rather than "transcendent" or "supernatural" is deliberate. The moderns gave a deistic sense to these terms such that immanence and transcendence, natural and supernatural exclude each other. This view became so prominent that it made a backdoor entry into scholastic theology and it took the heroic efforts of Henri de Lubac to expose it. But this deistic view continues to dominate philosophical discussions even today.[8] This manner of understanding transcendence becomes impossible when it is seen through the prism of nature mysticism. The original meaning of transcendence (from *transcendere*) is to cross the boundary. When boundaries are seen as space-time markers, that which is experienced in nature mysticism can indeed be seen as transcending the boundaries of space and time. "Flower" and "sand" are in space-time objects but not the "object" experienced in nature mysticism. Since the distinction between immanence and transcendence is a distinction between the locus of experience and the "objet" of experience, there can be no transcendence without immanence! Transcendence is experienced in and through a space-time locus. It is this view of God and the world that is present in the recent encyclical of Pope Francis where the Eucharist is seen as the culmination of the mystery of the Incarnation whereby God comes to us not from above but from within so that we might encounter Him in the intimate depths of this material world.[9]

Its implication for matter-spirit, body-mind relationship is the same. John Hick calls it the fifth dimension of reality, as against the four dimensions of space and time. In other words, what goes by the name of mind, spirit, soul, and so on is not another reality alongside the material reality of the body as dualism holds. We are not spirits who happen to have bodies, but embodied spirit or spirit-in-the-world, in the terminology of Rahner. But spirit in the world in English sounds very much like a ghost in the machine, the kind of dualism that is being repudiated here. A good way of conceiving the body mind relationship is provided by psychiatrist Diane Powell who has coined the term "mobius mind". A mobius strip is made by giving a 180-degree twist to a plain strip of paper or cloth before connecting its ends. The twist results in a loop where the inner and outer surfaces of the strip are not separate but continuous with each other. Similarly, "the material turns over into the mental, and the mental turns over into the material, but neither can be fully explained by or reduced to the other."[10] Another way of conceiving the relationship is in terms of a holographic image where the whole image is present in every bit of its parts.

When we understand ourselves as necessarily embodied, fasting is a way of affirming that embodiment by aligning our body and spirit, a way of tuning the one with the other. The basic point McKnight makes in his book is that we commune with God through our bodies. It is not a matter of will power, as in ancient dualism; nor is it a matter of indifference to the body as in modern materialist monism. It is a matter of making the body a vehicle of the spirit and the spirit acknowledging its embodied character. In the words of McKnight, "For this kind of body image, fasting is natural. Fasting is the body talking what the spirit yearns, what the soul longs for, and what the mind knows to be true. It is body talk – not the body simply talking for the spirit, for the mind or for the soul in some symbolic way, but for the person, the whole person, to express himself or herself completely."[11]

Notes

1 Cited in Audrey Truschke, "Dangerous Debates: Jain Responses to the Theological Challenges at the Mughul Court," Modern Asian Studies 49, no. 5 (2015): 1339.
2 Lionel Stokes, *Prayer and Fasting: A Primer* (Bloomington: iUnivere, Inc., 2013), 29.
3 http://www.polarlight.org/Pages/HistoryofFasting.aspx; see also, http://www.greekmedicine.net/hygiene/ Fasting_and_Purification.html (accessed October 10, 2015).
4 http://www.religion-online.org/showarticle.asp?title=1155 (accessed October 10, 2015).
5 See Dave Williams, *The Miracle Results of Fasting: Discovering the Amazing Benefits in Your Spirit, Soul, and Body* (Tulsa: Harrison House, 2004).
6 Apart from spirit-body dualism, Santhara practice is also intrinsically linked to the other aspects of Jain beliefs such as causing least harm to other creatures. Eating a strawberry has more harmful karmic effects than eating a mango, because strawberry has more seeds and therefore, kills more possible lives.
7 Bede Griffiths, *The Golden String* (London: The Harvill Press, 1954), 9.
8 See for example, Berger's view of the Biblical God. Peter L. Berger, *The Social Reality of Religion* (Hammondsworth: Penguine Books Ltd, 1973), 121; Mario De Caro and David Macarthur, *Naturalism and Normativity*, Columbia Themes in Philosophy (New York: Columbia University Press, 2010).
9 Pope Francis, *Laudato Si'*, no. 236.
10 Sudhir Kakar and Jeffrey J. Kripal, eds., *Seriously Strange: Thinking anew About Psychical Experiences* (New Delhi: Viking/Penguine, 2012), xxix.
11 Scot McKnight, *Fasting: Ancient Practices* (Nashville: Thomas Nelson, Inc., 2009), 11.

18

Body, Suffering, Death and Afterlife

John Peter Vallabadoss
St. Joseph's Capuchin Philosophical College, Kotagiri

Abstract: Our bodily experience enhances the understanding of human life with predicaments of suffering and death and drives us to postulate the afterlife. Reflections on life with pain and suffering focus on the nature and cause of suffering and death and aim either at alleviating suffering or postponing death. We try to come to terms with suffering and to overcome fear of death. The search for the transcendence of suffering ended with the hope for deliverance either in and through life or after life. The conception of the 'after-life' through myths, cults, poetics, ideas and beliefs portrays the human quest to pass over the empirical existence. The paper attempts to reflect on: Suffering in the body, Death of the body, After-Life with/without the body, and to analyse the meaning of the human quest for understanding life in the body with suffering and death. We attempt to clarify if the notion of the 'after life' is basically centred around human identity and continuity of life even after the bodily existence and making sense of life lived in the body.

Keywords: suffering, death, empirical existence, after-life, identity, continuity, resurrection of the body, transcendence, bodily existence.

Introduction

Human beings born with and living in the body are the only creatures here on earth to understand and make a reflection on their life in the body, before the death of the body. More than what is reflected on life in the body, reflection on death and afterlife has been occupying the human minds and a number of writings and belief systems of different traditions. The human predicament of life with pain and suffering has been focused very well. Human thought dwelt on the nature, cause of suffering and pointed out many sources of it. A life of suffering is regarded to be a burden, a bondage which is to be liberated. Humans alone can reflect on death while living. The conscious acceptance by humans about their suffering, difficulties and continuous losing of something in life ending with the loss of life itself, marks their difference from other creatures on earth. Other creatures also undergo suffering and death but not as consciously as humans do.

Death as considered a universal phenomenon which humans sought always to find ways and means of understanding and further transcending death to become immortal, occupied the minds of thinkers and religious leaders. Vedic prayers like, '*mrtyorma amṛtam gamaya* – lead me from mortality to immortality,' express the inherent tendency to overcome the fear of death. Myths, mystery cults, poetics, philosophical ideas and religious beliefs consist of the human desire for the ultimate quest of transcending the phenomenon of birth and death. Experiencing suffering, death and decay all around, sometimes humans viewed the world as a place of suffering and death, a vale of tears; life as bondage. The search for the transcendence of the world of suffering and bondage ended with hope for deliverance in and through life or after life.

The conception of the 'after-life' found in many philosophies and religions speak of the human desire for transcendence over the empirical existence of suffering and death.[1] The question of the 'afterlife' and doctrines of life after the bodily living, becomes crucial in many religious traditions that characterize the peculiarity and specificity regarding their concepts and belief of the given tradition. Discussions, debates, questions and counter questions emerge out of differences in the conception of the 'afterlife' in many traditions. The meaningfulness of empirical existence often gets defined by the conception of the 'afterlife'; in terms of liberation, salvation, ultimate freedom, deliverance, *mokṣa, paramukti,* mystical union with the Absolute, etc.

We attempt to gather our reflection on relating suffering, death and the afterlife with that of the understanding body, with the following phrases: Suffering in the body, Death of the body, After-Life with/without the body.

Suffering in the Body

The human aspiration to seek good and ultimate happiness in life is often paradoxically jeopardized by the human predicament of suffering. Human suffering remains the main focus of human thinking and writing as recorded in most of the religious, philosophical and cultural traditions. Suffering in the body ranges from trauma, disease, old age, dying, hunger to flood, drought, and natural calamities. Suffering has physical, psychological, social and cultural implications besides being metaphysical. The what of it is well known and explained but the why of it is complex. The human tragic condition in suffering expressed in various ways of art, drama and poetry, apparently becomes a problem with no immediate solution. Life seen as absurd and the human as a useless quest leaves humans with hopelessness. The pessimistic and cynical view of suffering in some thinkers is furthered strengthened by the fact that certain kinds of poverty and misery in the world are all human-made by the unbridled ambition of a few people who secure their own well-being at the expense of the weak and poor. All attempts to find solutions to this fundamental human problem end up in seeing apparent meaninglessness of human life. Life is all suffering and all that we find as happiness in life are all the more creating suffering.

The Buddhist claim of the insolubility and inescapability of suffering, as part of a chain of factors, teaches us to search for the authentic reality of the human beyond the impermanence of a suffering world.[2] Buddha's answers to life's perennial question of suffering began with being sensitive to human predicaments. His encounter with the old man, disease, the dead body and the recluse, caused an awareness of the basic realities of life. The entire gamut of Buddhist teaching stands on the four noble truths about suffering, its cause, the possibility of cessation and the way to the cessation of suffering, *Duhkha, Samudhāya, Nirōdha,* and *Mārga*. The Buddha says, "Suffering is my teaching; the origin of suffering is my teaching; the cessation of suffering is my teaching; the way to the cessation of suffering is my teaching. I teach them because they lead to that which is connected with welfare, truth that is *Nibbāna*."[3] According to the first noble truth, *Duhkha*, birth, decay, disease, death, union, separation, any craving, attachment, everything contains an element of human suffering.[4] Holding on to the theory of dependent causation, *pratitya samutpāda,* the Buddhist tradition puts forward an argument that if there is any sort of suffering in any form there must be a cause. As suffering is a pragmatic fact it must have a cause which Buddhists identify as 'ignorance.' From ignorance proceeds the desire, desire leads to activity and it brings in its turn rebirth, etc.[5] Hope is given by Buddha that there is a possibility of the removal of suffering if it has a source or origination. If the condition for suffering, the cause is ceased, there is a possibility of the effect being removed. The attachments are rooted out, meaning that when one succeeds in breaking the link of the chain of causation, one can overcome suffering and the goal of liberation is attained. Buddhists have not only given a hope for the end of suffering, they have also spelt out the eightfold path of 'Right faith, right resolve, right speech, right action, right living, right effort, right thought, right concentration.'[6]

Suffering symbolized the common plight of human beings. The middle way for Buddha is a rejection of extremes, be it a rejection of extreme austerity or extreme indulgence in worldly pleasures or a rejection of 'eternalism'[7] of the

Upanishads or the 'nihilism'[8] of Cārvāka. Buddha's basic teaching of the four noble truths (*chatvari ārya satyāni*), as exposed in '*Dhammacakkapavattana-sutta*' was against hair splitting metaphysical speculations on human life. The fact is in front of us, the plight of humans that he named '*duhkham*' (suffering). The goal is life without 'suffering.' And the means are purely ethical and meditational. The only difference in this matter between him and the other thinkers was a rejection of metaphysical speculation. Though an initial pessimism is there in Buddha's teaching on '*sarvam duhkham,*' this realization is the first criteria for enlightenment. The root cause of entanglement in the causal chain is ignorance which is the absence of liberating cognition, the four noble truths.[9] When one strikes at the root of this endless chain by removing the basic ignorance which is the wrong view of *ātman*, permanence and pleasure, one prepares the way for liberation. In the Buddhist understanding, suffering is removable. *Nirvāna* is the cessation of all suffering; annihilation of all that binds; the complete vanishing of thirst, an abandoning of all afflictions and the attainment of freedom.[10]

The Jain tradition adopted a positive view of life and its multifarious aspects of suffering and proposed a process of synthesis that would bring together the various aspects and values that will slowly and gradually develop in an individual's life into infinite knowledge and power and happiness. Bondage in the Jain understanding is the association of the soul with matter and liberation therefore should be the complete dissociation of the two. Passions of the soul which spring from our ignorance about the real nature of our soul, lead to association. Right knowledge alone can remove ignorance.[11]

In the Vedic-Vedantic tradition, the problem of suffering is sought to be solved by the distinction between spirit and matter. One solution is that the spirit is reality par excellence and tends to discount evil and suffering as unreal and transitory over and against the permanence and immutability of the self. The karma theory placed the responsibility for suffering completely on the individual and one's own past actions which left their seed in the subtle condition of matter which later produced its results in another life in a chain of beginningless *samsāra.* The whole life struggle insists in trying to escape from this bondage of *samsāra.*[12]

The Biblical narration of the origin of evil and suffering due to a choice from human free will and a violation of the Divine command, through pride and rebellion, found the value of suffering in two ways; Suffering as a punishment for one's own deed and also as ransom for one's own misdeeds as well as for that of fellow human beings. The suffering of the servant of God and that of Jesus serves as a perfect example of suffering for others. In Jesus' suffering, God identified himself with the suffering humanity and offered himself as a sacrificial victim for their wellbeing. For the Christian tradition, suffering is itself somehow a part of human activity and it is not to be transcended but embraced.[13]

Thus, human suffering, besides the human aspiration to seek good and ultimate happiness, remains the main focus of human thinking and writing. Human suffering pervades human existence, and much of it seems unavoidable. In all suffering from ill-will, weakness, thoughtlessness and selfishness, humans are both victims and villains. Most of them are due to unjust distribution, desperate uses of power and domination. A good part of human suffering is deliberately inflicted by human beings on their fellowmen. The poor and the oppressed suffer more than the other. The concept of a saviour in religious traditions also indicates the human conception of life in the body as prone to suffering and decay, which has to be redeemed.[14] Realistically in privation and suffering, the human discovers one's own naked existence and arrives at self-consciousness and the realization of his own reality and that which surrounds him/her. Solving at the riddle of human suffering, various possibilities are proposed. Suffering is a mystery and will remain a mystery for the finite mind of man.[15] All that is possible is to approach it from different perspectives and points of view. They express that the human life of suffering is neither useless nor meaningless but points beyond itself.

Death of the Body

If human suffering is ongoing at all levels of human life, death is also seen as a continuously occurring phenomenon in human existence. The climax takes place at the last death of the physical body. The problem of confronting death is perennial in all philosophical and religious traditions. Meeting death with an attitude of composure recurs frequently in religious writings. The experience of death is transformed by a particular view of reality.[16]

When the universe is thought to be static and permanent there is no need for transcending the transitory character of the phenomenal world. Zen tradition has not suppressed the transitory character of the world but given full attention to it. When there is a reminder of the impermanence of the natural world, there is no suggestion that impermanence and death are unnatural or repulsive. The brief existence of everything in the world gives us enthusiasm to discover the truth of life that change is the basic fact of existence. Yet looking at the dichotomy made between this world and ultimate reality there is an insight that the true essence of this phenomenal world is *nirvana,* devoid of all empirical attributes which are merely empty names. Seen as an enlightenment experience, it enables one to consider that there is no real substance to birth, suffering and death associated with the realm of nature. "Nature itself is without birth and without destruction, without going and without coming."[17] Knowing the emptiness of attributes ascribed to the phenomenal world, one would be able to face death with composure. In other words, the world possesses the ultimateness which humans aspire to attain. The enlightenment that one is born with everything and dies with everything helps to cope up with death. One's final departure from the phenomenal world in peace will only be a natural extension of his enlightened life-style.

In the Christian tradition, death is depicted as an accidental element in the natural order. There is an acknowledgement of the inevitability of death and the transitory character of human life. Certain consolation in death is brought forth in the suffering of Jesus. Generally the accepted notion is that the suffering that Jesus experienced on the cross has removed the tragic element from death for the faithful. In the dying cry of Jesus with agony on the cross, Jesus' humanity experienced a sense of alienation from God and the human nature of Jesus itself came out. The art of dying is to be considered as an ongoing quest for reality and as a preparation for the event of physical death. Those, who receive an insight into the nature of reality are able to transform their attitude toward death. This insight is associated with the conviction that the greatest value in human life is indestructible, and is the new kind of experience and approach to death. In Christianity, the belief is that the fullness of their salvation cannot be enjoyed as long as they remain in the mortal body. The assurance of life beyond the grave makes a clear cut distinction between the world and life beyond the grave, death being the great divide between the two.[18]

Dying is undoubtedly an issue and an integral part of the human quest for meaning. Death's power of challenging human's most cherished dreams, constrains us to pursue the meaning of existence with intensity. Dying becomes the last decision a human can make as a human. It turns out to be the last possibility of one's own self-realization. In some thinkers, to crave for death and a life beyond the grave suggests that there is a radical difference between life and death. In Zen the conviction that there is a dimension to humans that cannot be annihilated by death helps to overcome fear of death. Understanding death as the last chance to achieve the fullness of one's destiny enables one to grasp the meaning of the whole life itself.

Afterlife with or without the Body

The question of the 'afterlife' becomes crucial in many philosophical and religious traditions. The answers, beliefs and doctrines about the 'afterlife' characterize the peculiarity of the given tradition. Analysis of the experience of death lead to ways and means of overcoming it; whether it could be transformed by enlightenment as proposed by the Zen tradition, or by the suffering of Jesus in the Christian tradition, or by realization of the human self apart from body as in the Vedantic tradition, to name a few.

In Indian idealist traditions like the Vedic-Vedantic tradition, the cases of Naciketas and Savitri as in *Katha Upaniṣad* and in *Mahābhārata* present the theme of immortality and quest for final liberation. At least two famous figures in this tradition have had conversations with Death and Yama, and both these encounters are quite celebrated. Naciketas famously has a dialogue with Death in the *Katha Upaniṣad.* Savitri also has a conversation with death, in *Mahābhārata*, at the end of which she saves the life of her husband, Satyavan. Both manage to put Yama, the god of death, in a predicament. Yama dispenses boons to both of them, but asks both of them to choose some other boon, when Naciketas wants to know whether there is survival after death or liberation, and when Savitri wants her husband to be brought back to life. Both however have their way in the end, and present the theme of immortality and the quest for final liberation.

The dead are purified in the realm of Yama (Mahabh.13.111.92ff) and the dead are again slain (Mahabh. 8.92.10). Naciketas asks to be able to return to his father (Katha Upa. 1.1.10) and for knowledge of the sacrificial fire that leads one to heaven (Katha Upa. 1.1.13). Yama is happy to grant these two boons. Finally when asked for knowledge about death, Yama is reluctant to grant this boon. He offers other choices like wealth, long life and pleasure. But Naciketas refuses them and replies that all these things are ephemeral (Katha Upa. 1.1.26). Then the teaching of the secrets of life and death starts. Once knowledge of the secret treasure is attained freedom from death is attained. In most traditions, the body is separated at death and the immortal soul survives death, either in eternity of hell or heaven, or waiting for dispensation to be born again.[19] There is an assertion that lives continues even after death, without the physical body.

The African worldview perceives that the dead do not go to another world but change their physical mode of existence to that of a spiritual one and there is no polarizing dichotomy between the world of the living and the world of the dead. In the network of relationships, all are interconnected to each other. The dead remains connected as an ancestor as one's life is defined through belonging to a community. As an ancestor, one continues to be part of the community.

Transmigration

The theory of transmigration as one of the answers has been shared by many thought traditions, expressing human beings' undying quest for the fullness of reality and the truth of life itself. Transmigration means the passage of the soul from one body to another. Other terms used are, rebirth, reincarnation and metempsychosis. Reincarnation is used in a specific sense of the passage of the soul from one body to another in the same species, while transmigration could include other species also. The upaniṣadic sages interested in the destiny of the human and their condition after death formulated the eschatological theory.[20] The journey of the soul after death has different descriptions in the Upaniṣads. *Bṛahadāranyaka* (6.2.15) explains it as knowledge of the path.

One should know that his/her life itself is a sacrifice and is offered again by the gods at one's death. The knowledge of this leads one to the world of Brahma to be eternally there. Those lacking this superior knowledge, attain the world of the moon where they enjoy the fruits of their good works until they are exhausted only to return to this earth to be born again as human beings. The *Chāndōgya* (5.4-10) teachings resembles the same with few additional details of the nature of rebirth, of how one enters the womb of a species according to the degree of goodness and wickedness they acquired while living. Kaushitaki Upaniṣad (Kau. Up. 1.) explains how the knowledge of Brahman saves the soul from rebirth. After death everybody goes to the world of the moon where their esoteric knowledge is tested. Failure in the test results in a return to the earth. Similarly Prasna Upaniṣad proclaims that the knowledge of Atman wins the world of Brahman. Those who seek Atman with faith and austerity will not be born again. (Pras. Up.1.9-10)

The reason for transmigration is the ignorance to think that this world is everything and there is no other world. (Kath. 2.6) Neglect of knowledge and attachment to sacrifices and rituals cause rebirth. (Brah. 6.2; Cha. 5.10; Pras. 1.9; Mundaka. 1.2) The fundamental reason for rebirth is the desire other than the knowledge of Atman or Brahman. (Mund. 3.2; Brah. 4.4; Pras. 3.3). Secondly the determining factor of rebirth is one's own actions. According to the degree of goodness or wickedness one acquired till the time of his/her departure, the nature of one's next life is determined. (Cha. 5.10; Kau. 1.2; Kath. 3.7; 5.7; Mund 1.9-10; Sve 5.7; Maitri 3.2)

The Vedantic tradition reinstating the existence of three bodies, *śarīratreyam*, accounts for the body as necessary for transmigration. A popular fifteenth century text of Advaita vedānta, *Pañcadasī* of Vidyāraṇya, describes the human personality as composed of the three bodies, the physical or gross body, *sthūlaśarīra,* the subtle body, *sūkṣma-śarīra,* the causal body, *kārana-śarīra* and alternatively of five sheaths, *pañcakōṣa,* containing the elements of food, vital airs, mind, intellect and bliss. There is a correlation of the bodies with the sheaths (*Pañcadasī* I, 15-23), physical is with food, subtle is with vital air, mind and intellect, causal is with bliss. The subtle body is the mechanism through which the embodied soul, disembodies at death, and then proceeds to re-embody itself. At the moment of death the subtle body along with the causal body leaves the gross-body and moves on to acquire another gross-body. The subtle body is said to be surviving death and is transparent and invisible, and perhaps has to be accepted as material. Transmigration reveals the basic intuition that the soul is immortal and spiritual and it can realize itself fully and forever by attaining the unlimited.[21]

Transmigration is terminated by the true knowledge of Atman or Brahman. Those who know the Atman become passionless, perfect, and are liberated from death. (Mund. 3.2) Brahma-knowers, become merged in Brahman and are liberated from rebirth. (Sve. 2.7) Transmigration reveals the basic intuition that the soul is immortal and spiritual and it can realise itself fully and forever by attaining the unlimited.[22]

The question of 'life after death' has been another interesting issue many traditions from ancient times onwards have tried to answer. Discussions, debates, questions and counter questions emerge out of differences in the conception of 'afterlife' in many traditions. The meaningfulness of empirical existence often gets defined by the conception of the 'afterlife'; in terms of liberation, salvation, ultimate freedom, deliverance, *mokṣa, paramukti,* mystical union with the Absolute, etc.

Meaningful Bodily Existence

The question we raise on the meaning of life could also imply for questions on afterlife. All answers maintain that an essential element of human beings survives death and the kind of existence depends on the life before death. Understanding death as the last chance to achieve the fullness of one's destiny enables one to grasp the meaning of the whole life itself.[23] So, death is not the end of life; rather a birth into a new form of life. There is continuity and discontinuity of life; Discontinuity in terms of the physical and continuity in terms of the moral and spiritual realms. Immortality, transmigration, reincarnation, rebirth, resurrection are different answers provided by various traditions.[24] The human soul, seen as the root principle of life is believed to be immortal, surviving the bodily death and becoming indestructible by nature. A number of arguments have been put forward in establishing the immortality of the soul, like human desire for eternal happiness, etc.

All arguments on immortality are associated with the moral life of humankind, the moral order, the prevalence of goodness and justice, the universal human desire for happiness. Death is not the end of their quest for happiness. Craving for happiness is so deep rooted in humans that its realization is possible at one point of time. The question of now and hereafter offers a psychological hope contributing to the wellbeing of human life. They make people optimistic and highly goal-oriented and to lead a meaningful life. Hope becomes a permanent force in every human being, a driving power as long as we are alive. Faced with the reality of death, human beings have often drawn a sense of hope from a belief in life after death. It makes an argument that beliefs in afterlife enable meaningfulness of life in the body.

Indian materialists like Cārvākas, Vaiśeṣikas, Ajñanavādins, Bhūtavādins and Ajīvikas and dualists like Tantric and Sāṁkhyas, insist on the importance of the physical body and the material world. The contempt for the body and for materialism lead to prejudices that one who focuses on bodily and material existence is hedonistic, pleasure-oriented, low in thinking, perverted, and who little understands the higher values of human existence. Their philosophy of 'this-worldliness' is of practical everydayness. Their doctrines find meaning of everything here and now. For instance, Cārvāka's doctrine of the 'consciousness of matter' (*bhūta-caitanya-vāda*), another name for 'consciousness of sense organs' (*indria-caitanya-vāda*), does not deny consciousness but denies only that it can be independent of the body. They regard consciousness as a mere product of matter and as always found associated with the body and is destroyed with the body's disintegration. 'Matter secretes mind as liver secretes bile.' Their denial that there is nothing existent beyond this material world and no survival of anything, no other world, and no God is a result of their assertion that all that exists is only matter. So, a destiny beyond this world has no basis in the true nature of reality. Such a conception calls for giving due importance to life in the body and living the present meaningfully.

Conclusion

The universal recognition of mortality about life in the body has been recorded in most traditions. An earth-bound, ego-centred consciousness looks at death as a threat while the idea of afterlife presents death as a door to life with God and the people of God. Instead of fear and trembling, the believer longs for it. As believers and truth seekers humans cannot deny their beliefs nor stop searching for truth. Questions of life, death are basically about identity. Afterlife beliefs, perceptions and claims are all creating possibilities for new forms of identity. 'Life before death seems to need a life after death for meaning and significance… life before death is significant and every effort must be taken for the wellbeing of each individual and community.' The question of suffering, death and the afterlife is reflected in how we make sense of life lived in the body.

Notes

1 Francis Vadakethala, "Editorial," *Journal of Dharma* 6, no. 3 (July-September 1979): 215.

2 B. K. Matilal, "The Enigma of Buddhism: Duhkha and Nirvana," *Journal of Dharma* 2, no. 3 (July 1977): 305.

3 Ryudo Yasui, *Theory of Soul in Theravada Buddhism*, 155.

4 Richard De Smet, "Guidelines in Indian Philosophy," *Divyadaan: Journal of Philosophy and Education*, 23, no.1 (2012): 126.

5 Swami Vikrant, "The Buddhist Idea of Man," *Jnanodaya: Journal of Philosophy*, no. 2 (1992-1993): 5.

6 Sudha Gopinath, "Buddhism – I," in *Indian Philosophy – I, BPY – 001*, eds. Gracious Thomas and George Punthanmarkel (New Delhi: Indira Gandhi National Open University, 2010), 291.

7 The entire vedantic traditions have a view termed as 'eternalism' by the Indian philosophical writers. It means that there is one unchanging, permanent principle called the 'self,' the *ātman,* which is eternal.

8 By 'nihilism' of Cārvaka, we mean their assertion that there is no permanent, unchanging principle called '*ātman*' and life ends with physical death.

9 Matilal, "The Enigma of Buddhism," 304.
10 See Y. Karunadasa, "The Buddhist Doctrine of *Anatta*," in *Buddhist Thought and Ritual*, ed., David J. Kalupahanna (Delhi: Motilal Banarsidass, 2001), 1-15.
11 see Vincent B. Sekar, "Consciousness: A Dynamic Psycho Cognitive Process from a Buddhist, Jain Perspective," *Suvidya* 3, no.1 (June 2009): 53-64.
12 John B. Chethimattam, "Editorial," *Journal of Dharma* 2, no. 3 (July 1977): 246-247.
13 Robert Neville, "Suffering, Guilt and Responsibility: Christian Responses to Suffering," *Journal of Dharma* 2, no. 3 (July 1977): 248-250.
14 Ibid, 249.
15 Chethimattam, "Editorial," 247.
16 James Breckenridge, "Religion and the Problem of Death," *Journal of Dharma* 6, no. 3 (July-September 1979), 217.
17 Philip B. Yampolsky, *The Platform Sūtra of the Sixth Patriarch* (New York: Columbia University Press, 1967), 174.
18 Breckenridge, "Religion and the Problem of Death," 224.
19 Chethimattam, "Editorial," 246.
20 Gabriel Aranjaniyil, "Transmigration in the Upaniṣads and the Greek Thought," *Journal of Dharma* 6, no. 3 (July-September 1979): 244.
21 F. Max Muller, *The Six Systems of Indian Philosophy* (London: Longmans, 1903), 174.
22 Aranjaniyil, "Transmigration in the Upaniṣads and the Greek Thought," 254.
23 Vadakethala, "Editorial," 216.
24 Jose Nandhikkara, "Life after Death: Quest for Meaning of Life before Death," *Journal of Dharma* 37, no. 4 (October-December 2012): 387.

19

The Buddhist Concept of the Body

Kurian Alumkal
Carmel Hill Philosophy College, Thiruvananthapuram

Abstract: This paper intends to elaborate upon theoretical and practical approaches to the 'Body' in Buddhism. It bases itself on the *Abhidharmakōśa* perspective of Vasabandhu on its theoretical approach and the '*upāya*' approach of the *Madhyamaka* as the model approach in the practical Buddhist analysis of the body. For the theoretical analysis we expose the Buddhist concept of the human person, starting from the historical milieu of Buddha and basic characteristics of his unique vision. We present Buddha's milieu as *Brahmiṇic* (*Vedic*) world-vision where the basic metaphysical perspective is emphasis on 'permanence.' Buddha's unique vision springs up from his keen observation of the contradiction in the *Brahmiṇic* (*Vedic*) world-vision and the consequent formulation of the Buddhist world-vision that emphasizes 'change.' Actually the rational analysis of reality flows from these basic perspectives in these world-visions. Our contention here is that ultimately 'permanence' emphasizing *Upaniṣadic* world-vision or 'change' emphasizing the Buddhist world-vision is designed to achieve the goal of life which is *mokṣa* or *nirvāṇa* (liberation). The means for this liberation presented by both world-views are strikingly similar where body and its awareness is the central point which is practical. From a practical perspective the *Madhyamaka* concept of '*upāya*' is central in our understanding of the body. This is a tradition that springs up from Nāgārjuna's *Madhyamaka*, as interpreted by Chandrakirti and later Śāntideva. Śāntideva's *Bodhicāryāvatāra* is the basic text here, with the key question "will a sick person have any benefit merely by reading about medical treatments?" and the key vision that body itself is an *upāya* or medicine which is relative.

Keywords: theoretical, practical, analysis of body, Abhidharmakośa, Vasabandhu, upāya, Śāntideva, Bodhicāryāvatāra, Brahmiṇic world-vision, permanence, Buddhist world-vision, change.

Introduction

This paper has two parts. This division is based on the classification of Buddhism into theoretical (metaphysical speculative part) and practical (exposition of the means for *Nirvāṇa*). Though Buddhism has its origin in the intuitive awareness of Buddha and the communication of that awareness to his disciples, with the characteristic mark of considering metaphysical speculations as '*dṛṣṭi*' that must be termed '*avyākṛtas*' which divert us from the main focus, in the course of time it was turned into huge metaphysical systems by his disciples. Thus, we have different systems of Buddhist schools and a variety of Buddhist religious groups.

The first part of this paper deals with the question 'what' is 'Body' in Buddhism from a theoretical perspective. It is an exposition or review, so we take up the Buddhist analysis of the human person as it is accepted mostly in all Buddhist schools. Here *Abhidharmakōśa* of Vasabandhu is the basic text and we analyse it. This analysis is in the historical context of Buddha's milieu where the trend was Brahmiṇic (Vedic). Here we do a comparative exposition of basic metaphysical perspectives in the Brahmiṇic and Buddhist worldviews. When we study them we see that they go hand in hand with only one fundamental difference that makes all the difference; namely, emphasis on permanence in Upanishads and change in Buddhism. We also answer the 'why' of this 'what' interpretation as Buddha's vision that sees a contradiction in the Brahmiṇic vision which he saw as existing when he started philosophizing.

The basic Vedic vision about the nature of the universe and of human life is that they are permanent, free, and happy. In reality though, they knew that life in this world, be it normal activities, relationships in society, or even our own body and mind, always brings dissatisfaction. All phenomena are impermanent and constantly rising and falling, coming and going. Why did a permanent, free and happy existence create such an impermanent and uncomfortable world? This is the great contradiction. However, the Vedic intelligence ignored the contradiction, may be because of their basic 'seeing' (looking glass perspective). Their concern becomes the ending of their suffering in order to regain the permanently blissful state of the Brahman/god. Hence, their theory of liberation arose. But Buddha began with the basic vision centred on change, may be because of his basic 'seeing' (looking-glass perspective) and his 'rational' analysis of Nature and Person.

In the second part we concentrate on the same question: What is body? But this is in the context of 'practical Buddhism.' Here the concept of '*upāya*'[1] is central and we approach the body as '*upāya*' in the Buddhist pursuit of achieving the goal of life. Here we take up *Bodhicāryāvatāra* of Śāntideva as the basic text that emphasises practice over theory. We read in No. 109: "What is the use of merely reading the words? Will a sick person have any benefit merely by reading about medical treatments?"[2] Again, how to use the medicine, body? Chandrakirti uses the analogy of the medicine as relative. A doctor administered a powerful remedy which would remove all the ailments of the patient, but could not afterwards be expelled from the abdomen. Do you think that the patient would be really cured? No, he would suffer even much more than he did suffer before. The body which is relative itself is relative.[3]

Abhidharmakōśa of Vasabandhu

About every Buddhist personality and their works, lot of opinions are there, both for and against. Among them Vasabandhu and his text *Abhidharmakośa* standunique as all scholars agree on the text and its content and its author's name as Vasubandhu. Whether there is only one Vasubandhu or two or three Vasabandhus is a scholar's matter of debate. Though the Buddhist tradition goes for one Vasubandhu, most scholars of modern times go with the theory of two Vasubandhus. The elder Vasubandhu, the brother of Asaṅga lived in the 4th century CE and the younger Vasubandhu is the author of *Abhidharmakōśa* who lived in the 5th century CE. But recently we see again a swinging back to the Buddhist traditional understanding in the works of Alex Wayman, for example. According to him there is only one Vasubandhu, brother of Asaṅga, who lived in the 5th century CE and his first work was *Abhidharmakōśa* and its *bhāsya*. After his conversion to the *Mahāyāna*, he composed the commentary on the *Mahāyāna Saṁgraha*; and after the death of Asaṅga he composed his other *Mahāyāna* works and secondly of Yogācāra texts like *Vimsatika* and *Trimsatika*. He became a famous teacher and died at the age of eighty.[4]

Since Buddha was a very charismatic personality with the conviction about Metaphysics as perspectives that misdirect us, he answered metaphysical questions in his characteristic way and the answers were convincing, for his personality stood high with his charisma. Buddhists, after the*parinirvāṇa* of Buddha, were forced to answer questions logically in order to give convincing answers to metaphysical questions of rival visions of reality. As time changed, the teachers felt the need of analytical exposition. Thus, by the 5th century CE, we have the *Abhidharmakōśa* type of books. *Abhidharmakōśa* is a basic text in the Buddhist tradition which explains theoretical aspects of Buddhism with the categories of *skandas, ayātanas, dhātus*.[5] This book harmoniously synthesized all the great doctrines accepted by different Buddhist Schools.

The text contains nine chapters of which eight in verses are known as each *kōśastanas* and the ninth *pudgalaviniṣecaya* (denial of the soul) is in prose. This Sanskrit text has Chinese, Tibetan and Japanese language versions, modern French, German, English, Hindi, Singhalese and Modern Japanese language translations and studies available.

Abhidharmakōśa's Concept of Human Person

Immanuel Kant, one of the authorities in the Modern Western Philosophy made a basic distinction with his classification of reality into noumena and phenomena. When we start studying Indian Philosophy one basic classification that will clarify many of the inconsistencies is *vyavahāra* and *paramārta* levels of reality as Brahminic traditions understand or *saṁsāra* and *nirvāṇa* levels of reality as it is understood in Buddhism[6] from ancient time onwards. *Vyavahāra* (*saṁsāra*) is the world as we see it now, our experiential world. *Paramārta* (*Nirvāṇa*) is that which is open to those who are '*dārśanic*' or initiated or those who have received realization. The Upaniṣads are talks of those belonging to the second category. They use mystical language to explain what they realized to those in *vyavahāra.*

Almost all religious philosophers speak of the body and soul when they speak of human beings. In the Upaniṣads, the concept of soul or self is explained in mystical language that culminates in "*Nēti, Nēti*" (Brhad II 3:6; IV 4:22; Tait. II 7; Katha III 15) or "that in which all the contradictions are reconciled" (Brhad IV 3:22; IV 4:3; Trait II 6; Katha II 20; Īsā 5) that which transcends all thought and speech and is indescribable and the ineffable Self (*Ātman*), which is identified with the supreme reality (Katha II 16, IV 5-9). In the final analysis this has nothing to do with egoistic ideas, for only at the shedding of all egoism do we reach at this realization.

Coming to the *Bhagavadgīta*, this is exposed in the form of the Universal spirit dwelling inside all beings (B.G. X 20, XIII 17, II 24, XIII 32, XV 15, XVIII 6). Now a return back from this manifoldness to the One is Life's purpose.

But Buddhism since it uses a more rational language than mystical, developed the concept of *Āryasatyas* to explain their vision. All that they speak about reality can be explained as the analysis of the four following truths: *sarvamdukham, dukhasamudāya, dukhanirōdha and dukhanirōdhamārga.*

They will first reduce all the positions of the other systems into one group that basically takes up the dualistic concept of burden (*bhāra*) and the carrier of burden (*bhārahāra*), a modern equivalent to the 'ghost in the machine' or 'pilot in a vessel'[7] images of Rene Descartes. The Buddhist's alternative way of speaking about it is the elements of existence (*dharmas*). But the classification of this body into five set of elements represent elements of different moments of one's life[8] and someone may experience it only through the 'mindfulness of body.' Actually the human person is nothing but a conglomeration of the constituent elements of a personal life.

The five elements are one material (*rūpa*) and four immaterial – *vijñāna, vedana, saṁjña and saṁskāra* or *chetana*. It is interesting to note that the Upaniṣads also speaks of five sheaths – *Annamayakōśa, Prāṇamayakōśa, Manōmayakōśa, Vijñānamayakōśa* and *Ānandamayakōśa* but they are basically believers in the soul and Buddhism is just opposite, they reject such concept of soul but the rest of the analysis go hand in hand. It is the same type of arguments, the goal is also same as *nirvāṇa* or *mukti* or *mokṣa* but metaphysical foundations are distinct. According to *Abhidharmakōśa* what actually exist are elements (*dharmas*) and different names are given to the conglomeration of elements like: sentiment being (*sattva*), man (*nara*), Manu's progeny (*manuṣya*), son of Manu (*mānava*), a person (*puruṣa*), an individual (*pudgala*), a vital source of life (*jīva*), a soul (*jantu* or *ātman*) and the like.

Statements like "that is the name of this venerable man, he belongs to such a caste and such a family, he eats such food, this pleases him, he has reached such an age, he has lived so many years; he has died at such an age" etc. are nothing but mere words, mere conventional designations. In the pudgala or individual, everything is impermanent, conditioned and is of dependent origination. Buddha's words from *Bimbisāra Sūtra* are quoted: "O monks! The notion of 'myself' and of 'mine' is a childish notion or uneducated and ignorant people, who are misled by current expressions. There is no Self, nothing mine, nothing except the separate elements of the suffering of life in their ever-changing apparitions" Bhikkuni Śila's reply to Māra, the Evil One, is also significant in this connection when she says: "O Māra, you are misled by false conception. Here there is no sentient being and the mass of aggregates or elements is void of self. Just as a set of wooden parts receives the name of 'carriage,' so to the mass of elements we give the name of *Being*."[9]

Practical Buddhism as Practice of 'Mindfulness of the Body'

Second part of this essay has its basic clue from Buddha's refusal to answer metaphysical questions. For him these questions are '*avyākṛtas*', no answer can satisfy hearer because of the basic temperamental differences, so we have to reject these questions and answers and be practical. Buddha got the title 'skilful doctor' by successful application of this method. Buddha, because of his personality stood above all questions, in front of him either question become non-questions that doesn't need an answer for satisfaction or his personality itself became answer. But as time went on, his disciples were not able to answer convincingly as Buddha did or in their effort to understand Buddha, they exposed the metaphysical foundations inherent in Buddha's teaching. From practical angle Buddha's principle behind his 'use' of everything for liberation was titled as *'upāya'* or '*Upāyakausalya.*'[10]

An interesting simile we see in *Questions of King Milinda,* where we see Greek King Milinda asks the Indian Buddhist Monk Nagasena "Is the body dear to those who have gone forth (monks)? The monk replies that it is not. "Then why" replies the King "do you treasure it and foster it?" The monk answers by comparing the body to a wound received in battle, which is anointed and bandaged, so that it might heal. Similarly, although the body is 'not dear' to monks, they protect it as a means of promoting the holy life.[11]

Since body in itself neither good nor bad; it can be used positively or negatively. In itself it is indifferent. But our attitude towards it, our mentality with which we use it makes it do harm or help for liberation. If we ask the question, what is the relevance of body positively in Buddhism; we must answer that by speaking about the reason for their denial of the self (soul). Why they denied self and how they defend our life experience of continuity? Here we have their basic ingenuity of classification of reality into *saṁsāra* and *nirvāṇa*. *Saṁsāra* is our experimental world in which we have experience both of change and continuity. We cannot but speak of personality here. But once the talk centred on *nirvāṇa*, as Buddhist understand their three metaphysical truths stands basic. Everyone can experience *dukha* and *anityam*, but *anāntmam.* Metaphysical foundation flows from these experience because of the basic logic that they apply to form theory.

Bodhicāryāvatāra: A Guide to Bodhisattva Way of Life

From Buddha onwards, Buddhism was a practical religio-philosophical trend, which presented certain practices for truth-realization. This practice is basically a meditative introspection occurring within a specific social and behavioural environment. Certain conduciveness in the *Saṅgha* (community of seekers of *nirvāṇa* as a body), with Dharma (Buddha's teaching as body) and Buddha (the empirical, historical person, his inspiring life as body that energizes as in *stūpa*, prayer places, pilgrim centres etc.) prepare monks for life's goal attainment. *Bodhicāryāvatāra* of Śāntideva is one classical text that presents practices for the attainment of Buddhahood in 10 chapters.[12]

The Buddhist practice, basically the practice of mindfulness always happens as an experience in our bodies. Basically it is "to experience the breath in the body" it is a realization of the world found within our body.[13] Buddha always emphasized "within this very fathom-long body, with its perceptions and inner sense: lies the world, the cause of the world, the cessation of the world and the path that leads to the cessation of the world."[14]

There is a basic distinction between the concept of "Body Consciousness" as understood in Western culture and the Buddhist. In one word we can present the Western as an orientation focussed on the image of body as an external object that can be used, but the use is of the type of modern advertising industries that triggers the building up of fashion centres, local gyms, cosmetics centres, hair style creating centres etc. This is a materialistic type of objectifying the body. The Buddhist understanding is that this type of objectification disconnects us from our own sense of aliveness and consciousness, which can come from inside out. Once we start to experience subjective awareness from inside out, we begin to learn that the body is awareness itself, a "process" rather than a "thing."

Basically Buddhists overcome dualism of the body and awareness of the body with the concept that "the body itself is bodhi (awakening)" or as Zen Master Dogen puts it, "mindfulness of the body is the body's mindfulness." Actually the mindfulness of the body practice is an invitation for us to open to the awareness which is already present in the body. Practice is not directing or creating something. The beginning and end of practice is the awakening of what is already there – within this very fathom-long body. The difference is explained with the classical example of the distinction of the person who gets angry and speaks out "O! I was angry."

Buddhist literature distinguishes a variety of different "bodies" – the energy body, the bliss body, the transformation body, the diamond body, the karmic body, and the awareness body. It is possible for a person who meditates to experience all these different bodies, often as a flow of energy on field of awareness[15] on their path of realization.

One question stands out at the end: where all these ways of explanation leads to? If we look at Buddhism from the angle of *Bodhicāryāvatāra* of Śāntideva, it all leads to a type of mystic intuition which is a living experience. But for us this is a problem for understanding and therein lies the problem too! For these are matters of experience and not of explaining in words. There is a legend centered around Śāntideva that while he was reciting the *Bodhicāryāvatāra* and as he reached chapter 9 verses 35 he started to rise up to the sky and disappeared. This legend has a sense in it for it is speaking of the fruit of complete *nivirtti* or detachment; the verse is this "*Yadānabhāvahnabhāvah mateḥ santuṣthatepuraḥ. Tadanyagatyabhāvena nirālambhaprasamyati// when there is neither 'is-ness' nor 'non-is-ness' existing before the mind; there being no other course, the mind, without a support, will become tranquil.*"[16] The need is: the mind freed of all 'is' and 'is not' conceptualizations and the consequent clinging, then, just like fire without fuel gets stilled in absolute tranquility, equanimity and the complete *prasānti* (absolute peace) mind too enters.

Conclusion

Mahāyāna Buddhism, as it is developed in Madhyamaka of Nāgārjuna, Chandrakirti, Śāntideva and so on leads to a philosophy without words, the philosophy of *śūnyatā*, the philosophy of *tūṣṇīmbhāvaḥ* (silence). It is a type of seeing through all metaphysical construction works of metaphysicians, be it realistic or rationalistic; idealistic or absolutistic. This 'seeing-through' is not different from the construction; otherwise it will be a new construction! Thus it is only awareness about the construction. The fact of the body, experience of body-consciousness, vision of the body as *upāya* or medicine which is relative remains as facts! So, also Śāntideva's experience!

Notes

1 See my essay on "The meaning and significance of *UpāyaKausalya* in Buddhist Tradition," in *Journal of Sacred Scriptures* 6, no.1 (January-June 2012): 97-107.

2 Śāntideva, *A Guide to Bodhisattva Way of Life: Bodhicāryāvatāra*, trans. Vesna. A. Wallace and B. Alan Wallace (New York: Snow Lion Publications, 1997), 55. This book is available at http://hoavouu.com/images/file/AkMNdk9R0QgQAAoD/shantideva-bodhicaryavatara-wallace.pdf (accessed January 20, 2016).

3 As quoted in Stcherbatsky, *The Conception of Buddhist Nirvāna, along with Sanskrit Text of Mūlamadhyamakakārikā* (Revised and enlarged by Jaidea Singh.Varanasi: Bharatiya Vidya Prakasan, n.d.), 82.

4 See Marek Mejor, "The Problem of two Vasubandhus reconsidered," in *Untying the Knots in Buddhism: Selected Essays*, ed. Alex Wayman (Delhi: Motilal Banarsidas, 1997), 115-148. http://www.indologica.com/volumes/vol15-16/vol15-16_art19_MEJOR.pdf (accessed January 20, 2016).

5 Modern study of this can be found in the works of Theodore Stcherbatsky especially in his *The Central Conception of Buddhism: and the Meaning of the Word "Dharma"* (Delhi: Motilal Banarsidas, 1923), 1-31.

6 Both in Brahmiṇical tradition and Buddhist tradition this division is there. Accepted culmination of Brahmiṇical tradition is Advaita Vedanta that speaks of three levels of reality: *pratibhāsic, vyavahāric* and *paramārtic*; final traditional Indian school of Buddhism is Yogācāra that speaks of three fold division of reality in the same fashion. Yogācāra developed much early to Advaita Vedanta.

7 Rene Descartes, *Meditations on First Philosophy*, Sixth Meditation (London, Cambridge University Press, 1911 edition of The Philosophical Works of Descartes, translated by Elizabeth S. Haldane), 29. (Available at http://selfpace.uconn.edu/class/percep/DescartesMeditations.pdf).

8 Sukomal Chaudhuri, *Analytical Study of the Abhidharmakōśa* (Calcutta: Sanskrit College, 1976), 230.

9 Ibid., 228-229.

10 '*Upāya*' or '*Upāyakausalya*' (skilful means) is used in different senses. In common sense use, we have the word 'caturupāya' – *sāma, dāna, bhēda* and *danda*. A teacher uses on student to make them understand. *Upāya* in the Buddhist context generally can be understood as everything that has no intrinsic value, but only extrinsic value. All that is useful when it helps for attachment of *nirvāṇa* are expedient means (skilful means or *Upāya*). See Joy A. P., "The meaning and significance of *UpāyaKausalya* in Buddhist Tradition," in *Journal of Sacred Scriptures* 6, no.1 (January-June 2012): 97-107.

11 Stephen Collins, "*The body in Theravāda Buddhist Monasticism*," in *Religion and the Body*, ed. Sarah Coakley (Cambridge: Cambridge University Press, 1997), 197.

12 The translation of Wallace contains an introduction and one section titled 'contextualization of Bodhicāryāvatāra' that explains in nutshell what each chapter deals with. He himself was a monk and mostly his hearers are monks who are oriented for the goal (bodhisattva's path to enlightenment) for which he presents the means of six perfections (*pāramitās*) of generosity, ethical discipline, patience, zeal, meditation and wisdom. First seven chapters are preliminary aims at developing first four *pāramitās*. Eighth chapter is meditation for cultivation of altruism and the spirit of Awakening and the Ninth on Perfection of Wisdom,

from the *prāsangikamādhyamika* angle. Tenth chapter is the conclusion. See Śāntideva, *A Guide to Bodhisattva Way of Life*, 12ff).

13 Gil Fronsdal, "*The Body at the Center: Mindfulness of the Body in the Practice – Instructions of the Buddha*," http://buddhiststudies.commongroundmeditation.org/mindfulness-of-the-body/resources (accessed January 15, 2016).

14 Ibid., (accessed January 15, 2016).

15 Gill Fronsdal, *Issue at Hand: Essays on Buddhist Mindfulness Practice* (New York, Barnes & Noble, 2001), 47-53; available at http://www.insightmeditationcenter.org/documents/iah/IssueAtHand4thEd.pdf (accessed January 20, 2016).

16 Paramanda Sharma, *Santideva's Bodhicaryavatara* (Delhi, Aditya Prakashan, 1997), http://www2.hf.uio.no/polyglotta/index.php?page=fulltext&vid=24&level=2&cid=46496#N1109rn (accessed January 20, 2016).

20

The Body in Śaiva Siddhānta

Andrew Anbarasu
St. Eugene High School, Kombadimadurai

Abstract: Life in the world is possible only through the existence of the body. But the body is seen to be the mainculprit in terms of human suffering. The pleasures or the joys of the body are rather seen as stumbling blocks on the road of deliverance. It is because of this reason that the body is looked upon as a burden, which through meditational techniques and ascetical practices, has to be done away with. It is this negative psychological attitude towards the Body which dominates the philosophy of Indian tradition. Here in this paper, I would like to present the philosophical views on the concept of body in Śaiva Siddhānta and cultivate a positive approach towards understanding the body which is a gift given by God for our earthly existence.

Keywords: Śaiva Siddhānta, *mokṣa*, *sādhana*, yoga, *svadharma*, *mantirameni*, *deha*, Tirumular, Andal.

Introduction

We live in a world where the body is celebrated: fitness overemphasized, a culture of the fashion show, spending extravagantly on one's body. We can say that the body is adored. Life in the world is possible only through the existence of the body. The body by its very nature is the medium for the insertion into the world. The body is the means of expression and action in the world. But, today, the body is used, misused, misunderstood and abused as means for pleasure. Some people treat the body as a business object, a means for attractiveness in advertisements.

The human being is a bodily being, a body-self. St. Paul describes the body-person as a temple of the Holy Spirit (1 Cor. 3:16, 6:19). The final destiny of the human person is to be with the Lord forever not only in a disembodied state, but with the body, a transformed body. The body is for the Lord and the Lord for the body and all are invited to glorify the Lord in the body (1 Cor. 6:13). Yet, in the Christian tradition, the body is considered as a help for the encounter with the Lord. The body is a sacred weapon to have a fruitful encounter with the Supreme Being.

Here in this paper, I would like to present the sacredness of the human body from Indian philosophical traditions, a special reference to Śaiva Siddhānta and to cultivate a positive approach towards understanding the body as a gift given by God for our earthly existence.

A Philosophical Understanding of Body in Indian Traditions

The human body is composed of the physical structure of a human organism. It consists of the various systems, organs, tissues and cells. The size is largely determined by genes. According to *The New Oxford English Dictionary*, the combination of individual atoms, molecule polypeptides and cells in human body is a source of its emergence. The body is real and has materiality but at the same time, it is socially constructed. This understanding of the body makes us know our power, knowledge and our relationship in a new light.[1] Elizabeth Grosz who researches embodiment claims: the body is understood as concrete, material, animal organization of flesh, organs, nerves, muscles and skeletal structure, which are given a unity.[2] The body has been redefined by the claim that physical form is not a natural reality but a cultural concept: a means of encoding a society's values through his or her shape, size and ornamental attributes. The body is produced by the meeting of physical drives and society's supervision of those drives.[3]

The most common word used to refer to the body in Sanskrit is *deha* or *deham*. *De* means to protect and *aham* means the Self. *Deham*, thus, means that which protects the individual Self (*Atman*). The physical body not only protects the Self but also assists it in various ways during its continuation upon earth as a bound soul.[4]

The alternative word in Sanskrit for the body is *śarīra*, which is probably coined from the root word, *śarāh*, meaning five, to denote the presence of five elements in its formation. However, *śarīra* is used to refer to the bodies of both animate and inanimate objects since the five elements are present in both.

Body in the Vedic Period

In ancient Indian society, the knowledge of the body, in both its physical and subtle dimensions, had reached a level rarely equalled elsewhere. It still remains the center of interest for *ayurvedic* healers and yogis. We think today that this practical knowledge was developed and transmitted over the centuries in two kinds of circles which were centers of deep research; that of the healers and that of the ascetics. These two groups have the common orientation of placing themselves outside the circles of the Brahmin elites, and this from the earliest Vedic period. The contact with the body and, more generally, with any object affected by pollution or disease or, worse still, with human and animal corpses, is seen as being beyond bounds for Brahmins. As a matter of fact, the purity-pollution factor heavily structures *Brahminic* society and is the corner stone of rites and sacrifices and of the distinction between communities and classes (*jātī, varna*).

Body in the Upanishadic Period

The body is called *śarīra,* it is also called *deha* and the human being in its existence on earth is referred to also as *dehin*, the embodied. The individual soul is at times presented as being surrounded by a succession of material sheaths or envelopes (*kōṣas*), more and more dense, which constitute its organs, and restricted in different degrees, its sphere of action and range of knowledge. Starting with the outermost and moving inwards there are five *kōṣas*, namely *annamayakōṣa* (food-formed sheath), *prāṇamayakōṣa* (etheric-formed sheath), *manomayakōṣa* (mind-formed sheath), *vijñānamayakōṣa* (consciousness-formed sheath) and *ānandamayakōṣa* (bliss-formed sheath). These layers can also be said to be different attributes of atman, which both reveal and conceal it, the attributes being materiality (gross body), life, reasoning, consciousness and bliss. Rather than a dichotomy between the body and soul, this seems to present a gradual 'materialization' of the inner spirituality.

There is a close relation, parallelism or homology between the microcosm (the human being is made up of *śarīra* and atman) and the macrocosm (consisting of the universe and Brahman). The cosmos is composed of the same matter as the body and vice versa, the only difference being one of scale. Thus, the flesh is a small-scale version of earth (soil) and stones a large-scale version of bones. At death, the various elements that make up the body return to the cosmos. Because, of the close affinity between the two, it is believed that by manipulating one, an individual can bring about a corresponding effect in the other.

Some of the Indian Philosophical schools attribute to each person three bodies, namely, the gross body (*stūla śarīra*), the subtle body (*sūkṣma śarīra*), and the casual body (*kārana śarīra*).[5] Some speak only of the gross body and the subtle body. The gross body is made up of the five gross elements, namely, earth, water, air, fire and ether. Flesh, blood, bones, muscles, bile, saliva, semen, etc., are some of its constituent elements. At death, the gross body goes back to the various elements like water and air from which it has been formed. The subtle body (*sūkṣma śarīra* also called sign body, *liṅga-śarīra*) is made up of the five organs of perception, the five organs of action, the five vital forces or winds as well as the mind (*manas*) and intellect (*buddhi*).[6] Part of the *sūkṣma-śarīra* cleaves to the *atman* at death and transmigrates with it. The causal body (*karma śarīra* or *para śarīra* which means over body) stores the experience of all the actions performed during one's earthly existence. It transmigrates with the atman and determines what type of existence one will have in the next life.

Although the general attitude towards the body is negative, there are also statements which indicate a positive attitude towards the body. Thus, we are told that our body is the earth waking to consciousness and that the body is the abode of the Supreme Being in which the divine consciousness abides. The *Yogasūtras* of Patanjali propose bodily postures as a help for the attainment of spiritual freedom. According to Ramanuja, all bodies and individual selves together constitute the 'body of the Lord.'[7]

The physical body is lived as an emanation or expression of the self. The body is the revered vehicle which allows each living being to play its role during its existence and to accomplish its *svadharma* (his or her proper duty or vocation).

The Indian tradition, through the breath and yoga, touches an energy field that mediates, not only between the body and the spirit, but also between nature and the human and the human and the divine.[8] Much of oriental spirituality evolves round the mastery of the energy field. This is why the body has to be cared for. It has to be integrated.

The Role of Attention in its Approach to the Body in Ancient India

Neither yoga nor any psychosomatic techniquewill be viable without the light of attention (*smṛti*). Besides it is noteworthy as the same word *smṛti* refers at the same time to attention and intelligence as well as to remembrance and love. The triad attention - memory - love is meaningful in many ways that is for each one to cover. Traditionally the following powers are attributed to *smṛti*: acting out of inertia (*tamas*); taking care with intense attention; acting in a state of attention.

We know that the body holds an important place by means of various techniques and practices; with the energy of attention, it becomes a body that is disciplined, controlled, directed to its essential function and suited to live the direct experience reality.[9] Another interesting element concerns the intuition of a continuity body breath (energy)-consciousness. The body appears as the house of being, the locus of consciousness.[10]

Body: Expressive of Wisdom

Indian tradition thinks of the body as a universe made up of complex networks at the same time physical and psychic, in which the body, breath and spirit are intimately related. In its physical dimension the body is constituted by the five great elements, earth, water, fire, air and ether, which form the exterior cover. The more subtle, interior cover is made up of the canals through which the breath-energy of life flows and of the various *chakras* which are the bases and modes that structure the central axis of the body.[11]

It is equally the place where the emotions are stored, the *vāsana* (residual impregnations or hidden unconscious memories). And as a matter of fact we are made up of innumerable strata, levels of identity, which can flower forth on the occasion of an experience. An innate wisdom is inscribed in our bodies, that of *ritam*, the cosmic order, which can become accessible again.[12] The fact of coming into contact again with oneself, also through the body, seized in its different dimensions, also plays an essential role in the process of transformation, of interior recognition.

Body in Bhakti Tradition

In the Agamic or Bhakti tradition the body as microcosm reflects the universe, the macrocosm. Integrating the body one integrates the universe. The layout of the temple is such that as one walks from the entrance to the sacred center, one moves from the basic to the summit chakra, integrating the whole body with the universe. The body in worship, in song and dance, integrates the senses, the emotion, reason and insight. In the Vaishnavite tradition the world is seen as the body of God, who is the Indweller. In the *avatars* God takes on a human body as a mediation of a salvific loving relationship *Vishnu* is supposed to have a subtle body form even without the *avatars*.[13]

Śaiva Siddhānta and Its Philosophy on Body

Śaiva Siddhānta is the system of *Saivism* which is the pre-historic religion of India. This system is not only logical but also scientific. It was not founded by any particular person and it does not have a date of origin. According to Sir John Marshal, "Saivism has been recognized as the most ancient religion which is living in the world. The term *Siddhantam* was first used by the great Saint Tirumular in his great work, *Tirumandiram* verse 1421. The goal of Śaiva Siddhānta is to get rid of all impurities.[14] In the name of God and religion, it does not divide or dissect people. The propagators of Śaiva Siddhānta are broad minded and noble hearted. They taught that God is *Love* and *Love* is God (*Anbe Sivam*).

Meaning of Siddhantam

This term *Siddhantam* is composed of two words, they are: *Siddha* and *Antam*. *Siddha* means the establishment of truth. *Antam* means the end. So, *Siddhantam* means end to the ends, an absolute intellectual finality. *Siddhantam* is the systematic way of life in Śaivism.[15] The Śaiva Siddhānta is the philosophy of

Saiva religion which relates to the established conclusion of the ultimate truth in religious matters.

Basic Truths and Literary Sources of Śaiva Siddhānta

Śaiva Siddhānta explains the triple realities: God, Soul and its Bondage. It also elaborates spiritual matters involving the soul. What is God? What is His nature? What is the purpose of this life? What is the reason of creation? Who am I? What is our relationship to God? These are some of the questions that are answered in this philosophy.

The Śaiva Siddhānta tradition draws its authority from the 28 Saiva Agamas. The first guru of Śaiva Siddhānta was Nandinatha who lived around 250 BC. He left behind a compilation of twenty six Sanskrit verses called *Nandikesvara Kasika*. The next prominent personality of this tradition was Tirumular who composed *Tirumandiram* in Tamil. His work was carried forward by subsequent generations of devotional saints such as Appar, Sundarar, Sambandar, whose works are preserved in *Tevaram*. Manikkavasagar contributed to Śaiva Siddhānta. His work is known as *Tiruvasagam*. Later *Tirumurai* by Nambi Andar Nambi and *Siva-gnana-bodham* by Meykandar are some of important works in Śaiva Siddhānta philosophy.[16]

The Philosophy of Human Body in Saiva Sidhantha

According to the *Tamil siddhas* the aim of *yoga sādhana* is *kāyasiddhi* or the perfection of the body. Let us understand the *siddha* conception of the human body, which is unique and which is not accepted by any system of Indian Philosophy; it is an unacknowledged postulate in Indian tradition.

In Tamil *Siddha* philosophy the human body has acquired an importance, it had never before attained in the spiritual history of India. According to the *Siddhas*, an adept's experimental field is always himself and his body, which contains in itself an immortal essence. The ordinary human body can be and should be transformed into a divine body and must be made an aid to liberation. The *siddha* view of body as a *mokṣa sādhana* is known as *kāya sādhana*. In *Tirumandiram* we come across a number of verses praising the importance of the human body as a ladder to *mukti*.[17] In one celebrated verse Tirumular calls the human body as the abode of God. God rejoices in the body of the Good those who are of good speech, deed and thought in their hearts.

He also says in another poem that the Lord is in Body, let us not despise it.

Dump fools are they
Who as Mala (impurity) despise the body;
Other places as holy
They go about seeking;

They who consider: "Good this is"
And in it seek the Lord,
Shall experience macrocosm entire,
In their body tenacious.[18]

Siddha literature, the various parts of the structure of the temple are designed as features of the human body. The Tamil *Siddhas* understood the human body as a threshold, a passage to the ultimate reality. Sivakkiyar is fond of using the expression threshold, that is "*vāsal*" in Tamil and he calls the human body as a threshold where God resides. The concept "threshold" is one such mystical thing. It is a boundary between two worlds, the ordinary, profane, world and the sacred world beyond. It is a point where we pass from one mode of being to another, from one level of consciousness to another. The term "*vāsal*"[19] used by the Tamil *Siddhas* stand for the moment when we ourselves open up to new depths of our being. They say that one need not go to places of pilgrimage or study *śāstras* when the threshold is in oneself. The idea of the body as a microcosm of reality received a spiritual, mystical connotation in the Tamil *Siddhas* as against purely physical denotation of it in the other traditions. The inter-relations of man's body and the universe (that is Reality) have to be realized by spiritual endeavor. *Kaya sādhana* is such an endeavor. Another important aspect of the *siddha* view of the human body is *nyasa*, which consist of feeling the God or powers representing God in different parts of the body.

Siddha literature we come across the following types of bodies - the *stūla-deha*, the *yoga-deha*, the *siddha-deha*, the *pranava* or *mantra deha* and the *jñāana* or the *divya deha*. Turning the *stūla-deha* into *divya-deha* is *kaya sādhana*.[20] Sivavakkiyar explains the transformation of the physical body into a divine body on the analogy of a worm turning itself into a butterfly. Let us state briefly the various stages involved in *kaya sadhana*. *Stūla śarīra* is the unripe, ordinary, physical body not disciplined by yoga. It is a "deceptive threshold", and one has to "open" it, that is, go beyond it to achieve *kāya siddhi*. Sivavakkiyar says that people should protect, immortalize and preserve the body through the method of yoga just as they would protect a beautiful lady of the house. When the *stūla śarīra* is disciplined by yoga it becomes ripe or *pakva*. Pambatticcittar uses the term "*pudam*"[21] in Tamil which is the equivalent of "making one ripe" *pakva*. Agathiyar Pancacaram speaks about removing the unwanted elements from the body through the process of burning, (*kuṇḍalini agni*). Once the *deha* is hardened by yoga, the internal forces help the *sadhaka* to arouse the *kuṇḍalini* in him, which passes through six *adhāras*. It is a process of the acquirement of yogic powers, *siddhis*, leading to a *siddha deha,* where the body can do and be anything at the will of the *sadhaka*, since it does not have to adhere to the spatio-temporal laws or the laws of space and time of the ordinary body. After the attainment of *siddhis*, the *siddha deha* is turned into a *mantra deha* called *pranava tanu*. The *prananva deha* is a body consisting of the sacred formula "AUM." It is the body of *nada* or sound. This yogin's body is accompanied by certain mystic sound vibrations in the form of a mantra called "AUM" *namasivaya*". The yogin's body at this stage is different from the mantra, that is, the body gets transformed into a sound-form, mantra-form. This body is called *pranava* or *mantra deha*. We find a description of this body, *mantirameni* (*mantra deha*) in *Tirumandiram*. The human figure representing the *pranava deha* is called the *mantirameni chakkaram* in Tamil siddha literature. In *Tirumandiram* we find a description of how the fifty one letters of the alphabet constitute the various parts of the body.[22]

According to the *siddhas* the man with the *pranava deha* is a *jīvan-mukta*, "the man liberated while living." In *Tirumandiram* we find a description of the characteristics of a *jīvan-mukta*. In siddha philosophy there is no *videha-mukti* (post-mortem liberation) but only *jīvan-mukti*; for *videha mukti* is, at best, only a hypothesis. A *jīvan-mukta* does not possess a personal consciousness, but a witnessing consciousness. Even though he acts in the world, he does not have the sense of "I act." He sees all the usual things in a miraculous new light as he has entered into the heart of reality. As a Taoist thinker has said, "the perfect man employs his mind as a mirror. It grasps nothing; it rejects nothing. It receives, but does not keep.' In *siddha* philosophy a *jīvan-mukta* does not die to attain liberation, but is transformed into the very mode of liberation, viz., the *divya deha*.[23] When the *jīvan-mukta* gets into *divya deha* he becomes one with eternity, a paramukta. The "either-or" category of logic regarding his existence or non-existence does not rise in the case of a siddha who has attained the *divya deha*. *Divya deha* is a situation in which one is participating in immortality from now onward and from this present world; and immortality should not be convinced as a survival, post mortem. The attainment of *divya deha* is not *videha mukti*. There are standing examples against *videha mukti*, such a Saint Nandanaar, Saint Manikkavasagar, Sri Andal (merging with the lord at Srirangam), Sri Caitanya and Sri Ramalinga Swamigal, who have attained *divya deha*.[24] It is highly interesting and instructive to note the process which the great yoga master Sri Kṛṣna adopted for transforming his material body into a *divya deha* when he desired to leave the world. He, in concentration, executed a yoga process termed "*agneyi- yoga-dhrama*", i.e., the process of radiating inner fire, by which he reduced his body to a subtler form, and with that body he left the world.

The *divya deha* is called *cinmaya*, "the body of light.' It is a "body" of infinite space, *vettaveli*, a vast expanse without any determination. At this stage the "body" glows with the fire of immortality and is called "the body of light,' *oli udambu* in Tamil. As Tirumular says figuratively even the "hairs" of this transmuted body will shine. When a siddha attains *divya deha*, he attains *Sivahood*. Hence, *divya deha* is referred to as *kailaya deha*. In Siddha mysticism the liberation of the soul is not conceived as a *puruṣārtha*; rather we have the concept of *jīvan-mukti* or liberation within the span of life in the form of attained immortality.

Without entering into the details we may say that in siddha literature we come across three methods by which the human body can be transmuted into immortality. First, there is the method of alchemic process (containing siddha medicine) which, instead of being performed in the laboratory, takes place in the body and consciousness of the *sadhaka*. We find a reference to the method of preparation of the greatest of medicines (*muppu*) by the advocating of which the body will turn into *divya deha*, an immortal golden body. The second is the method of *kundalini yoga* which is the method adapted by all Tamil Siddhas. A third method suggested is called *ulta sādhana* "contrary practice" which states that the sex sentiment properly cultivated may lead man back to the very heart of reality. When sex energy is sublimated and transmuted the *yogin* rises above the sense of identity with physical body. This state is technically called *urdhareta*. *Agastiyar gnanam* and *Tirumandiram* speak of the third process and assure us that there is no death for a man who adopts it perfectly.[25]

A Philosophical Reflection on the Sacredness of Human Body

Wealth, friends, property, and even wife lost, can be acquired again, but the human body is different: once it is lost, it can never be got back, no matter how hard one may try. Human life is most precious, highly sacred, beautiful and invaluable. It is therefore the prime duty of every individual to take the greatest possible care of the body. The body is an indispensable vehicle for experiences. Without it nothing can be done, not even a simple task. The human body is, therefore, more precious than worldly wealth and such other material acquisitions. Life must be sanctified by making proper use of the body and engaging it in sacred actions.[26] Time gone will never come back. Once the Ganges merges in the ocean, you cannot get back even a drop of its sacred water, likewise, once life ebbs out and the body is gone, it cannot be recovered.

The human body is also a clock marking time and the passage of life. It tricks away the seconds, minutes, days, weeks, months, and years. A human person knows that life is ticking away and yet he does not bother to enquire about the real purpose of life. No one can say when the clock will stop. It is, therefore most essential to make proper use of life while it is still available. The body is the vehicle for the journey of life. If the vehicle is not properly maintained, then one must be prepared to face serious problems on the way.

The body has been gifted in order to serve others. We must firmly resolve not only to take care of ourselves but also others. Unfortunately, human persons today do not know what service means. The essence of all the eighteen *Purānas* can be summarized in two short sentences: help ever, hurt never.

Though God has given the body for service man does not seem to understand what help means, being ever immersed in selfishness. Every thought, every word, and every action is driven by selfishness. The human person has become a puppet in the hands of selfishness and self-interest. How can a puppet ever be called independent? Selfishness must therefore be totally rejected and selflessness must be wholeheartedly embraced. Then alone would the real purpose of the human body and human life be realized.

We must make an effort to realize that the body is just an instrument given to us for a specific purpose, and must further understand that purpose. The body must be used only for performing good deeds. We must lead a virtuous life. In the end, we must give up the body with good thoughts. Let us not assume that the body has been given for enjoyment, comfort seeking, beautification, and useless pursuits of that nature. Indulgence in pleasure seeking, comfort and luxury can be dangerous. God has not given this body for indulgence. Let us safeguard our body by all means and take full care of our health, but use our body solely to perform good actions.

Conclusion

As a human being is a being created in the image of God, he is also related to having or being a human body. However, the image of God is not understood exclusively in terms of human embodiment, but the body is a necessary thing for the human being to live as the image of God and for the fulfilment of the obligations to realize the image of God in our earthily life. St. Paul asked in his first letter to Corinthians: "*Don't you know that your body is a temple of the Holy Spirit which is in you, which you have from God?*" In his second letter to Corinthians, Paul comes right out and says it plainly: "*We are a temple of the living God; even as God said, 'I will dwell in them, and walk in them; and I will be their God, and they shall be my people.*'"

God loves our physical body and it is very precious to Him. Jesus showed God's love for our bodies when He healed so many people. God states His care and love for our body in Psalm 139 where he says, "*we are fearfully and wonderfully made and that our physical bodies are amongst the concern of His thoughts*." God has made a future for our bodies when He will resurrect them from the dead. God dwells in our physical bodies and calls them His temple. Our bodies like temples are sacred sites where God dwells. Other people should be able to come to us as temples of the living God and meet God there.

Notes

1 Victor Ferrao, "Politics of Body: Enabling and Ennobling our Embodied Selves," *Mainstream* 32, no. 2 (1998): 282.
2 Ibid.
3 Many Maxwell, *Human Evolution: A Philosophical Anthropology* (New York: Columbia University Press, 1984), 26.
4 See V. Jayaram, "Human Body Symbolism in Hinduism," http://www.hinduwebsite.com/symbolism/thebody.asp (accessed March 15, 2016).
5 Jose Kuttianimattathil, "Body: Eastern and Western, 606-612," *Vidyajyoti Journal of Theology* 74, no. 8 (2010): 610.
6 Ibid., 612.
7 Ibid.
8 Colette Poggi, "Body in Hinduism 75-84," *IGNIS* 41, no. 4 (2011): 78.
9 Ibid., 79.
10 Ibid.
11 B. Bhattacharya, "Body Divine, 82-85," *Kathiroli* 63, no. 2 (1958): 83.
12 Poggi, "Body in Hinduism 75-84," 84-85.
13 Ibid.
14 Subodh Kapoor, *A Short Introduction to Saivism* (New Delhi: Indigo Books, 2002), 14.
15 Ibid.
16 Ibid.
17 Tamil Priyan, *Pathinattu Siddhargalin Mukiya Padalgalum Vilakangalum* (Chennai: Narmadha Publication, 1998), 37.
18 Tirumular, *Tirumandiram: A Tamil Scriptural Classic* (Chennai: Ramakrishna Math, 2013), 334.
19 T. N. Gnanapathy, "Tamil Yoga Siddha Research Project: The Basic Difficulties (Part 3)," http://www.babajiskriyayoganet/articles/art18-tamil-yaga-siddha-research-project-3.html (accessed March 25, 2016).
20 Ibid.
21 Ibid.
22 Motilal Pandit, "Body as the Symbol of the sacred 94-114," *Living Word* 98, no. 2 (1992): 112.
23 Ibid.
24 Tamil Priyan, *Pathinattu Siddhargalin Mukiya Padalgalum Vilakangalum*, 48.
25 Tirumular, *Tirumantiram*, 336.
26 Jeyaraj Ambrose, "Body: A Sanctified Dwelling of the Divine 27-39," *IGNIS* 41, no. 4 (2011): 28.

21

A Meditative Reflection on the Human Body
Body as Media of Dialogue and Communication

James Purathail
INDOCERT, Aluva

Abstract: The human body, which images the soul, which is its form, and God, who is its Creator, is a mystery, which, in order to be sufficiently grasped, is to be meditated upon. It is believed and speculated to be a living and Trinitarian image of God, which reveals in and through it love and thought, images of feelings and emotions. It reveals its transcending contact with the world and along with the soul it shares and reveals transcendence remaining in communion with every encountered reality. Hence, the body is media par excellence in its multifarious functions and expressions. I, as an embodied existence, can be proud of and thankful for my body, which I am free to love and care for, and through which I am present to myself, to the World and to God.

Keywords: body, image of God, animated, transcendence, soul, communion, process, movement, language.

Introduction

In order to understand the mystery of the human body, it has to be meditated upon as it is the case with the human soul. The soul is spiritual and invisible. It can be known only through a meditative reflection. The body, however, is visible and as such it can be subjected to experimentation. But the visible body constantly involves itself and co-operates with the spirit or the soul in its functions and operations. The body *images* the soul in that it is *animated* through it. Thus, the soul becomes almost visible through inhabiting the body, through its animation of the body. It is a mystery to be pondered upon. A mystery can be unravelled only through a meditative reflection. Hence, my presupposition and attempt to expose this paper as the fruit of a meditation![1]

Animated Body

The human body has no existence without its union with the soul, which is spiritual. The soul as *anima* – the animating principle – is subsisting life. Life is a dynamic movement. It constantly vivifies the body and gives it a dynamic presence and appearance. Appearance, more than being a phenome, is a manifestation, an ongoing revelation. That which reveals itself is the soul, the life-principle.

It is both body and soul together that make the human existence unique. That which is unique overcomes multiplicity. Here the dichotomy between body and soul is overcome by revealing the uniqueness of a human person. The problem of one and many is the most basic of all philosophical questions. The human body is one, and hence unique, because the soul finds it's abode in a particular body; or, better formulated, a body becomes capable of giving abode to the unique spiritual reality called the soul, by being *formed* by it.

The most basic philosophic and spiritual presupposition that reveals the relationship between the human and the Divine is the biblical statement that man is created in the image of God. God, being a pure spirit, deprived of all materiality and divisibility, sheds his image on man in a very mysterious way. What is this image of God? Has the Spirit an image? An image belongs to the material realm. Only matter can be *imaged*! How then can God shed his image upon man? This is the mystery of all mysteries related to man who is believed to be created in the image and likeness of God. What is the ontological basis or presupposition behind the biblical conception that man is created in the image of God? Is God's image in man the same as the human soul? Or, is it a model according to which the soul is *formed*? What is the ontological reality of this image? So, we begin a meditative reflection. I try to visualize the Divine in me through a meditation of my body and at the same time try to see the body through my soul.

A Trinitarian Image

God's image is the image of his being, knowledge and love, and these constitute the mystery of his Trinity. The Trinitarian image of God is transmitted to us through the soul that vivifies the human body, or through the union between soul and body. This image constitutes the being of man, of which the moving force is the movement of knowledge and love. Thus, man is the living image of God. By being a Trinitarian image it becomes conceivable with a logical contour. An idea has such a contour. A conceived and delivered word has this contour.

Now, by switching to the realm of images and imagination, I would say that the human body is like a canvas on which a beautiful picture can be painted. The body is therefore the *surface* on which the invisible will be pictured. It is also like a projecting screen on which living images can be *projected*. It is even like the visible sky where the infinite wonders of the universe are constantly being displayed. Man's face is like the sky with the unending manifestations or revelations of the universe. How many images come and go on the face of man! All that takes place in me, in my soul, will be revealed through my body. The body is also like a flower that blossoms before the sun. The sun gives light, warmth and life to the flower. The human body can radiate light and warmth and reveal the wonders of life. It constantly reveals all that I sense and experience; it is constantly revealing hope, love and the yearning for peace.

Man's face is constantly facing something or somebody. The *facing* makes it a face! Every being is facing the rest of beings. This is the principle behind the all-embracing relationship, behind the principle of universal relatedness and relativity. Everything is ultimately facing the absolute and central being, which we call God, who is like the sun for a flower. The divine centre is the centre of attraction. Here I see that my bodily existence is constantly sustained by the *imaging* presence of God.

Life and Movement

The most basic thing that characterizes human body is movement – the movement of life, the movement of growth, the movement of transformation. Movement makes the divine image, that represents his inner being, dynamic and at the same time *suggestive*. Man remains all the time a being to be *interpreted*.[2] His inner being is in an ongoing revelation. It is his inner being that is being revealed through his body. We can even say that the human body becomes visible through the revelation of his spirit.

The human is not one among many in a multitude of things. Man is in a *moving* relationship with them and towards them. This relationship is revealed through the constitution of his body, which is adapted and suited to *reach out* to others, namely with the help of his legs, hands and other parts of the body, especially with the head which is the summit of his awareness, knowledge and love.

Every movement of the human body is revealing and communicating something. In that it receives and gives information, it becomes an instrument of communication. By its very nature the human body is communicative. So, every part of the human body communicates that which is taking place in the interior of the human being, which is his soul. In other words, man's body reveals all that is hidden in his soul. The spiritual is revealed through the material body! The spiritual (soul) becomes visible and the visible gets the qualities of the invisible! There is an invisible communion of the human body with the rest of the universe through the spirit that dwells in it and which is present everywhere, beyond space and time.[3]

Being Thoughtful

The human thought is the final product of a long process of various physiological and psychological experiences, which are revealed through impulses, emotions, reactions, desires, repulsions, hopes, expectations, sweet or burdening recollections, love or hatred etc. The process of these experiences will be revealed through my body like in a movie film. The body will manifest all these varied emotions as the revelation of the psyche, the soul. There is a constant effort of the soul to express itself. It can produce the *image* of its thought only through these emotions and expressions of feelings. So, the body communicates the thought of the soul through emotive reactions which are proper only to the body, which is subject to change and modification. An actor, for example, professionally produces the various emotive expressions. An orator gives to his word eloquence, modulation, depth and softness as it may be suitable. Joyful experiences open our heart and correspondingly expand the body in its various areas of expansion. Sorrowful experiences, on the other hand, cause the shrinking of the body in many respects. In both these situations it is the body that is revealing the inner state of the soul.

The Body and the World

Again, it is the body that is in constant contact with the rest of the world. This *being-in-touch* with the world is revealed through the body. So, the body is the medium of all sorts of communications. The world at large is material. It, however, reveals values that can only be detected by the soul, for example, being, goodness, truthfulness, beauty and harmony. Thus, it reveals equally its spiritual dimension. By being a mediator between the world and the soul the body becomes a medium of communication within existential and ontological perspectives.

The body is the possibility for the soul *to be in the world*, which is the sum-total of the experiences of limitations, transitions, growth, decay and death – as regards the human body. The soul is bound to experience the *body-in-transition*; thus the soul knows the world as it passes away in the process of being and becoming. The soul can know the world only through the body. This knowledge, this process of knowing, is also a mystery. Death is also an experience the soul is making through the body. Death as the last stage of the process of life – along the path of birth, growth, maturing, and decline – is an experience of the soul received from and through the body.

Death as a gradual process is experienced as aging with its various stages. The body experiences compulsory transition and transformation. The facial and other bodily expressions reveal a lot about the passing life. Childhood, youth, middle age and old age are rich in experiences and expressions. It is the fault of comparison that makes or shows one or the other stage better or worse. Life at every stage is beautiful and rich in meaning. The ideals or values that are expressed vary in each of these stages. In early stages, namely in childhood and youth, hope and happiness may be dominating man's attitude towards life. In later stages reminiscence, satisfaction or despair may be taking the upper hand. However, in every stage there is the maturing of thought.

Being in Process: Rebirth and Revelation

There is a process of reception or negation - selection or rejection with regard to the interaction of the body with the universe. There are two basic attitudes in this respect which can be termed *using* and *enjoying* (*uti* - *frui* - in Latin). The world can be looked upon as the sum-total of things to be *used* or to be *enjoyed*. These terms stand for the so-called *being mode* or *having mode* respectively. The body tends to possess and the soul tends to enjoy.

The continuous and lasting experience that the body makes is the experience of a process and of a transition that is the essence of its being. It culminates in the compelling and irresistible experience of death, to which all beings are constantly tending, even hurrying. This experience, however, is mitigated by the recurring experience of rebirths that overcome death, or push death farther away. Every moment is new, because at every moment there is the birth or manifestation of being, a new beginning or a new revelation of being. Joy at every stage is this experience that man makes. The intimacy with the world and the experience of transcendence make human life rich with insight and knowledge. Hence, the *embodied* existence of man becomes the measure for the understanding of the world.

The experience of regeneration – a new beginning – culminates in the conviction that resurrection is the ultimate realization at the end of life's pilgrimage. It is the convincing triumph of the spirit over the matter, of the soul over the body; or better said, the redemption of the matter through the spirit. The redemption of the body is through the soul. Here start the religious beliefs. Religion is not merely an ideological speculation about *life-after-death* or the *after-life*; it is rather a balancing attitude of life in this world. It tries to see the harmony of everything and a harmonious culmination and blending of everything in oneness.

The Philosophy of Communication

The inner thrust for union with everything, materially and spiritually, is the basis of all communications. Communication is the human effort to become one with everything. It is first of all a process of knowing and of transferring that knowledge. It presupposes that everything is knowable, that there is the presence of Intelligence in everything, even though in an infinity of grades.

Intelligence in man is guided and supported by love. Love leads to universal union.

The body in its totality is in a process of constant communication. Every expression of the body is communicative. These expressions can become cultured, refined, studied, transformed and scientifically formulated as imitation and acting, as language and rhetoric. The most communicative function of the body is language – the ability to speak and sing, to write or to give out meaningful signs. Man's body is a psychological arena, where these are displayed. Man's body and bodily behaviours reveal or betray the inner state of the soul, which is affected by the body and by the fact of *being-in-the-body*. All these behaviours have to be observed in the totality of expressions and to be interpreted.

The Instrument Par Excellence

The body is a fantastic instrument with innumerable functions. Any part of the body can become an instrument to do an action or to reach out. Let us think of the innumerable works that are being done through the body, how the external world is reached through the body!

The ability for transcendence enables the human body to develop further instruments to interact with the world. Hence, the invention of instruments which revolutionized the world and made the human effort hundreds of times more efficient! The human body now *touches* the farthest end of the universe! So, the world becomes a reality *at-hand*!

Body and Transcendence

A living body reveals the possibility of constantly going beyond its limitations, which means its possibility of transcendence. It can overcome distances in space and go even ahead of time. Man can rise above the restrictions of his environment and modify the world to a certain extent through his knowledge and positive interference. He can reveal his transcendence towards a greater human and divine milieu. The soul gives the body the possibility to become spiritual, which is the ultimate possibility of matter. Matter is potency or possibility itself. Every possibility can once be actualized. The belief in the resurrection of the body is an existential hope which can be extended to the whole of creation, which, according to St. Paul, 'sighs for its redemption' from its materiality, from its inclination to degeneration. The body as possibility possesses these. Everything of matter hopes for and *tends* to become spiritual so that ultimately everything becomes one. Here I find the meaning and extent of transcendence. Transcendence, then, is higher and wider than 'presence', which has, in some way or the other, the implied connotation of time and space. Thus, we see how the human body *yearns* to come in *communion with everything*.

Religion and Religious Language

The human body, in union with the soul, enters a new and higher realm of experience when it faces the fascinating fact of the unity of everything. The inexpressible can gradually be expressed as God or the Divine. As the experience of the rising sun arouses hope and joy in our heart, so is with this experience of fascinating light and attraction. The adoring attitude of the body reveals a new dimension of the communicative function of the body. Here originates a new kind of language which can be termed as religious language. This language is richer with the functions of faith and imagination, hope and expectation. It opens a wider horizon for both body and soul. The human body expresses itself through prayer, meditation and contemplation. It reveals the ultimate realm of transcendence and it is expressed and communicated through the body, which *touches* the Infinity!

Beauty: The Ultimate Revelation through the Body

The human body reveals a wonderful unity, truth and goodness of the whole reality through the unity it experiences. This fullness, which is effulgent and radiating, reveals beauty. Beauty implies fullness; beauty reveals order and harmony. These are the ultimate meanings and messages of the body. Beauty has a wonderful power of radiation to reveal itself through the body. Beauty is the last word the body speaks.

We are inclined to call a body beautiful because of its complexion, because of the harmonious proportion of its various parts, the natural and studied demeanours, the manifestation of inner harmony, peace and joy etc. – everything revealed through the dynamism of life. The variation and gradation of beauty will take place because of the greater or lesser radiation of these values. We can say that beauty is something internal and it essentially pertains to the soul as its source. Beauty can be *imitated* or *copied*. Behind this there is a desire to 'appear' beautiful before others, but not the effort to *become* beautiful! Beauty is something that communicates or reveals being itself.

Love and Care for the Body

When we realize the richness and the wonderful ability of the human body we will be positively convinced to love our body and to care for it. It is to be loved, as it is the instrument of love for the *incarnate* being. We are allowed to cherish the body and keep our body in its proper beauty. The body is not to be considered a slave to the soul or to any austere religious discipline. Instead, body should radiate the inner world of light, truth, hope and love and bliss. The body is a mirror that reflects the inner and outer world. Thus, it can reveal itself as the image of God, the temple of God and the bride of the Divine!

Emerging Conclusions

This meditative research was a rewarding revelation of my *embodied* existence for me. I am filled with a positive and enriching appreciation of my body. I am now proud of being gifted with a body. My body is not a cell of loneliness, death and dissolution; it is rather a door that opens itself to wonderful revelations within and without. It is my possibility, the possibility to reach out. It is in and through my body that I remain in constant touch with life itself. It is in my body that I experience the birth of thought and word and then I speak it out. My body is the language of my soul. It is in my body that I encounter and experience God and the Divine world. Thus, I enter into the *possibilities* of my body as in a temple! In me and in my body I am able to experience the unity of everything, the harmony of everything and the beauty of everything. Now I rejoice in being myself, in being the abode of the Spirit and of the spiritual, experiencing unity in everything.[4]

Notes

1 I primarily meditate upon my own body, on my bodily existence. This meditation starts with observing my body, and then I interiorize this vision. I also observe other bodies, which are more 'visible' to me. I am also fascinated about the female bodies in contrast to my male body. The female body reflects the female personality and individuality. It is at the same time a mirror of my male existence, as both bodies are fascinated by the mutually related or relatable existence. This vision enlarges itself to the hemisphere of the female world and allows a di-polar vision of the human body, pointing to the dialogical nature of human body.

2 The process of interpretation is the process of meditation, an interior journey.

3 Here, I experience the transcendence of my body through the spirit. My meditative insight leads me to a cosmic vision of the human body.

4 This was a meditation of my body, of every human body, which was guided by philosophical, mystical and spiritual insights. There are a lot more to be excavated through practical and repeated observations. It has to go on all through our life!

Statement of ACPI Research Seminar on "Philosophizing the Body: Challenges and Opportunities"

The 40th Annual Research Seminar of the Association of Christian Philosophers of India (ACPI) was held from 22nd to 25th October 2015, at *Vijnananilayam: Institute of Philosophy and Religion*, Janampet, Eluru, Andhra Pradesh. Ninety-three participants from different parts of India came together to deliberate on the theme, "Philosophizing the Body: Challenges and Opportunities." We, the members of the ACPI, affirm the following:

1. Our bodily existence has material, social, spiritual and psycho-somatic dimensions. We need to continuously discover and unfold the meaning of each of these dimensions of bodiliness more deeply.
2. We are not our bodies or have bodies, but are bodily beings. Our bodies are constitutive of our identities as persons. Embodiment has a symbolic character, both of finitude and transcendence – it is a mystery to be lived and not a problem to be solved.
3. We reject a reductionist or mechanistic understanding of the body, which leads to objectification, reification and commoditization of human beings. While we do not absolutize the body by fostering crass materialism, we also do not relativize it by fostering a disincarnate spirituality.
4. Our embodiment is both enabling and disabling. The therapeutic interventions and enhancement possibilities offered to us by technology may be used cautiously, keeping in mind the dignity and rights of persons.
5. We need to appreciate the beauty, worth and dignity of our embodiment in its everydayness. The media tends to portray a distorted and instrumental perspective of being bodily, which has an adverse impact in how sexuality is understood. This has serious

consequences in the areas of gender, interpersonal and family relations.

6. Equality in gender relations needs to be upheld, entailing a rejection of all forms of discrimination, degradation and subordination. While respecting sexual or biological differences, we need to be aware of the many subtle or unconscious ways of subjugating and manipulating the other, especially in their bodies.
7. Devaluation and subjugation based on colour and caste – other forms of body-based discrimination – also need to be addressed and eradicated.
8. We are called to discover and live out wholesome Indian and Christian values while celebrating our cultural and religious differences. This entails the befriending of other persons and communities in their unique bodily expressions and forms of life.
9. Suffering and death are part of the process of bodily existence. At the same time we are called to reduce unnecessary suffering and unnatural deaths. Life after death is brought to its fullness in the wake of a wholesome embodied life.

Contributors

A. Pushparajan (anjelpura@gmail.com), Professor and Head (Retd.), Dept. of Interreligious Relations, Madurai Kamaraj University, Coordinator of the School of Philosophy and Religions in the same University, has authored 30 books, contributed over 300 articles in research journals, and presented over 400 papers in national and international seminars, symposia and conferences. Been a Consulter to Pontifical Council for Faith and Culture; Awardee of Charles Wallace Fellow in Dept. of Religions and Theology, University of Bristol UK; Invitee to the UN Peace Summit of the Religious and Spiritual Leaders; Member of the Founding Meet of World Council of Religious Leaders; Member of the Governing Body of the Indian Council of Religious Leaders; and Member of the Governing Body of the NBCLC. Presently, resides in Bengaluru, giving guest lectures in his fields of specializations: Interreligious Dialogue, Gandhian Theology / Spirituality and Ecosophy and Eco-Spirituality and Family Spirituality.

Andrew Anbarasu (anbuomi@gmail.com) is a Catholic Priest belonging to the Pontifical Congregation Missionary Oblates of Mary Immaculate (OMI). He is a Professor of Philosophy and presently Head Master of St. Eugene High School, Kombadimadurai, Sivagangai District, Tamilnadu. He has done M.A. (Philosophy) from Indira Gandhi National Open University (IGNOU), M.A. (Christian Studies) from University of Madras, M.Ph from Dharmaram Vidya Kshetam , Bangalore and a B.Ed from Tamilnadu Teachers Education University. He served as Dean of Philosophy at De Mazenod Institute of Philosophy, Perambakkam, Tiruvallur District, Tamilnadu. His areas of interest are Indian Philosophy, Hermeneutics, Philosophy of Religions and World Religions. He is a visiting Professor in many institutes of philosophy in India.

Ashley Miranda (ashsdb@gmail.com) is a Salesian of Don Bosco who teaches at Divyadaan: Salesian Institute of Philosophy, Nashik. He has also taught at Don Bosco Philosophate, Pyin Oo Lwin, Myanmar. He is specialized in Ethics but is also deeply interested in Contemporary Western Philosophy, Epistemology,

Philosophy of History, Postmodernism, Political Philosophy and Ecosophy. Since June 2015, Fr. Ashley has combined teaching of philosophy with work at the Salesian Community of *Bosco Samajik Vikas Sanstha*, Walwande a tribal hamlet 90 kms away from Nashik. This community is committed to working with the people of the villages around with a view to promote their integral development both individual and social.

Dolreich Pereira (dolreichpereira@gmail.com) is a Catholic priest of the Archdiocese of Bombay. He teaches philosophy at St. Pius X College, Mumbai. He did his philosophical studies at Institute Catholique de Paris in France and is currently writing his doctoral thesis at Jnana Deepa Vidyapeeth, Pune.

Felix Fernandes (felixsdb@gmail.com) is a Salesian priest. He holds a doctorate in Philosophy from the Salesian Pontifical University, Rome. His doctoral dissertation was based on the thought of Emmanuel Levinas, under the title "Levinas' Asymmetrical Relation: Its Relevance for Justice Relations." He also holds a Master's degree in Theology. Currently, he is involved in teaching philosophy at Divyadaan Salesian Institute of Philosophy, Nashik, India. Among the subjects he teaches are Anthropology, Philosophy of Education, and Contemporary Western Philosophy.

Francis Arackal (farackal@gmail.com) did his PG Diploma in Media studies from Griffith College, Dublin, Ireland, and Licence and Doctorate in Social Sciences, specializing in media, from Gregorian and St. Thomas Universities in Rome. He holds a Master's Degree in Philosophy from Nagpur University and Licence in Philosophy from St. Thomas University, Rome. He was Director of *Gyandhara*, Institute of Philosophy, in Orlim, Goa. He was both Professor and HOD of the Mass Communication Department in St. Joseph's College, Bangalore. He has published four books and many papers in reputed journals. He has a significant presence in online media with a personal website, blogs, and social networking pages offering comments on economic, political, religious, and social issues concerning the nation and the world. At present, he is Professor of Media Studies and Media research at Amity University, Gurgaon.

Gayatri Mendanha (gayatri@ssla.edu.in) holds masters' degrees in both English and Philosophy. She is currently an Assistant Professor at the Symbiosis School for Liberal Arts, Pune where she teaches courses in Literature and Philosophy. She is a visiting faculty at Jnana-Deepa Vidyapeeth. Her areas of interest are hermeneutics, women philosophers, modern drama and romanticism. She has written an article for a book, entitled *Kaleidoscope*, which comprises a set of critical articles, written by scholars in the field of English literature on literary works, published by Deccan Education Society's Fergusson College,

Pune. She has presented a paper at Jnana-Deepa Vidyapeeth for the ICPR Seminar on "Democratic We."

George Karuvelil (gkaruvelil@hotmail.com) is a Jesuit priest belonging to Patna Province, working as formator at Papal Seminary since 1999, and Ordinary Professor at the Faculty of Philosophy at Jnana-Deepa Vidyapeeth (JDV), Pune. An accomplished scholar who has published in prestigious national and international journals such as Journal of Indian Council of philosophical Research (JICPR), Theological Studies, Zygon: Journal of Religion & Science, besides Church-related publications like Journal of Dharma, and Vidyajyoti; presently he edits *Jnanadeepa: Pune Journal of Religious Studies*.

Gregory Mathew Malayil (gm6272@gmail.com) is a lecturer in the Faculty of Philosophy, Dharmaram Vidya Kshetram, Bengaluru. He has two Masters' Degree (Physics and Philosophy) to his credit. He secured a Doctorate in Physics from Cochin University of Science and Technology. His areas of academic interest include Cosmology, Consciousness and Science-Religion Interface.

James D. Chellappa (jameschellappa@gmail.com) is a member of the Church of South India. He is the Founder and Principal of Christian Academy for Advanced Theological Studies (CAATS), an Interdenominational and Ecumenical/Evangelical Seminary situated in Nagercoil, Tamil Nadu. He teaches Christian Theology, Philosophy of Religions, and Contemporary Theology.

James Purathail (purathail.james@gmail.com) is a priest belonging to the Little Flower Congregation. He holds a Master's degree from the Pontifical University Angelicum, Rome and a PhD from Pontifical Gregorian University, Rome. He has been teaching in Little Flower Seminary, Aluva where he also served both as Rector and President. Currently he is the Director of INDOCERT, Aluva and continues his teaching as a visiting faculty in Little Flower Seminary and in St. Joseph's Pontifical Seminary, Aluva.

John Peter Vallabadoss (petercapu@gmail.com) is Dean of Philosophy at St. Joseph's Capuchin Philosophical College, Kotagiri in Tamil Nadu. He has a doctorate in Indian Philosophy for the thesis "*Mayai* in *Tirumandiram:* An Ecological Perspective," from the University of Madras. His area of specialization is in Saiva Siddhanta and Indian Philosophy. To his credit, he has scholarly articles in philosophy journals and edited volumes. He has been Consultant in Philosophy at IGNOU, New Delhi; and as Registrar and Professor of Philosophy at Vijnananilayam (Institute of Philosophy and Religion), Eluru. He is a visiting faculty to JDV, Pune and other philosophy institutes across

India. He is presently Secretary of the Association of Christian Philosophers of India.

Johnson J. Puthenpurackal (johnsonjp@rediffmail.com) is a Heidegger-specialist with a Ph.D. from the University of Louvain (Belgium). He is one of the pioneers of the 'Association of Christian Philosophers of India' (ACPI); until 2015 he has been in its administration for eighteen years; under his leadership the ACPI brought out several publications, the acme of which was the two-volume *ACPI Encyclopedia of Philosophy*, of which he was the Editor-in-Chief. To his credit there are several studies published. Presently, he is President of *Vijnananilayam: Institute of Philosophy and Religion* (Janampet, Eluru, A.P.), where he has been resident Professor of Philosophy for the last twenty-five years. He has given lectures in many Institutes and presented papers in numerous seminars.

Keith D'Souza (keith@jesuits.net) teaches Philosophy and Religious Studies at St. Pius X College (Mumbai), and is visiting Professor at various other institutions. He has a B.Sc. (Physics) from St. Xavier's College in Mumbai, an M.A. (Philosophy) from the Mumbai University, a B.Th. and a M.Th. from JDV (Pune). His Ph.D. in Philosophy is from Marquette University in Wisconsin, USA, with a specialization in philosophical hermeneutics. He has published more than thirty-five articles in the areas of hermeneutical theory, socio-political philosophy, religious studies and various philosophical themes. He is currently on the Provincial Team of the Bombay Province Jesuits, a member of the Bombay Philosophical Society (Mumbai University) and the President of the ACPI.

Kurian Alumkal (alumkaljoy@gmail.com) is a Catholic Religious Priest belonging to OCD Malabar Province. Presently, he is Dean of Students in the Carmel Hill Philosophy College, Thiruvanathapuram in Kerala. He obtained Master's degree in Philosophy with gold medal from Banaras Hindu University and took his PhD in Philosophy from the same university, specializing in Buddhism. He teaches in different philosophy and spirituality centres too.

Kuruvilla Pandikattu (kuru@kuru.in; kuru@jdv.edu.in) is a Professor of physics, philosophy and religion at Jnana-Deepa Vidyapeeth, Pune, India, since 1996. He has three Masters' Degrees (Physics and Philosophy) and two Doctorates (Philosophy and Theology) to his credit. He has been actively involved in dialogue between science and religion. Presently, he is the treasure of ACPI. Author of more than 26 books and 112 articles, Pandikattu is a Jesuit priest belonging to Dumka-Raiganj Province, India. He has been involved in organising more than twenty national and international conferences on science-religion dialogue and visited more than fifteen countries and attended more than hundred conferences on philosophy, theology and science-religion dialogue. Because of his creative and committed writings, he has been in the editorial board of five journals. He is a renowned author, spiritual leader, motivational speaker and research guide. His main topics of research are: anthropology, eschatology and transhumanism.

Nishant Alphonse Irudayadason (nishant@jdv.edu.in) is a professor of Philosophy at Jnana-Deepa Vidyapeeth: Pontifical Institute of Philosophy and Religions (JDV), Pune, India. After having completed his doctoral studies on Derrida and Ethics at Université Paris-Est and in Insitut catholique de Paris, France, he has been actively pursuing academic life. He is currently the Chairperson of the doctoral programme in the Faculty of Philosophy at JDV. His regular courses include Research Methodology, History of Contemporary Philosophy, Ethics, Politics and Hermeneutics. He has presented research papers in many National and International Conferences. He has authored two books, edited one book and penned more than 30 articles in National and International Journals as well as in edited books. He is a regular contributor to contemporary political analysis in "Light of Truth," a bimonthly published from Kochi, Kerala.

Noel D'Costa (noelcost75@yahoo.co.in) is a diocesan priest of the Archdiocese of Goa. He teaches Philosophy of Science, Cosmology, World Religion and Science and Technology at the Patriarchal Seminary of Rachol, Goa. He holds a Master's degree in Interfacing Science, Philosophy and Religion from the Jnana-Deepa Vidyapeeth, Pune. He is also the Convenor of the Inter-Religious Dialogue in the Archdiocese of Goa. His areas of interest are Philosophy of Science, Cosmology, World Religion, Historiography, Science and Technology.

S. Sekar Sebastin (sekarsebastin@gmail.com) is a priest of the diocese of Trichy. He holds a M. Phil in philosophy from Annamalai University, Chidambaram and a Doctorate in philosophy from the Pontifical University of St Thomas Aquinas, Rome. He has been teaching philosophy at Sacred Heart Seminary, Poonamallee in Chennai since 1999. He was the Dean of the department of philosophy for seven years and at present he is the Registrar at the same institute. He is a visiting faculty to several institutes of philosophy in India. His areas of interest include Moral Philosophy, Philosophical Anthropology, Postmodernism and History of Western Philosophy. He is author of two books and has written more than thirty articles in the areas of postmodern trends, Levinasian thinking and ethical studies.

S. Stephen Jayard (sjayard@gmail.com), belonging to the diocese of Tiruchirapalli, is a Professor in the Faculty of Philosophy, Jnana-Deepa

Vidyapeeth, Pune, since 2008. His PhD in *Philosophy of Science* is from the Central University of Hyderabad, had the Post-doctoral research on *Science and Values*, at the Lonergan Institutes, Washington DC and Boston College, Boston, USA and Regis College, Toronto, Canada, He is a visiting faculty at various Institutes of Philosophy and Religion in India and abroad. He has conducted workshops on 'Integrating Science and Spirituality' and sessions on motivation for the faculties and the students in Schools and Colleges, published several articles in the National and International journals, and five books; including *Towards a Theory of Rationality in Science: A Plea to Reasonableness* (2012) and *A Book That Cannot Be Titled* (2015).

Victor Ferrao (victorferrao@yahoo.co.uk) is a priest of the Archdiocese of Goa, and teaches at Rachol Seminary, Goa. He has doctorate in Philosophy from Jnana-Deepa Vidyapeeth, Pune, with a specialisation in Philosophy of Science. His primary interest is in the area of Science and Religion Dialogue. He has attended as well as organised several international as well as national conferences in this area. He is the Co-founder of Science-Religion Sangam, a science and religion dialogue movement in Goa. He is a co-coordinator of the special study centre of IGNOU at Rachol Seminary. He has published five books and several research papers in reputed and peer reviewed journals and has been an active member of the ACPI.